# SALTLED BREAD

The True Story of Two Good Friends

As told to Sarkis Buniatyan

By

Gagik Buniatyan

# SALTLED BREAD

## The True Story of Two Good Friends

As told to Sarkis Buniatyan

By

Gagik Buniatyan

GOLDEN AGE MEDIA

**Back to Culture**

**First printing in English, 2007: 3,000 copies by Torchlight Publishing Inc**
**Second & Third printing in Bengali, 2012: 3,000 copies by Saptarishi Graphics Inc**
**Forth printing in English, 2012: 1,000 copies by Print Point Inc**
**Fifth printing in Hindi, 2014: 5,000 copies by SRST BBT Bhaktivedanta Book Trust**
**Sixth printing in English, 2015: 1,000 copies by Golden Age Media Inc**

Cover design: Sarkis Buniatyan
Design and Layout: Jahnudvip dasa & Manideep dasa
Library of Congress Cataloging-in-Publication Data

Buniatyan, Sarkis, (1990)
Salted bread : The True Story of Two Good Friends / as told to Sarkis Buniatyan by Gagik Buniatyan.
p. cm.
ISBN-13: 978-0-9779785-6-4 (SB.: alk. paper)
1. Buniatyan, Gagik–Imprisonment.
2. Sachisuta Das, 1964-1987–Imprisonment.
3. Hare Krishnas–Soviet Union–Biography.
4. International Society for Krishna Consciousness–Soviet Union. I. Title.

BL1175.B86B86 2007
294.5'512–dc22, 2007001632

You can contact the author at: divinecouple@gmail.com

This Edition is Printed & Distributed Exclusively by **Golden Age Media**

Salted Bread is available at special discounts for Bulk purchases. For more information, please contact:

**Back to Culture**

**Golden Age Media (Nandagopal Jivan das)**
New Delhi, INDIA
Mobile: +91-8506805060
E-mail: ngjd.gkg@gmail.com
Nandagopal.Jivan.GKG@pamho.net
Web: www.goldenagemedia.org

# DEDICATION

This book is dedicated to my dear father, Sarvabhavana das (Gagik Buniatyan) and his best friend Sachisuta das (Sarkis Ohanjanyan, 1964–1987) who risked and sacrificed their lives to spread the Krishna Consciousness Movement in the former Soviet Union. They were tortured in a Russian prison camp for two years, and as a result Sarkis died just one month before his release.

**Sarkis  Ohanjanyan**          **Gagik  Buniatyan**

*He reasons ill who thinks that a Vaishnava dies,*
*While thou art living still in sound.*
*A Vaishnava dies to live*
*And living spreads the holy names around.*

# ACKNOWLEDGMENTS

I would like to thank my mother and all my friends who inspired me to write about my father's experiences, as well as my dear teacher, Mother Sukhada of Alachua Learning Center Charter School in Florida, USA, for giving me the idea for Salted Bread and encouraging me to write this story. Without her encouragement, my father would probably never have found time to share his experiences, and this book would never have been published. I also offer my gratitude to some anonymous donors for helping to publish this book.

My sincere thanks go to Bhaktivignan Goswami for encouraging and supporting us in many ways; Urmila devi dasi and Bhaktin Sharon for editing; Pancha Tattva Prabhu for his kind help with the cover of the first school edition; Radha Damodar Prabhu (Don Delaney) for editing the first publication and expanding Salted Bread; Bhakta Charlie for spell checking, encouraging, and helping in many different ways; and finally Satyaki dasa and my publisher Advaita Candra dasa, who kindly agreed and cooperated with us to publish this book, and Jahnu das and Mani Deep for interior design and layout.

**Sachisuta (Sarkis) Buniatyan**


My heartfelt thanks goes first of all to Nandagopal Jivan das (GKG) and Golden Age Media team for publishing this Original Edition of my book 'Salted Bread' as well as HG Mohan Rupa das (GKG) (TP-ISKCON-Delhi) and HG Sarvasakshi das (GKG) for their encouragement and guidance to Nandagopal Jivan das and his team, HG Ajay Nath das (GKG) for improved cover design art work and arranging the design and layout and Sangini Radha devi dasi for her support of her husband, Nandagopal Jivan, in his service to Srila Prabhupada and His divine movement.

May you all be blessed by Lord Sri Krishna.

Thank you very much for your support and cooperation...

**Sarvabhavana das**
Sweden, 2015

# FROM THE EDITOR

Religious persecution is nothing new, and those willing to suffer and be martyred for their faith have always been among us. Yet this account of the dedication and difficult struggle of Krishna's devotees in the former Soviet Union is especially inspiring and moving. Sarvabhavana tells his story simply. He writes as if a willingness to endure torture for a spiritual mission is ordinary. Yet, when we travel with him on his search for meaning, his time in the army, his selling of scripture, his time in prison, and his visit to India, we wonder what we would do in similar circumstances and ponder the depth of our own faith and dedication.

It has been a great privilege to edit Sarvabhavana's account of the Krishna Consciousness Movement in Armenia. Readers curious about religious movements, Soviet history, and human psychology will find it fascinating. Those who wish to deepen their internal and external dedication to the mission of Lord Caitanya will find it nourishing and strengthening.

**Urmila devi dasi**

# CONTENTS

# INTRODUCTION

This true story, which I have named Salted Bread, is an unusual and painful, but at the same time encouraging story that I have heard from my father throughout my life. Sometimes, when my father would talk to his friends or our guests, they would ask him about his coming to Krishna consciousness and how he and the other early recruits to the Hare Krishna Movement developed Krishna consciousness in the then former Soviet Union. I used to listen to him with great attention and interest. He told these stories, of what he likes to call his "painful but blissful past," in many ways with different moods and emotions. Sometimes he would describe things very briefly without getting into details, and sometimes, depending upon the listener and the purpose, he would speak about many details for a long time. Sometimes, when reporters or devotees who were writing about this subject would come to us, the conversation would go on for a much longer time. Hearing over and over about my father's experiences in jail, I felt very sorry about how heartlessly police officers tortured him for no reason. When I compared his past tribulations with my bedtime stories from the Vedic literatures that Mom or Dad would tell me every day, especially about Haridasa Thakura and Prahlada Maharaja, I started to see my father in my childish mind and heart as a hero, and a very dedicated devotee of Lord Krishna and Srila Prabhupada.

Sometimes, I used to ask my father questions about the 730 days he spent in a Soviet prison. Sometimes he would be so emotional that I could see his tears, as well as sudden changes in the tone of his voice and the color of his face. I remember him becoming especially emotional when anyone asked him about his friend, Sachisuta das (Sarkis Ohanjanyan), who left his body on December 26, 1987, in one of the cruelest Russian prison camps (YU-25/B in the Orenburg Territory). My dad and Sako, as my dad used to call him, were best friends from their childhood, and they loved and respected each other very much. They were in kindergarten together and went to the same high school. They served in the Russian Army for two years, and after that they joined ISKCON—the International Society for Krishna Consciousness (also called the Hare Krishna Movement)—together in Armenia. Unfortunately, due to Soviet laws, they were taken to jail soon after joining ISKCON for the so-called crime of printing and distributing the holy scriptures from India, such as the Bhagavad-gita, that were secretly translated into the Russian and Armenian languages.

Many people, after hearing of my father's past, asked him to put his life story in writing, but he didn't have time to write it down. He never seriously considered it because, as he used to say, he did not consider himself a good writer, and he didn't know if anyone actually needed to read all these painful stories. Many events have been forgotten in the course of time, or as he says, no longer evoke the same feeling and emotions when he talks about them. But, even after so many years, what I am about to tell you is far beyond my imagination —sensitive, sad and encouraging, too. I will try my best to retell everything I have heard from my father, and I hope this will help my readers to become more serious about Lord Krishna's teachings and philosophy. This story is written as my father told it in his own words, with his voice. I am just the recorder.

I would just like to add that, as a result of the personal sacrifice of these early devotees, eventually the Krishna Consciousness Movement was registered officially in Russia and today there are more than one hundred large and small ISKCON Hare Krishna temples in the territory of the former Soviet Union. I offer my humble respects to all those sincere souls who sacrificed their lives for these great achievements.

You may ask why I named this book, Salted Bread. The answer is that during my father's two years of imprisonment he used to eat mainly three slices of bread a day. All ISKCON devotees are strict vegetarians, and as he describes, "There was nothing vegetarian available in jail but bread. But, no one will be able to eat just bread by itself for a long period of time, especially bread of such poor quality. So, in order to make my mouth produce water to swallow that type of bread, I had to add salt to it."

According to my understanding, eating bread and salt for such a long period (730 days) is a very difficult task, and as you will learn from the book, this was one of the most painful experiences of all for my father. So, for that reason, I named this book Salted Bread.


**Sachisuta (Sarkis) Buniatyan**
**Sri Nityananda Trayodasi**
14 February 2003
Alachua, Florida, USA

*"Humility; pridelessness; nonviolence; tolerance; simplicity; approaching a bona fide spiritual master; cleanliness; steadiness; self control; renunciation of the objects of sense gratification; absence of false ego; perception of the evil of birth, death, old age and disease; detachment; freedom from entanglement with children, wife, home and the rest; even mindedness amid pleasant and unpleasant events; constant and unalloyed devotion to Me; aspiring to live in a solitary place; detachment from the general mass of people; in between accepting the importance of self-realization; and philosophical search for the Absolute Truth—all these I declare to be knowledge, and besides this whatever there may be is ignorance."*

*–Bhagavad-gita, 13.8-12*

# REVIEWS

"Salted Bread" is a book of extraordinary historic significance, not just to iskcon, but to the whole world. It chronicals a massive turning point in the history & development of the Hare Krishna movement which is impacting the entire planet on a huge scale! First, the martyrdoms of the devotees must be compared to that of the early christians who were thrown to the lions in stadiums but would not give up their faith. Secondly, the devotee martyrs must be compared to prahlad maharaj, who was tortured by his father but never compromised his Krishna consciousness. Directly by their sacrifices, the former soviet union devotees now comprise one of the largest group of ISKCON devotees in the world!

This book is a "must read" for those who want to know the true history of this great movement! In delhi some devotees produced a full-length drama based on this book which was a masterpiece. Someone should produce a feature-length film based on this book. It is rich and "can't put it down" reading!

Respectfully submitted,
**Bhakti Madhurya Govinda Swami** (ACBSP)
(formerly Makhanlal Das)

---

"Salted Bread" is a book worth reading not only for the devotees of Lord Krishna but even for those who aspire to come closer to the God, the goal of every religion. The story of the author and his best friend to maintain the God consciousness inspite of so much of physical and mental torture is really inspiring and hope giving.

Your servant,
**Gauranga Das**
**ISKCON Chowpatty**

In a culture that often demonizes religion for its fanaticism, Salted Bread offers a stirring real-life counter-narrative of fanaticism directed against religion, or more particularly against a minority religious group by an atheistic government.

By acting as a voice for the victims of atheistic fanaticism, this heart-wrenching book shows the dehumanizing depravities that can be rationalized by prejudice, propaganda and xenophobia.

In addition to this message for the broader society, Salted Bread offers a poignant portrait to practitioners - a portrait of faith amidst atrocity, undying inspiration amidst unspeakable desperation and the final redemption from hopeless adversities. It calls us all to cherish the gifts of the freedom to practice that we presently have and urges us to do what we can to assist for the restoration of similar freedom in places where that freedom is even today threatened or curtailed.

Most importantly, the simplicity of the writing style of Salted Bread underscores the gravity and the glory of the theme - devotion can not only survive but also be strengthened through distress when there is determination. Grace works in inconceivable yet unstoppable ways to keep the human heart moving in its march towards the divine heart. By offering our obeisances to and meditating on the examples of those who have endured torture, even to the point of martyrdom, for the sake of faith, we can all pray that we can gird our faith for the challenges it faces in our individual situations and take our heart closer to the Lord of our heart.

Your servant,
**Chaitanya Charan Das**
**ISKCON Pune**

# CHAPTER ONE

# The Beginning

*"O best among Bharatas, four kinds of pious men begin to render devotional service unto Me—the distressed, the desirer of wealth, the inquisitive, and he who is searching for knowledge of the Absolute."*

*–Bhagavad-gita, 7.16*

I think that everything happens for a reason, whether what happens is good or bad. Often we think, "Why is this happening to us, but not to others?" In my humble way, I will tell you the truth, the way I understand it, because you are special, dear reader. Everyone is special and unique in his own way; it just takes some time to realize that you are special. Sometimes, it takes many long years, sometimes even a lifetime, to understand that.

Often God's plan for us is so unpredictable that it is very difficult to understand why everything is happening, but as we all know well, to accomplish any plan there must be some preparation. My dad told me many times that he could not believe how things happened so perfectly and timely and how everything was so well-planned by Lord Krishna for all His devotees. Here is his story, just as I have heard from him:

My dear son Sachisuta, I will start my story with my birth in the small town called Meghri, Armenia, on the 26th of August, 1964, where I had a very ordinary childhood. My mother worked for the post office, and my father worked in a factory that made fruit preserves and jams; so, we were not rich or poor but a middle-class family. I was growing up just like anyone else in my town, associating with children that had almost the same mentality, and almost no difference from each other in the way they led their lives. Such sameness was always boring, and therefore I was never satisfied, but rather searching and dreaming about finding a special, different lifestyle. Sometimes I would try to open my heart to some of my friends, but either they wouldn't understand what I was telling them, or they would laugh at my ideas. My greatest fortune in childhood was to have one very good, close friend named Sarkis Ohanjanyan, who fortunately shared my understanding about life in general and would discuss my ideas happily. He was exactly two months older than me and was born on June 26, 1964. We used to call him Sako, and throughout this story I will usually call him Sako because that is the name that I remember him by. We had been friends in kindergarten, elementary school, and high school together, and I do not remember any incident of fighting or misunderstanding between us, except over insignificant things.

Sako was expert at many different things, and many times when we got into trouble of all sorts he would come up with a solution and protect me as if I were his younger brother. I remember particularly an instance when we were in the ninth grade, when we were about fifteen years old. Sako was quite a good gambler; he used to make a bit of money by playing a card game similar to poker. One day, we had some visitors who wanted a game so we went to their motel room. The three guys were quite a bit older than we were, about thirty, but we agreed to a game. At first, Sako pretended to be losing, and the guys became a little excited and careless. They were also drinking alcohol and smoking marijuana. Then, when almost all our money was gone, Sako began playing well and winning. The guys got angry at the turn of events. One of them walked to get water so he would see Sako's hand (cards) and signal his friends. I pointed that out to Sako at which point all of them became very angry and started a fight. We tried to escape. I ran out of the room, down the stairs, and out to the street, but Sako, who had most of the money, was held in the room. Three guys followed me and knocked me down. They were kicking and punching me. I could hear the cursing and fighting upstairs, too. Then, Sako jumped out the 2nd floor window and over the balcony rail. He held onto the rail, and even though it was still a great distance, dropped to the pavement, pushed those big guys aside, and helped me out. We ran until we could catch a cab. We were all bloody, and our clothes were ruined. But Sako said, "Don't worry, Gago (that's what he called me), we will buy some new clothes and eat in a nice restaurant today and have some fun, okay?" On the way out he was able to grab all the rest of the money and so had lots of money in his pocket. Sako was very generous; when he had money he shared it with everyone. We went to a store and bought some new clothes. We then went to the public bathhouse and cleaned up. After that we went to a fine restaurant to eat.

There were many adventures and narrow escapes like this, and I could always be confident of a successful outcome when my smart friend was with me. No adventure was unthinkable with him by my side.

We had a great love of nature, and spent much time in the beautiful Armenian mountains and forests. We had several guns, but not for killing animals. We had been vegetarians since fifteen years of age, and considered animals as our good friends, so there was no question of killing or eating them. We used our guns strictly for targeting bottles or other objects and for our personal protection.

Like most Armenians, we were brought up to eat animals, so, in general, people we met were very surprised to find out about our vegetarianism. My commitment to giving up meat-eating, and to a life of Ahimsa, or non-violence, started with a hen and a neighbor.

Once, I was alone in the house with my mother when my next door neighbor came in carrying a hen. She asked if my father would kill it for her so she could cook it for her guests. My mother said that my father was out, and she couldn't butcher chickens either. Then, the neighbor asked me to help. I had never killed any bird or animal and had no idea how I would go about doing the job. But when I explained my inexperience, my mother and neighbor started to prod and encourage me by teasing that such a grown-up gentleman as I would certainly already know how to kill a bird. I decided to show that I was, indeed, a competent gentleman. I followed them to a corner of our garden.

They placed the unfortunate bird on the ground, instructing me to press down her wings with my right foot and her legs with my left foot. Then, while holding a sharp, blazing knife in my right hand and her head in my left, I started the terrible act. As soon as I touched the knife to the bird, her whole body started shaking as she squirmed mightily to escape. Then, when the hen apparently realized freedom was impossible, she relaxed and closed her eyes, as if waiting for the death that hovered only moments away from her.

At this point, I started to have some doubts about the job. "Perhaps I can release her," I thought. I hesitated.

My mother and the neighbor started screaming, "Cut it! Cut it! What are you doing?" In response, I moved the knife up and down without pushing it into the hen. I was trying to please them without doing any real damage to the bird. My hairs were standing on end, and my body started to shake. My nose felt hot, and my ears were ringing.

I accidentally nicked the hen's neck with the sharp knife as I was moving it. Blood stained the snow-white feathers. I started to think, "What am I doing?" As I saw the blood spreading out from the wound, I immediately released the hen and threw down the knife. The bird flew away, crying. Perhaps it landed in someone else's garden, but we never saw it again. As she flew away, the women started to curse and criticize me for not being gentlemanly enough to kill even one small bird.

Looking in my mother's eyes, I said that I was never again going to eat anything with blood, even if I died from hunger. She could cook meat for me, I told her, but I would not touch it. I have kept that vow to this day.

My mother was not pleased to have to give one of our own hens to the neighbor, and the neighbor left in frustration to find someone else to butcher her new bird. I had a lot of conflict for some time with my parents and other relatives over my determination not to touch any meat product, what to speak of eating it. Gradually they understood the futility of trying to change my mind, and I became an advocate of a vegetarian diet. I began to tell anyone who would listen that since there are so many fruits, vegetables, and grains God gave us in the world, there is no reason to spill the blood of innocent animals and birds. Even the Bible supports a vegetarian diet, since the original foods God gave were grains and herbs.

Sako and I also used to love reading books and always had something interesting to talk about from our reading. We would often spend a lot of time in libraries and bookstores. We were searching, though we did not know exactly what we were searching for. But from time to time we would find something interesting and discuss it together. We felt encouraged that we had found something interesting, and for a while that would help us to go on little by little towards our unknown target. Religion and ancient scriptures were our main interest, and we could not quench our thirst even though we read all the books that were available at that time from the library.

Sometimes we took special trips to the far mountains to visit very old churches and temples. It was fun to see these old buildings, neglected for hundreds of years. We would take photographs of them for our collection. Some of the buildings were extremely beautiful and unusual, and we would think sometimes about how to protect them from becoming damaged and destroyed. Since they were far away from where the general public could see them, sometime vandals would break into the buildings, even by taking out one stone at a time. Slowly these churches came to look very sad, and in some cases were even very dangerous to walk in.

We would clean the churches as much as we could, and write a request for the next visitors that they would not destroy the buildings, which had historical value as well as being houses of God. I do not know how much our signs were helpful, but at least we were trying our best and doing some service to the Lord. Once we had even tried to clean up a big church in our town that was extremely dirty because for many years no one ever thought of doing any type of cleaning or maintenance. Probably the Soviet regime had a lot to do with this type of neglect, but whatever the reason, that church was in a very critical condition. Some people, if we can call them that, were using the church as a toilet, which made it impossible to stay there for a long time.

Christian paintings on the walls were defaced, and some pieces were taken away. In their place there was dark black paint, many times showing very ugly and shameless scenes of boys and girls—and in most cases priests and girls—having affairs. Right at the entrance there was a big stone which was covered with blood and some parts of different animals and birds that were so-called sacrificed to God. It was terrible and a stinky place actually, and all the bottom portions of the walls, as well as many beautiful priceless old paintings, were completely black from the candles that had been lit as offerings to God by so-called believers. From the wood that was connected to the two main pillars was hung a long rope. Children had made a swing there, playing in that dirty place, sometimes all day long.

So anyhow, we decided to start cleaning the church late one night so no one would see us there or criticize and tease us. We would start cleaning after 10 or 11 pm, and finish by 4 am, so no one would see us coming out of the church with big tools. We had preached to some of our classmates who were our closer friends, thinking they could understand us and we could trust them to join us. So, they came to help, too.

It took us a long time to clean all the dirt from the church and make it look all right. We had cleaned all the black walls with sandpaper and broken glass pieces and took out and cleaned up all the feces. It was terrible to breathe all the dust there. We were unable to breathe properly although we were wearing some protection over our noses.

My grandfather was living nearby at that time, and we used to take and bring back his tools every night. After a while we had successfully accomplished our cleaning and placed a nice poster with a hand written note on it with a request: "Please let's maintain cleanliness in this holy place."

It was pretty nice looking after such heavy work. But to our surprise, one day we walked in and saw that our poster had been turned over. On the other side was written all kinds of bad words about us like "one who cleaned the church..." and so on, and someone had defecated right on the middle of the altar. Similar to how it had been previously, ugly paintings and bad words were written on the walls.

This was a very discouraging and disgusting experience for me and Sako. I could see the tears coming down his cheeks, and he hung his head and hands down helplessly. I embraced him, and we both breathed heavily and cried loudly in the church for about ten minutes. Then he sat down on the steps of the altar, and while placing his hands on his knees, hung his head and cried loudly. The echo of my friend's sufferings in the empty church created a special atmosphere, and I had a feeling as if, not God Himself, but perhaps some subtle entities like angels were present there and weeping with us. As for myself, I was walking around and trying to see what else had been done to the church and crying. After a while Sako started to walk out without even looking in my direction. I started to follow him, and we sat down outside, next to the gate where we started to smoke a marijuana cigarette and talk about all we had experienced in there. We decided that we would never again clean that place, and let the vandals go to hell.

I asked him, crying and intoxicated, why does God allow these people to do such awful things? I was very upset with the whole situation and trying to figure out why all these things happen in this world. I asked Sako why ignorant and bad people take birth on this planet. Why was God not breaking the hands of these crazy people who are destroying His own church, His own house where people should come for worship instead? Sako just wiped his tears, and looked like he was not even hearing me. We started to walk towards our home and continued our discussion there till late night. We were trying very hard to get answers for our questions but could not find them, and it was giving both of us much pain.

We read the Bible and other Christian books and came to the conclusion that they were very informative and nice but not at all enough to answer all of our questions. One of the most valuable things we found was the ten commandments of God, and we often discussed about them.

We could clearly understand that God's sixth commandment, "Thou shall not kill," was not only about humans but for animals and birds, our younger brothers and sisters, as well. This point was absolutely clear to us since God said also to Adam and Eve that He had given all the animals and birds to them so they will protect them.

We were always having the same opinion about this very clear point and thinking that God was intelligent enough to mention only one word containing only three letters "man" at the end of this short sentence if He really meant, "You shall not kill man." But since He didn't say so, then it was absolutely clear for us because animals and birds also suffer when you kill them and similarly blood was pouring from them too.

Anyway, this was one of the main points that would keep us very far from meat eating. The Bible had become the main book on the table near my bed. I would never go to sleep without reading at least one or two pages from it. I loved Jesus and his teachings and was always searching for more books to read about him. Armenians are the first who accepted Christianity as the official government religion in the year 301. I used to love reading about my country's rich religious history and traditions. From time to time I thought of going to Echmiadzin, which is the seat of Christianity in Armenia. Sometimes, I dreamed about staying and studying there, dedicating the rest of my life to Jesus Christ just like Grigor Narekatsi and many others.

Unfortunately, during the Soviet regime it was easier to find anti-Christian literature than anything positive. However, even after knowing this bitter truth, I still searched in the local libraries for any book which would contain even a little amount of information about Jesus and Christianity. In the course of my search, I read some books in which the writer documented hundreds of negative incidents that took place in churches and different religious organizations in the past several hundred years. Such history impacted me so that I started to have many doubts about religion in general. These books were like poison for my mind, and I was totally confused and lost.

Despite all this poisonous information, from time to time I felt some strong desire to stay in Echmiadzin, giving up my mundane lifestyle and devoting everything I had to Jesus Christ. But, there was an unsolvable problem even if I had faith in the institution of Armenian Christianity. The Armenian Christians did not follow a vegetarian diet. I felt sure that I could give up all my bad habits to become a priest. But I was not sure if they would understand my commitment to the sixth commandment of the Lord not to kill any living creature. It is a tradition in the Armenian Church to sacrifice different animals. All the priests are meat eaters. Convincing them that the commandment, "Thou shall not kill," didn't only mean murder of humans would have been impossible, and would only have created trouble for me. Armenian priests would either consider me crazy, or an un-bona fide speculator.

Anyhow, when things got a little hectic at home once, I ran away and went to Echmiadzin to meet someone to whom I could open my heart and ask all the questions I had accumulated for years. I left one Sunday morning without telling my plan to anyone except my best friend Sako. He was the only one whom I could trust to share my feelings, and he was the only one who could understand me. He came to tell me good-bye, and we separated from each other with tears. I could see him standing at the bus stop until the bus rounded a bend.

When I arrived, it was sunny and still morning. The liturgy was going on with organs and a choir in a big, beautiful church. There was a divine atmosphere there. The fragrance of all the candles and incense seemed to take me to a different dimension, especially because I was fully intoxicated. I listened to the celestial music and felt totally disconnected from this material world. From time to time during the liturgy, I looked at the decorated dome ceiling while praying to the Lord to show me some path to Him and help me to find the right person to talk with.

After carefully watching all the priests, I chose one old man to be the person I would tell what I was planning to do. After the ceremony was over, I quickly went out and stayed next to the church door, waiting for the priest to come outside. Soon, he started to walk towards me, at which point I started to shake and my face turned red. Maybe I was worried about what he would think if he knew I was intoxicated.

I pulled myself together and started to walk behind him. As soon as I was next to him I asked if I could speak to him briefly. He said he had little time, so I requested ten minutes. But, when I asked if we could sit on the wooden garden bench in front of the church, he wondered if it would be a serious conversation. "Yes, Father," I replied, "very serious, and concerning some important decision to take about my life. I have honest questions, and am expecting honest answers from you, sir."

"Okay, I will try my best," he told me, and took his seat on the red painted bench. The red reminded me that I was living in a communist country where there is no religious freedom.

I immediately went to the heart of my problem, thinking of how we had little time. "From my very childhood I have been sure that God exists," I told him. "But I have many unanswered questions which are like arrows in my young heart, disturbing me day and night. I do not have anyone in my town to share with and get the right answers. If I get satisfactory answers, then I may consider staying here in Holy Echmiadzin to study and dedicate my life to God."

"What are the questions that are disturbing you, son?"

"What is the real meaning of the sixth commandment?"

"It is very simple to understand. One should not murder and spill innocent blood. This body belongs to God, and one should take care as if it is the house of God. One shall not kill; it's as simple as that," he replied.

"Why then did God not say one more word to make it even clearer for ignorant people like me?"

"Which word? What do you mean?"

"If it was only about killing people, then God would have said, 'You shall not kill men or humans,' but instead He says, 'You shall not kill,' and to me it equally applies to the birds and animals. What do you think about this point, Father?"

He looked at me very strangely with wide-opened eyes. It seemed he was not expecting such a question from a fifteen-year-old boy. He started to scratch his head and touch his half-gray beard for a while. "Animals don't have a soul, my son, and there is nothing wrong with killing them.

They are part of our daily food, and if we do not eat them, then they will multiply out of control."

I then presented him with all the arguments I knew for vegetarianism. I said, "So how it is that God ordered Adam and Eve to protect animals in Eden? And how is it that animals feel pain as we do, but they have no soul? When we are trying to kill a sheep, it is trying its best to protect itself, defending its life till the last moment. They also have babies to whom they give milk, and their baby is as dear to them as I am dear to my mother. So why can people eat a sheep's baby but not me? I have heard that people must be vegetarians according to the Bible, and that the first people ate only fruits, vegetables, and grains at creation as the original food for a human body. Also, we have teeth and stomach like other vegetarian animals. Isn't it violence, Father, that because of humans killing animals, some species are almost lost from the face of the world? And, why are people so cruel, even killing other people? Even in the name of God, such killing goes on, so that there have been so many wars between people who think of themselves as pious believers."

"Hmmm, what is your next question?" he asked, and looked at his watch.

"You see, I decided to give up my worldly life and fully dedicate myself to the Lord, our God, but recently I read some books wherein they were criticizing almost all the religions. The books said that religious leaders were leading very sinful and worldy lives, committing many illicit activities but still wearing holy clothes and preaching to the public. Is this true, and is this happening also here in Echmiadzin? I want to give all I have, including my heart, to God and become a priest here. Worldly life has lost its meaning to me. What do you think, Father?"

He hung his head and was silent for quite some time. I didn't know what to do or say. My childish heart was burning from curiosity about what he was thinking to tell me. I felt my face to be burning hot and red like a tomato. I felt bad that I might have embarrassed him. After some time, he started talking slowly to me without looking me in the eyes.

"You are certainly a very unusual boy, my son. Your questions are very unusual, too, and they make me wonder about some things that I have never considered thinking about before. No one ever asked me about such things, and they never came to my mind. How old are you?"

"I am fifteen. I like honesty very much and would never like to be cheated by anyone, especially when it has to do with religion and church. I am searching for an absolute truth and I am sure I am going to find it somewhere, someday—if not here, then somewhere else. If you can help me, please do so, and I will appreciate it very much. But if you can't help, please tell me straight. I can never possibly forgive anyone who would cheat me under the name of God."

"Hmmm, I am afraid I won't be able to give you the right answer to your first question at this time, but I will think about it, and perhaps discuss the matter with some other priests who I am sure also never thought of this issue of killing animals for eating. About your second question, here is what I can tell you, son. Bad things are happening everywhere, including in churches and similar places, but one should never lose his faith in God and must continue his prayers and lead a sinless life. God will certainly listen to your prayers and show you the right path, my son. Please keep praying and you will get the answer, but I don't think you will find what you are searching for here."

He stood up and placed his right hand on my shoulder and told me, "I wish you all the best, son, but this is not the right place for you, since no one will understand you, and you may get frustrated and end up in a difficult situation."

He turned his back toward me, and started to walk faster than before towards the main gate of the church, leaving me alone standing in the courtyard. I didn't know what to do or think. At first, I wanted to run after him and ask what I was supposed to do now, whether to go back or stay. In the next moment I understood that he had already told me everything he could.

Tears started to pour from my eyes as I sat down on the same bench again without looking at anyone who was walking to and from the church. I felt, however, that everyone was looking at me. I intensely prayed to God asking for help. My hands were shaking, and I had a heavy headache. I do not know how long I sat there, but it felt like more than two or three hours. I felt extremely hungry and my stomach started to hurt a lot, as it did when I was emotionally stressed.

I stood up to walk without knowing where I would go, but I felt dizzy and sat down again. I felt this was my last day and all my dreams would never become reality. In that lonely and helpless state, I noticed that the sky was filled with black clouds and it had started to rain. Everyone was running to get out of the rain, but I continued to sit as if nothing was happening. It seemed that even the clouds were crying for me. My own crying then increased as I saw that no one was left to sympathize with me, and even if someone came, they would simply think I was wet from the rain rather than from tears. Finally, I noticed that the cigarette box in my pocket was getting wet, and so I stood up and started to walk slowly towards the main gate of the church courtyard to a place where smoking was allowed.

As I passed by people, I had a feeling that they knew everything in my heart and mind. I was thinking that perhaps the entire world knew what a helpless condition I was in. I went to the nearest small shop to sit under a big umbrella, order some food, and smoke. By evening I had no other option but to catch a train back to Meghri, where I assumed my parents' punishments were waiting for me, as usual. I was already preparing answers to all the questions they would ask.

I sadly thought that everything was lost for me, that there was no point to search for the absolute truth anymore. Yet, another feeling started inside. Somehow I was periodically able to remember things I had read that were true so far in my life. I decided that nothing was finished and I had to keep searching. I considered that these bad things were happening so that I would collect my strength to fight for what I wanted to achieve.

After getting rebuked by my parents the next day, I called Sako to tell him everything about my meeting with the priest in Echmiadzin. At first he was sad, but then started to laugh and told me the same thing that I had been thinking the previous night—that after this bad thing, there is good waiting for me.

I stopped reading the Bible for a while and read some other books instead. My faith needed urgent repair. At that point Indian philosophy and yoga came to help me to understand life better, with answers about why we are in this material world and have to suffer so much. In this way, one important life chapter closed as I entered a previously unknown realm of thought.

One day, Sako came to my house with a wide smile on his face; I knew he must be bringing me some good news about our main interest—Eastern philosophy, something that we liked a lot. I used to love India from my very childhood. Every picture I saw about India, every book I read about it, every story or piece of music I heard from there, was so sweet and dear to my heart. My fondest dream was to one day take a bath in the sacred Ganges River, visit all the ancient temples, and climb the Himalayan Mountains to meet the great yogis there. Walls in our rooms were decorated only with pictures taken from the Russian magazine India, a good source of encouragement for us at the time. We used to read poems and books by Rabindranath Tagore and parts of the Rig Veda, Manu Samhita (Laws of Manu), and much more from Panchatantra, all of which were nicely translated into Armenian or Russian languages. One of our most favorite things was watching the latest Indian movies. We loved them very much, and sometimes would come out of the cinema hall crying. We used to buy tickets for each other, making surprise arrangements before or after the movie to have some fun.

We had never missed any Indian movie that played locally, and some of them we even watched three to five times without ever getting tired of them, especially if Hema Malini, Dharmendra or Amitabh Bacchan was acting. Hema Malini was like our angel, and we learned and I am still learning a lot from her these days. Our radios were always tuned to Indian stations, and we knew exactly what time each show would be, although we did not understand anything in Hindi. We loved the sound of the sitar and flute so much that we could not live without hearing it every day.

Anyways, we were very close friends, and we would share any small article related to India with great pleasure. We were sure that our destiny had a lot to do with India and Indian philosophy. Sako bought a blue hand-made book titled Astanga Yoga. It was very difficult to read, and we could hardly see the pictures at all because this was probably the seventh or eighth photocopy. He had paid twenty-five Russian rubles for the book, which at that time was a lot of money for a young kid. (A ruble then was about US $1.25.)

We started to read the book very carefully, and we were trying to understand as much as we could to apply to our daily lives. We changed our diet suddenly and started to fast every Saturday, and sometimes we ate only fruits for one or two-week periods. We were sincerely trying to become yogis and were practicing some asanas (stretches and postures) at home, but we were still not satisfied. We were searching for some higher level of consciousness, but we did not know exactly what to look for, or where.

We were also influenced by the counter-culture of the time and took drugs such as marijuana, hashish, etc., under the name of yoga and Indian culture. Soon we were very sure that without intoxication one could not achieve the highest goal of life. So, mostly you would find us intoxicated and in a dreaming mood all day long.

Soon, we started to have a very interesting group of new friends, some of whom were as much as two or three times older then us, which had its beneficial as well as harmful effects. One of these was Senik, a very humble person. He was well known in our town as a learned man. He was expert in Tibetan medicine, yoga, and world history, and he used to talk to elderly people to learn more about the past. He would always find interesting books and share them with everyone; his books were everywhere and with everyone. Anyone he would see he would ask when he would get his book back. He was also an expert in taking drugs, so we had learned that from him too. Senik and I became very close friends, and we had started to travel all over Armenia to see historical sites, which gave us great pleasure. I placed a picture of Lord Vishnu from an incense box on the dashboard of his truck next to his picture of Jesus Christ.

Once, he found a book about Ramakrishna's philosophy, and we decided to go up on the mountains to read it, spend some time there, and at the same time collect some hashish. This was in August of 1982. We had just smoked some marijuana, and he asked me to drive his truck so that he could read the book to me. We were driving on a very dangerous area, and the road was very rough and narrow. At one point, I lost control of the truck. It turned over on its side, and we started to roll over down the hill about five or six times. Somehow, by the grace of the Lord, the truck stopped at the middle of the hill, but unfortunately upside down. Our legs were stuck under the heavy weight of the engine, and some hot water started to drip down and burn Senik's foot. We were screaming helplessly from the pain. After the dust had cleared, I opened my eyes and the picture of Lord Vishnu's smiling face was right in front of my face, and a picture of Jesus was in front of Senik's face! We took that as an omen that everything was going to be all right.

The first ten minutes were really scary, but after that we were just talking and sharing about how and what we felt when the truck was rolling over. We could not see each other, but our legs were together and we could touch each other, although we could not turn at all to either side. When I told Senik that Lord Vishnu was right in front of my eyes and smiling at me, he told me that Lord Vishnu is the one, without a doubt, who protected us when we were going down the hill! After a while, we figured out that there was not enough air. I took a hammer, which was right next to my left ear, and broke the window so fresh air started to enter the cabin.

Soon many villagers came to help us. Some were crying, and some were screaming. But we were just talking and sometimes even joking. We could not make even the slightest move in the smashed metal, so there was no option but to meditate on Lord Vishnu for about three hours before the emergency medics arrived and cut the door off with a hacksaw to take us out.

At first they placed us on the soft green grass and gave us some first emergency help, including some injections, after which they took us to a hospital. We had both lost some blood and had some twists and concussions. Both of us had our parents and relatives come there, crying and thanking God for protecting us. After the doctors took us to our rooms, one of our friends came and told us that two police officers wanted to ask us some questions. If they found that we were under the influence of illegal drugs, they may give some trouble to Senik for corrupting a minor. So, I decided to climb out the hospital window with the help of my friends and hide for some days until I was feeling better.

Senik was in worse condition, and it took him some months to recover completely. Plus his truck was totaled. But, he never complained to me about anything and instead told me many times, when I was apologizing to him, that this was God's arrangement. He said, "We were not supposed to read that book because it was nothing but impersonalistic philosophy!"

That book was left behind, but we read many books from the Vedas in the next few months. In our search, we came to know that Krishna is the Supreme Personality of Godhead and there are some mantras that one should chant to get His mercy, but as to what mantras, we did not have a clue!

We had one other friend who was even more knowledgeable and older then Senik, whose name was Misha. He was an expert in many different fields, and was a teacher of history and English. He knew much about Eastern philosophy and culture. We were learning a lot from him and enjoying his company. He had a family with three children. His wife was a teacher of English. We often gathered in his house, which was on a country site, and had very unusual, interesting, and fun conversations about the East.

We had come to know many other interesting people through Misha, one of whom was Sahak. Sahak was about six years older than I and a distant relative of my brother's wife. He was a nice, kind, and interesting person and was often on drugs, just like the rest of us. We had become very friendly and started to meet often in his house in Yerevan, the capital of Armenia. One day he told me that he wanted to introduce me to a very interesting man named Karen.

Karen was about his age and was famous in the city as "crazy Karen" or "Yogi Karen." So Sahak made the arrangements, and we went together to meet Karen in front of the central library. On the way there he started to tell me more details about him, I guess so that I wouldn't be surprised by Karen's strange attitude.

He told me that Karen had been practicing yoga for many years. He mostly walks barefoot in the city, and sometimes sits in the lotus position on the snow or ice in the park, while closing his eyes meditating on God. He is also a very strict vegetarian and knows a lot about Indian culture. I was burning with interest to see such a person, counting the minutes on the bus.

When Sahak and I met Karen, the first thing I had noticed was that he was standing on the library stairs in quite cold weather wearing summer shoes without any socks. He was tall with a little beard. My first impression was that he was very strange, even a little bit crazy. If I didn't know that we were there to see him, I would have preferred to walk a little distance from someone like him.

As soon as we came close to Karen, Sahak introduced us, and naturally I extended my hand for a handshake. To my surprise he didn't even react, and my hand stayed in the air without the handshake, as Karen asked Sahak what he could do for us. Sahak said that I am his friend, and that he brought me there to talk a little bit about yoga and its benefits.

That was enough for him. He started a forty-five minute lecture about yoga, speaking fast and sometimes joking. I was having a hard time following all his points, but what I could grasp was very interesting and informative. After some time, he stopped talking and asked me if I understood what he had just said. Mechanically I told him yes. Then, when he asked me what I understood, I was a little bit in trouble. So then for about thirty-five minutes more he spoke to me about how actually I do not understand him at all. He seemed even a little bit angry, but with whom, I really didn't know.

At the end he took out one small book from a soft velvet bag. He started to open it slowly, while saying that we are very fortunate in Armenia to see the first Bhagavad-gita in English. He showed it to us with a big smile, saying that this is something that contains everything possible that any man needs to know in this lifetime. He added that there is an absolute truth and highest level of all knowledge.

We both tried to take the book from his hand to see it closely, but he moved it away and told us that since we are very sinful guys, we shall never touch this holy book. He said we could only touch it when we gave up smoking and some other bad habits. I told him immediately that I am a vegetarian, but he was not satisfied with that. He told me that monkeys and elephants are also vegetarians and I'll have to give up drugs.

"So please show us more closely," I demanded once more. He brought the book very near, holding it with both hands. I saw a beautiful picture of Krishna and Arjuna on the chariot. That sweet picture is always in front of my eyes at any time I like. I was so happy to see that book, and started to think where and how to get a copy of it. I could never have imagined that just two years from then, I would not only have that book and a Russian translation of it, but would also give it to hundreds of other people in my country. In fact, after some time Karen would buy those books from me.

Then in November, I had to go into the Russian Army for two years. I really did not want to go to the army but had no choice. Sako and I both were called at the same time. Unfortunately they took us to different cities, and we could only contact each other through letters. The work was hard, the barracks were too cold in the winter, and I was quite unhappy. I hate cold weather. On the good side, I found new friends in the army who more or less shared my views. One of them was Romik from Georgia. One day, Romik and I ran away from the army when we were supposed to be on watch. We became AWOL (absent without leave) as the military calls it. We went to a store that sold unusual goods from all over the world. We had just gotten paid so we bought many candies, cookies, and other foods.

Then we saw the trays of frozen cut pineapple! Pineapple is rarely seen in Armenia, and we had never tasted it before. We bought a couple of plates of it and went out and ate it on the bench. I remember how sweet and sharp tasting it was! We crept back into the army camp and did not get caught, but my tongue was swollen for several days from the pineapple! I learned the military life and laws, as well as new ways of getting intoxicated with my new friends, a problem which went too far. My parents were wrongly thinking that if I went into the army then I would give up my smoking habit, but instead I had even started to inject opium.

One day, I got a letter from Senik wherein he was saying that he knew of the potency of the Hare Krishna mantra and that I have to chant it as much as I can under any condition and circumstances. He sent me that very same picture of Lord Vishnu that I had meditated upon in his smashed truck. I then carried it in my pocket through the entire duration of my army time. I was advised by my friend to chant the mantra also whenever I felt very cold and it would help a lot. He said that I should stay sober and free from any intoxicant, meditate on the picture, and chant the Hare Krishna mantra as many times as I could.

HARE KRISHNA HARE KRISHNA KRISHNA KRISHNA HARE
HARE HARE RAMA HARE RAMA RAMA RAMA HARE HARE

Being vegetarian wasn't so easy there, and I was having a very hard time. Sometimes my captain or commander would come and stand next to me and force me to eat meat like the others, but I would refuse. As a result he punished me, and sometimes they would even beat me badly and send me to a 'kartser,' a specially designed cold room where punished soldiers were kept.

Sometimes chanting was helpful, sometimes not. But time was passing, and I returned from the army after two long years. This was winter of 1984. I could hardly wait to see my friends again. Sako wrote that he would not be released from the Army for a few more weeks, but Senik came to see me on the day I returned home. In one of his last letters, Senik mentioned that he had several very interesting pieces of news for me, so I was very anxious to hear them. After a party, he took me to his new car, and we went to the park where we started to share information and shower many questions on each other's heads. I started to fill up a cigarette paper with marijuana that I had brought with me from the army, but instead of seeing a nice smile on his face as usual, he told me that he had not used drugs for over three months already, having given them up completely. I could not believe my ears! That person who had smoked practically speaking all his life was now refusing it even after I had told him it was from Uzbekistan, some of the best! I started my cigarette and inquired as to how he had suddenly lost his mind, what kind of influence he was under, and from whom he had suddenly found courage to give it up. How could he stop using such an important element of life that is so essential in order to see God and have a relationship with Him? I was astonished and thought that he was teasing me, testing me, or playing a game.

Slowly and humbly as usual, with a big smile, he started to preach to me, saying how he had accidentally met some nice people called "devotees of Krishna." They had changed his entire life in a matter of two or three days. He told me about the Bhagavad-gita and vegetarian food. At the end of his explanation, he mentioned to me that all the devotees had heard about me and wanted to see me as soon as I am back from the army. My answer was very straightforward. I told him that everything those devotees are saying makes a lot of sense to me, but if they're against drugs that means I don't want to have anything to do with them! I thought that they must be simply ignorant people if they did not see an obvious connection between drugs and God. How is it that they do not see a connection between a bulb and electricity?

After a long and hot discussion, he convinced me to visit the devotees at least once, since he had promised them that he would bring me there as soon as I returned back from the army. Since he mentioned that in a couple of days there would be a big festival there, I agreed to go so that he would not feel bad. We planned to make our five-hour journey to Yerevan city the next day in his new car.

So I got my parents' permission, somehow, to leave for two days to Yerevan. They weren't so happy about it, but since I had just come back from the army, they had to consider that I was old enough to make my own decisions sometimes and let me go.

I met Senik at his house early the next morning. He was very happy to see me, as he asked me to help him put some boxes in the trunk of his car. They were heavy, and I asked what was in them. He said, "Oh, this is some fruit for Krishna. Since today is Gaura Purnima, the appearance day of Lord Sri Krishna Caitanya, a holy day, the devotees will offer it to Krishna on the temple altar. It is always nice to bring something to Krishna when you go to His temple. Any house where Krishna or any of His forms are worshiped is considered to be a temple of God."

"So," I said, "can I also take something?"

"Yes," he replied, "anything you feel like." I asked him to drive to my house after that, where I filled up a box with different fruits and brought it back out to the car. He smiled and told me how beneficial it was for me to offer fruit like this. He also told my mom and dad that we were going to take this fruit to Krishna; they would earn good karma since we are going to offer the result of their work to Krishna.

*If one offers Me with love and devotion a leaf,*
*a flower, fruit or water, I will accept it.*

—Bhagavad-gita, 9.26

## CHAPTER TWO

# Entering the Spiritual World

*Just try to learn the truth by approaching a spiritual master.*
*Inquire from him submissively and render service unto him.*
*The self realized souls can impart knowledge unto you*
*because they have seen the truth.*

*–Bhagavad-gita, 4.34*

All the way to Yerevan, either Senik was preaching to me, or we were listening to something new for me, sweet music. He called it "guru's tapes," meaning Harikesa Swami's tapes; he was the spiritual master and leader for the Hare Krishna movement's preaching in the USSR. I really felt attracted to the chanting and even sometimes sang along. Sometimes I would ask Senik to stop somewhere so I could have some marijuana, since he would not allow me to smoke in the car because there were some pictures of Lord Krishna there.

After a long journey, we parked outside of a nine-story building. He looked at me with a smile and dancing eyes and said, "So, are you ready to enter into the spiritual world?"

I told him, "I do not have to enter the spiritual world, since I am already in the spiritual world," meaning I was in a blissful mood after my last smoking. Slowly, I got out of the car; I was a little bit tired from the trip. We retrieved our boxes of "good karma," and started to walk towards the entrance of the building. My first observation was the sweet fragrance of incense—it was pleasant, and at the same time strange for a traditional Armenian apartment building. Usually when you enter such places the meat smell is the first factor you notice, but this odor was very different or perhaps, I thought, the meat smell was covered because of the incense.

As we walked closer to the elevator doors I started to smell something different. While we were waiting for an elevator to arrive from the ninth floor, I was looking at the corridor, which had a brown, stinky substance applied all over the walls. I could not believe it was so foul smelling! I asked Senik, "What is this nasty stuff on the walls?"

"Oh, this is cow dung! Our Atmananda dasa applies it everywhere. Since the cow is a sacred animal, its dung is very valuable and antibacterial. Anywhere you apply it, that place will be purfied. The cow is also considered our second mother since she is giving us so much milk, which is so essential for our life."

It didn't make much sense to me, but I accepted it as some new knowledge and tried not to offend that "sacred animal" in my mind any more. But I made sure I didn't take any deep breaths! We started to go up the elevator. The closer we were to the ninth floor, the louder was the sound of the strange instruments the devotees were playing—the drum and karatals (hand cymbals), accompanied by even louder singing. Finally, we were on the ninth and last floor and ready to enter to the "spiritual world."

Senik knocked on the door three times fast and three times slow several times. Soon after that, someone looked through the security view hole and opened the door slowly for us, while almost screaming, "Hariiiibollllll, Hare Krishnaaaaaaa! Come in. Please, come in. Welcome to Gaura Purnima." As we came in, a devotee of Krishna opened the door slowly and then shut the door again. He had to open it slowly because of all the shoes and socks that were strewn all over behind the door. Devotees do not wear shoes in the "temple room" of Krishna. Shoes are considered to be very unclean.

Senik smiled hugely as he introduced me to anyone who was available at that time in the corridor. The devotees were asking Senik if I am the Gagik he had told them about many times before. "Yes," he replied, "he is the one. He is the Gagik, my good friend."

"Come in, come in, please!" the devotee who had opened the door said. "We were waiting for you a long time, and are happy for the opportunity to meet you! My name is Atmananda dasa. Or you can call me Armen, whatever is easier for you." He was a funny, young man. As I first got to know him, he would always tell me all kinds of humorous stories, mostly at the expense of the KGB and scientists. From time to time he would criticize other religions as well. At the same time, he would preach very heavily. Later on, someone told me that actually Atmananda das was a scientist, but he threw his PHD and all his diplomas into the trash can after he became a Hare Krishna devotee. When at first he greeted us, I thought that he was a little crazy, or at least strange, and I wished somebody else would have been the first devotee I met. But later on I started to understand him better. Sometimes I went out with him to distribute spiritual books, and I started to like him. So anyway, we gave our boxes of fruits or "good karma" to some other devotees who were enthusiastically cooking in the kitchen, then went to the temple room where lots of people were singing loudly and sweetly.

When Atmananda opened the door, the first detail I noticed after the shoes was a beautiful altar with three small statues and pictures. In front of them were many large and small pots, one on top of another, full of already cooked food and attractive fruits. The room was filled with pleasant fragrances and a very unusual smell of cooked food that could drive anyone crazy with a desire to eat. That was the first most powerful influence of Krishna on me, and right away I started waiting for the moment that I would taste all this very sweet fragrant food.

I told myself it was worthwhile to come here. "Such nice food they're eating, these people!" I then entered the room and saw 35 to 40 people sitting down, clapping their hands, shaking their heads, and singing Hare Krishna. Senik paid obeisances, bowing down in front of the altar, and mechanically I followed him. This was the first time I had ever paid my obeisances and without even knowing to whom! I sat down, looked around, and examined every devotee very carefully. I had never experienced such an interesting atmosphere in my life, and I'd never seen such intense and meaningful faces. To me it seemed that each and every one of them had been chosen, one by one, by someone. I really liked almost all the faces.

Everyone was singing very enthusiastically. I do not remember how, but somehow I found that I was also singing and clapping my hands with them. The singing was going on and on, and more people were entering the temple room. I was thinking that it would never end, and was surprised at how this many people could fit in this small room. The cymbals and drums were so harmonious that I felt as if I were in heaven! Everyone in the room was swaying back and forth like waves in an ocean of bliss. Some devotees kept bringing trays of food and ringing tiny bells; they were offering the food to Krishna in that way and then leaving the room shortly thereafter.

Soon I noticed that the fruits I brought were also offered at the altar, and I looked round me to see if anyone else noticed that those were the fruits I had brought. I wanted everyone to know that I was the one who brought these fruits for Krishna for the first time.

Later on they explained to me that it is important to understand the meaning of obeisances. In a spiritual community, one acknowledges his or her submission to the spiritual master by bowing whenever one goes before the spiritual master or before Krishna's deity form. Here is the prayer, in Sanskrit and translation, that the followers of the International Society for Krishna Consciousness say when they offer obeisances:

*nama om visnu-padaya krishna-presthaya bhu-tale*
*srimate bhaktivedanta-svamin iti namine*

I offer my respectful obeisances unto His Divine Grace A.C. Bhaktivedanta Swami Prabhupada, who is very dear to Lord Krishna, having taken shelter at His lotus feet.

*namas te sarasvate deve gaura-vani-pracarine*
*nirvisesa-sunyavadi-pascatya-desa-tarine*

Our respectful obeisances are unto you, O spiritual master, servant of Sarasvati Goswami. You are kindly preaching the message of Lord Chaitanyadeva and delivering the Western countries, which are filled with impersonalism and voidism.

After singing for some time, I was very hungry, but the singing was never ending, so I had no choice but to sing with them till midnight. When everybody was very tired but still enthusiastic, one tall devotee named (Karen) Kamalamala das, the young brother of Atmananda das, came in and asked some people to help him to remove all the pots from the altar to the next room where they were planning to serve the food to everyone. He explained that now the food was called prasadam or the remnants from the sacrifice of food offered to Krishna. In fact, Krishna enters into the food and thus the food is Krishna and is totally different and transcendental from ordinary food.

The leader had stopped singing for this announcement, and I do not know how it happened, but I started to lead the singing. Everyone in the room seemed very happy with this except one lady named Gaganeshi devi dasi. After about 30 minutes she asked me, "Can you stop, please?" I felt sorry, but I could not stop since some other devotees were making signs that I had to continue. So I kept singing and singing. What finally forced me to stop was when someone came to the room and announced that the police, the KGB, were trying to come in. Because the devotees did not want to open the door, they were trying to break the door down! I stopped and went to the corridor to see what was going on. Some devotees were running from one room to another and hiding the books, typewriters, and other items. Senik came to me and told me that I do not have to worry—by Krishna's mercy, everything will be all right.

The KGB were still trying hard to open the door, and cursing everyone who was inside behind the heavy metal door. Three or four devotees were trying to hold the door so the KGB could not open it. Atmananda told everyone to chant Narasimha Pranamas, a Sanskrit prayer for protection, and many of them started to chant. Someone called Senik and whispered something into his ear. After that Senik came to me and called me into the other room and asked me if I still had any drugs left with me. I said, "Yes, I do have some in my sock." He asked me to throw it away before the KGB entered the apartment if possible, since it would be very bad for all devotees. This was very grave news for me and I did not like it at all, but he told me that if they came in and found it, then it would be a good reason to take all the devotees to the police station. People would say, "Oh, the Hare Krishna devotees are only smoking hashish and singing all day long!"

Oh, it was very painful for me to throw away so much of the "honey" as we called it! But it looked as if I had no other choice. I went to the bathroom and took it out from my socks and, oh my God, my hands were shaking and I did not know how to throw it away! After some minutes, I put some in my mouth and threw the rest in the toilet and flushed the water. This was my second sacrifice for Krishna. I did not want all these innocent people to suffer because of me.

After some time, the devotees decided that it would be better to open the door before they broke it down. As soon as they opened it, five angry men practically flew in and started to scream orders. Everyone was running to different rooms. One KGB officer closed the door and stayed there so that no one could get out. They started to search everywhere and anywhere; I did not understand what they were looking for so eagerly!

They started to register everyone's names and check their documents. Some of the KGB men were very angry and upset about something, but one of them was cool and relaxed. He seemed surprised to see us, and he was asking all kinds of questions of different devotees. So, it became like a crazy house—it was really noisy with five or six different groups of devotees in different rooms with many starting to preach to the KGB members. The only reason I could think of for why the KGB had come was that neighbors had complained about the noise from the late night singing.

The two brothers, Kamalamala and Atmananda, in whose house all this was happening, were demanding that the KGB produce an authorized document that showed that they were allowed to enter their home in the middle of the night, but the KBG did not give a proper answer. Perhaps they didn't have anything to show. One group of devotees was quieter in their preaching, which produced a beneficial result, because after a while I noticed that the KGB members were eating prasadam, food offered to Krishna.

One KGB man was saying that he had never had such tasty food and was glorifying it. Others said that they were not allowed to eat anything due to the specific instruction of higher authorities. They took some books and a box of papers and told all of us that we should never organize such a gathering again, because it is improper. They promised us that the next time we do so, and the neighbors complained, they would take us to the police station and demand a big fine. Atmananda was trying to pull some papers from their hands while they were going out, but they pushed him very hard against the wall and left.

After everything cooled down, the devotees started to serve the sanctified food, prasadam, as if nothing had happened just five minutes ago. It was a real feast! There were rice and vegetables, fried foods, cakes, and sweets, along with cool, sweet drinks. I had never, ever seen anything at all similar to this wonderful food! I liked the prasadam so much that I was thinking I could eat all the prasadam in the room by myself! I even started to mentally calculate how much everyone would eat and decided that there wouldn't be enough for everyone. But my calculations were very wrong, and as a matter fact, it was too much. Twenty more people could have been there to eat it all!

After the big feast, I was very satisfied, but at the same time so tired that I was thinking of nothing but sleeping. One devotee came to me and asked, "Would you like to rest here with us tonight? We have some spare sleeping bags."

"Yes," I told him. "I would like to rest, but what about the rest of you guys?"

"The ladies will rest in one room, and the other rooms and balcony are for the men. Somehow, we will make arrangements for everyone."

I was taken to an unfurnished room, and in a few minutes I was down inside a sleeping bag, which smelled like flowers or incense. For some reason, anything you touched there smelled like incense or some spicy fragrance. A few hours later, I suddenly woke up because I could hear a group singing in the temple room again. They were doing their "morning program." I was extremely tired and soon fell asleep again. I do not know how long I slept when a new, unusual to me, sound woke me up again. I could hear many devotees chanting together loudly

### "Hare Krishna Hare Krishna Krishna Krishna Hare Hare Hare Rama Hare Rama Rama Rama Hare Hare"

It was a sound resembling thousands of honeybees buzzing around their nest. I knew that this was the sound of many devotees practicing mantra meditation—they were chanting the names of Krishna on their beads and meditating intensely upon each syllable. It was interesting, but it was still before dawn! I covered my head with my sleeping bag and tried to go back to sleep, but I found that it was impossible. Soon several devotees entered my room and started their chanting there, too, so I had no choice but to wake up. After a while of lying there awake, I could hear a bell ringing. I guessed correctly that they were offering food to the Lord. So, I knew that next will be breakfast prasadam. I was not at all hungry, but I really liked the prasadam, so I decided to get up before it was too late.

As I got out of my sleeping bag and made my way to the temple room to eat, someone told me that it is better if I take a bath before entering the temple room. So I said I would take an early-morning shower, unlike my habit. I told myself, "When in Rome you have to do as the Romans do," as I walked into the bathroom.

It took me a while to make up my mind to take a shower so I was standing in front of the small piece of mirror, which was slicked with soap and hung on the wall. On top of the mirror was a sign that said, "You are not this body." It made me think, and I started to ask myself, "If I am not this body, then who am I?" I had not even scratched my head two minutes over this when someone started to knock on the door saying, "Hurry up, Prabhu, there are more people here waiting to use the bathroom!" I started to turn the left tap that was supposed to be hot water, but unfortunately it was not working and there was a sign saying "maya" on it. So I tried the next one and it was cold water. I knew someone was behind the door so I came close to it and slowly started to ask him, "There is no hot water, what should I do? And there is a note that says 'maya.' What is that supposed to mean?"

He immediately replied, "That means that out of illusion you are thinking that your body is your self! You let your senses tell you what to do, instead of being in control of your senses for austerity and self-realization! Now, please hurry up!" And they started to laugh at me sweetly from the other side of the door. So I did not delay any longer. I went back into the tub and opened the cold water, and for the first time ever on a cold winter morning, I took a cold shower. No matter how hard I was trying not to scream, still I started to make some kind of sounds that were very strange, like "Bbbrrrrrrr! uuuuuu Oh boy! Yiiiii!"

After my first austerity in Krishna consciousness, I quickly put on my clothes and came out. As soon as they saw me, they smiled and invited me for breakfast. Actually, I felt wonderful. Although I felt a little cold, it was so refreshing taking a bath in the morning. I asked them, "Do you take a cold bath every day?"

"Oh yes! It's an essential part of our practice. You see, a cold bath opens the pores and gets you very clean externally. Also, it clears the mind and wakes you up, doesn't it?"

"Oh, yes," I said. "I noticed that!"

"One should take a cold bath every day and chant sixteen rounds of the Hare Krishna maha-mantra on his beads. If you want, we can make some beads for you today so that you can try it out and see what you think of mantra meditation."

"Yes," I replied, "I would like to try it out. I am very much interested in Indian philosophy, yoga, and mantra meditation."

After a delicious breakfast of hot cereal, fruit, and milk, as well as lots of leftovers from the past day, Senik invited me to meet the devotee who was at that time one of the leaders of the Krishna devotees in Armenia. We went into a room I hadn't been in yet, where I was introduced to a young man with a full beard who was still lying in his sleeping bag. Although he was young, his beard was large, and my immediate impression was that he was intelligent.

"This is Sannyasa das or Suren," said Senik. Then, Senik turned to him,

"And this is my best friend, Gago. I told you about him many times."

"Yes, I remember," Sannyasa replied. "It appears he appreciates it here very much, doesn't it?"

"Yes, sure! I have never been in such an interesting place before!" I replied.

"I'm sorry about last night," he told me. "Did the KGB write down your name?"

"Yes, they did."

"So, that means you are already one of us. You are a Hare Krishna devotee!"

"I do not mind," I said. All the devotees, including myself, started to laugh softly.

"But, the fact is—now these people will start to bother your family members."

"What about?" I asked.

"I really don't know, but that is the first thing these men do if they find out that we have new members. They will try to spoil the relationship between parents and relatives so they can do something to stop you coming here."

"Why?" I demanded.

"They think we are dangerous people for this Communist country. They know we are connected to ISKCON (the International Society for Krishna Consciousness), and because the zonal leader, Harikesa Swami Visnupada, is an American, they think we are part of the CIA, Central Intelligence Agency!"

"This is too much!" I said. "All you are doing all day long is chanting Hare Krishna and eating very healthy food which has no violence in it!"

"Yes, they are crazy, do not understand, don't listen to anything we say, and whatever the KGB orders the police to do, they do it and that's it."

So, we had a long conversation and he gave me some hand-made books and papers. Everything he told me was very pleasing and reasonable. Honestly, none of the points were new for me. But, there was one issue we could not agree upon, and we had a long argument. His point was that one should never take any drugs since they are very damaging to one's spiritual life. My point was, "You say that we should use everything for God's service; there is nothing wrong in using the same God's creation—green leaves and drugs—as well. Senik used to tell me on the way to Yerevan that Krishna says in Bhagavad- gita that if one offers Him a flower or a leaf with love and devotion, He will accept. So what's wrong with offering Him some leaf of that wonderful plant which can help one to be connected to the Lord? One can take hashish or marijuana and chant mantras with love and devotion. Drugs make a person very subtle and sensitive; they take one to a different dimension and bring one very close to God! You are trying to convince others to come here and take this philosophy very seriously, yes? You are offering it to them and trying to convince them; but if they do not try to chant Hare Krishna, how can they feel what you are feeling? Similarly, you should try to smoke some marijuana and then chant the mantra so you will feel the difference. Like last night I was chanting with the devotees under drugs and it was so nice and sweet. You just try it once and you can tell me then how you feel. I am trying what you are asking me to do. Why don't you try what I am saying, too? How can you tell the taste of a fruit without actually eating it?"

Sannyasa dasa told me, "Our spiritual, master, Srila Prabhupada, said, 'There is no need to take drugs to find your spiritual life; your spiritual life is already there.' Further, Srila Prabhupada describes that the seed of love of God is in our heart, and it needs to be watered in order to grow. The 'water' that nurtures love of God is devotional service to God. One has to know what Krishna, or God, wants. If you give Him what he wants, then that is service. If you develop a relationship with God, then when you serve Him it is devotional service. But you have to know what He wants or else one may be simply watering the seeds of material desires. There are many material desires in the heart, and they are different for everyone. One person may desire wealth and fame very much whereas another may desire peace and quiet, but they are all material desires."

"But," I asked, "who knows what Krishna wants? I don't know!"

"Yes," Sannyasa dasa said, "The real purpose of life is to contemplate and find the answer to that question. The perfection of life is to please God. So, you should study the revealed scriptures and you should also follow the instructions given there. If you are sincere, then Krishna will send his representative, the spiritual master, to guide you at every step. Srila Prabhupada gives this example—if one is diseased, then one must have a correct diet as well as medicine. Right? The expert physician says, 'Don't do certain activities; don't eat certain foods.' Srila Prabhupada said that the four pillars of sinful life are meat-eating, intoxication, illicit sex, and gambling. These are sinful acts; everyone knows that. They are not pleasing to Krishna, and engaging in these activities only makes us more diseased. Material attachment is an impurity, a contamination. So, we give these activities up. That is our diet, and soon we find that we have virtues that were previously covered by those sins. The virtues are mercy, austerity, cleanliness, and truthfulness. The medicine that destroys the sinful contamination and strengthens our basic human virtues is the chanting of the holy name of Krishna and engaging in devotional service. Further, Srila Prabhupada says that each time we take prasadam, the remnants of the food offered to Krishna, we become inoculated against the attack of material contamination."

"Wow!" I said. "Why not take prasadam all the time, then?"

"Yes," Sannyasa dasa said smiling, "that's what we are doing. The process that Krishna has given us in this age is simple, because now men are short-lived, unfortunate and, above all, always disturbed."

"That's for sure!" I agreed.

"Krishna says in the Bhagavad-gita, Chapter Nine, Verses Twenty-seven and Twenty-eight:

Srila Prabhupada said, "Everyone eats three times a day, so he can offer his food to Krishna and he will always be in Krishna consciousness!" It was a long argument, and soon many other devotees joined, some just to listen. Sometimes Kamalamala would contribute some succinct examples and try to preach to me strongly, as well.

"Srila Prabhupada taught us to remember Krishna before drinking water, even," Kamalamala said. "By saying 'Sri Vishnu' before drinking water, we remember that Krishna says in the Bhagavad-gita that He is the taste of the water. Srila Prabhupada said, 'If all that you do all day is for Krishna, you will even dream about Krishna!' It is important to remember Krishna at every moment, because if one thinks about Krishna at the time of death, then he is liberated and stays with Krishna in his eternal abode."

"How do I find the person who knows what Krishna wants?" I asked.

"That is a very important question. The Vedic literatures describe a three-fold test. It's simple—one should clearly see that what the guru teaches is the same as the teachings of the scriptures, called sastras, and you should observe the results of following these teachings in his life and the lives of his followers, the sadhus. This is called 'the guru-sastra-sadhu principle.'"

"The more I hear about it," I said, "the more it seems that there is so much to know! It must take a long time to learn all the rules and details!"

"Yes," Kamalamala said, "Srila Prabhupada gave the example that if one is searching for gold then he must know the qualities and the place to look for it. There must be gold somewhere, but if you do not know the qualities of gold, then I can show you anything, saying, 'Take it, this is gold.' You see? And how much more valuable is the pursuit of our relationship with Krishna, or God?"

The devotees then gave me a set of wooden beads for personal chanting, or japa, and a bag to keep the beads from getting dirty. I kept it in my hand constantly and became very attached to it. Senik and I were supposed to return to Meghri, so we warmly spoke to each other for some time and then said goodbye to everyone in the late afternoon. They gave us some prasadam to eat on the way. I felt as if I was going away from a place where I had spent hundreds of years, and I really missed the devotees as we made our way to Meghri.

# CHAPTER THREE

# Right Time for Decision

*Abandon all varieties of religion and just surrender unto Me.
I shall deliver you from all sinful reactions. Do not fear.*

*–Bhagavad-gita, 18.66*

I did not know what it was, but something had really changed in me. All the way from Yerevan to Meghri, I was wondering what to do. I admired these people from my heart, but there was still the problem of my attachment to drugs. I thought, "How is it possible to live without drugs?" This was the only issue and nothing else; everything else they said was absolutely perfect and acceptable. Whenever I read Srila Prabhupada's books, it seemed that Krishna was speaking just for me, answering all my questions one by one. But I had to question my belief in the benefits of taking drugs. "What about my friends? What will they think about me? If I tell them that I am no longer taking drugs, they will laugh at me! At least, they will be surprised and upset and cut their relationships with me. What about my family and relatives?" All these questions circled in my mind over and over again, and I felt very unhappy. Sometimes I was so much into these thoughts that I did not notice that I was actually speaking out loud, and Senik could hear me.

Anyways, as soon as I entered the doorway of my home, I saw my mother sitting and crying. She seemed happy to see me, but I did not understand why she was crying. I hugged my mom gently and asked her what was going on, and in reply she only told me, "Thank you."

"What for, Mom?"

"You know for what."

"Please tell me what happened, Mom."

"Nothing special. Thank you for sending the KGB to our house. Seven generations of our family have never seen police in their homes and doorsteps. Now, thank you, you are the first to make that arrangement."

"I did not make any arrangement, Mom. What are you talking about?"

"They came and searched our house. They checked everywhere and made a big mess. They said that you have become a member of a dangerous cult that is working under the CIA and if we do not stop you, then they will put you in jail."

"This is nonsense, Mom! What were they searching for?"

"I do not know—some religious and illegal books, or something like that."

"Did they take anything from my room?"

"Yes, some pictures and books about yoga, the old books you had before."

"I do not know what you or they are talking about! I was visiting some really nice people who all day long worship God and sing nice prayers. They do not eat any meat and would not cause any trouble even to an ant!"

"Senik took you to these rebellious men, and now the KGB has come to harass us because of him!"

"No, Mom, they are not at all spoiled and rebellious! They are very nice people! They are even against drugs, and none of them are taking any drugs. Even I am thinking of giving them up too."

My mother's face changed right away, and she even stopped crying for a moment. It was a major issue for her and for my whole family—they had tried every way to convince me to stop taking drugs before with no results.

"So, now you are no longer taking drugs?" she asked.

"Well, I threw all that I had in the toilet after they explained to me that Krishna does not allow His devotees to take drugs."

"Who is Krishna?"

"Krishna is the Supreme Personality of Godhead."

"I never heard His name and I do not want to hear it again. All we know is Jesus, and that's all!"

"Yes, Krishna is the father of Jesus, as he says in the Bible, "I and my father are one." He was meaning Krishna. Krishna is the father."

It took me hours and hours to discuss all I had learned in the last two days. Later on, my father and my brother and his wife came, and I had to repeat all the Krishna philosophy that I knew again and again to them. I was exhausted. I could see that no one was happy, and I was sure that I could not live in their house any more, seeing their suffering every day. But at the same time, I did not know what to do and didn't want to just leave them. After all, I really loved my family and considered them as good, pious people. For example, I have never seen my father drunk or smoking a cigarette. Although they did not believe much in God, or at least never discussed anything about God in front of me, still they were very pious people in a general sense.

Every day, Senik told me that almost all the devotees were having the same problem with their family members as I was. "So it is normal for them not to be able to understand what you are saying or doing. It is sad here without devotees," he said. I felt that Senik was reading my mind perfectly. I could not say a word. My tears were stuck somewhere in my throat. I just nodded my head; I do not know how many times. I was feeling like a fish out of the water. I just nodded my head and remained silent.

"Do not worry," he said to me, putting his hand on my shoulder, "One day, I am sure you will go and stay with the other devotees forever. Just try to chant the Hare Krishna maha-mantra on your beads as much as you can, and Krishna will help you to make decisions so you will find your way out."

So that's what I did for a few more weeks while I was waiting for my good friend Sako to come back from the army. Kamalamala had told me that I should not even eat food cooked in the pots in which meat had been previously cooked, so I started to cook my own food in new pots. I had new problems with my parents because of my doing that. Everything started to become strained and unpleasant at home. My mother was very upset, feeling very offended that I was not eating any food she cooked or sitting with them for meals. Sometimes I had the problem of fasting if I didn't like what I had cooked, since I wasn't so expert with this new diet.

When Sako finally came back, it changed the situation a little bit because we were so very happy to see each other! We and our friends had a party, and then a fun time together for several days. We were taking drugs together, but I was not in the same mood as before. I could not avoid feeling that taking drugs was sinful. When Sako asked me what was wrong, I told him everything about my new friends and all that had happened. He was very happy to hear about the philosophy and ideas, but just like me, he was very sad that all the Hare Krishna devotees were against drugs.

"Is there any way we can take drugs but at the same time be Hare Krishna devotees?" he asked.

"That's what I was also thinking, and I have tried very hard to do that," I said. "In fact, in my opinion, these Hare Krishna devotees are very stubborn people and very egoistic. They are preaching to everyone to eat the fruit and then judge the taste, but when I offered them to taste the drugs once at least, they have refused. They simply told me that in the book it already says drugs are bad, so why do we have to try it out."

I told him that despite my quarrel with their prohibiting drugs, there are so many agreeable aspects of Krishna consciousness with only this one problem, so it is better than anything else I've found. I told him that I was just waiting for him to see if he wanted to join me in this. At first, he told me that he wanted to be where I am, but when I told him that I am serious about giving up drugs, he thought it would be better if he waited and thought about it a little more.

I then told him that I had an idea about going and staying there in the temple with the devotees forever, and asked him what he thought about it. He hung his head and didn't say anything. He was very sad and kept smoking during all our conversations. I could see that we were going through difficulties in our life leading to some important decisions. It was a cold evening, and we decided to go home without making any final decision. Yet while we told each other "Good night" and separated, both of us were upset, either with each other or with the whole situation.

After spending a few more days together like this, finally one day I told him that I had decided to go to Yerevan to the devotees. I asked if he had made up his mind. He told me that he thought that he would probably never give up marijuana, so it would be better if he didn't even try to live with the devotees. I asked him to at least visit them once just to see what it was like, but he was not inclined. So we embraced each other, tearfully saying goodbye.

After coming home, I started to prepare myself for the next day's trip to Yerevan. I was trying to take only whatever I considered nearest and dearest to my heart, but it ended up being too much luggage. I finally got down to one suitcase full of clothes and my personal necessities. At 12:30 am, I was lying down and thinking about all that had happened between me and my best friend, while smoking cigarettes in my room. Sometimes, tears ran down my cheeks, and I wanted to scream. I turned on the tape player, loudly playing George Harrison's "My Sweet Lord" so no one from upstairs could hear me crying. After a while, someone knocked on my door. "Who would be coming here at this hour?" I thought, because usually even my parents would not come to my room, even if my lights were on.

After quickly drying my eyes with a towel, I rushed to open the door. Sako was standing in front of me with a big smiling face, completely intoxicated! He looked at me and said loudly, "You know, I just realized that I cannot be without you! We were such good friends for so long and now we will allow Satan to separate us from each other? I came to realize that I'll come with you, wherever you are going!" He came in and embraced me with his long arms and started crying.

"I think I have to come at least to see those devotees once in my life; then I will know what to do, is that OK with you?"

We were ready to go the next morning. We did not tell anyone where and why we were going. All day while we were traveling, we discussed how we could please, or at least not offend, our relatives, while at the same time being devotees, but unfortunately we could not find any solution. When we arrived, I was very happy to introduce my friend, who I called by his formal name, Sarkis, to all the devotees. Everyone liked him from the very first contact, and I was feeling proud both that I was the one who brought him to them, and that I was so-called senior to him. It was the first time I felt how my false ego was screaming at me. I could not even hide my feelings and was thinking that the entire world now would come to know all my feelings. I left the room and went to the bathroom to look in the mirror to see if my face had turned red from my pride.

Sannyasa dasa was talking to Sako about the four regulative principles in the evening, and I was thinking, "Now Sako will use the same arguments that I did to support the use of drugs." But he started to say things that he had never told me before, such as that he agreed with everything the devotees said and how he saw a connection between himself, Krishna, and His devotees. He said that he was willing to give up drugs that very day and stay there with them, serve Krishna, and learn more about devotional life. My eyes opened wide as I could not believe what I was hearing!

That night, as we were preparing to sleep, I asked him if he was serious about what he had said to Sannyasa das. He told me that this is what he has been searching for all his life. In fact, he felt he had been searching for Krishna consciousness for many lifetimes already, and was happy to have finally found it.

"I am very grateful to you," he told me," for bringing me here. You saved my life."

I had no more questions to ask him. I knew very well that if he says something then he will surely do it. We were there for more than a week together, doing all kinds of devotional service and chanting with devotees, but my mind was at home with my parents, wondering how they felt and so on. During kirtana and service, I would forget everything about my other life. But as soon as I was free, I would start to think about all kinds of attachments. These thoughts created problems that appeared to be big obstacles in my devotional life. Sometimes I would even feel extremely sad.

Some of the devotees chanted Hare Krishna very blissfully on their beads, and some of them were falling asleep while chanting. It was funny to see how some devotees were trying to conquer their sleep but couldn't. They woke up and chanted from time to time and would then slowly hang their heads in sleep, an affliction they called "nodding out." I felt sorry for them; it meant they were working day and night with not enough rest.

I was considering that waking up every morning so early is the topmost austerity and was thinking that I would never be able to do so.

I started to think of drugs, my friends who liked to take drugs with me, and "How can I give up their friendship?" and so on. I started to think of Sako, as well. "If I go back to Meghri, then how will he feel, or what will his parents do to me?"

Then, as if he was reading my mind, he came to my room. He placed his hand on my shoulder and asked me softer than ever, "Are you ready to give your life to Krishna?" I did not understand why he was asking me that, but one point I was sure of—he had found something valuable that he would never give up.

I said, "I have to think about it. I actually have some important business to do in our town, so I am thinking of going back for a while. I'll be back. Do you want to come with me?"

"No, I'll be waiting for you here. Please come back, and if you do not mind, please give this letter to my parents. He handed me an envelope with bold letters on it saying:

"PLEASE CHANT HARE KRISHNA AND BE HAPPY!"

It was obvious that he took Krishna consciousness very seriously and he was advancing very steadily. I pictured him climbing up the spiritual staircase very fast.

# CHAPTER FOUR

# On the Way to Krishna

*That which in the beginning may be just like poison but at the end
is just like nectar and which awakens one to self-realization
is said to be happiness in the mode of goodness.*

*–Bhagavad-gita, 18.37*

I was very sad to go back to my parent's home, but I did not want to
start my spiritual life with cheating. I was having trouble waking up
early in the morning, taking a cold shower every day, and chanting
the mantra for such a long time. Sometimes it took me much longer
than two and a half hours to chant my sixteen rounds. I was having a
hard time concentrating my mind, so I felt that I was not ready yet to stay
with devotees. But when I was back with my parents, I started missing the
devotees intensely.

My parents were very unhappy with me and tried to make some
arrangement for me to start working somewhere. They were thinking that
if I started working, it might help me to stay away from "trouble." They were
still afraid that ISKCON was connected somehow to the CIA. Anyhow, they
convinced me to find employment, but I did not have any real interest in
the job. I was constantly thinking of Krishna and devotees and feeling as if
I had done something very wrong by leaving them.

Sometimes I would go alone to the abandoned church at night, which
was almost as dirty as before, and there, where I was certain no one except
God could hear me, I would cry very loudly. I would burn some candles and
pray to God to show me a right path that I could follow constantly.

I brought Sako's letter to his parents one evening and found that his
parents were very upset with me. They blamed me for taking their son

away from them and so on. His dad told me that if it had not been for me, then Sako would never have left them at all, so I was in big trouble. Soon, everyone in Meghri was looking at me strangely, which served to increase my need to be with the devotees and leave my home town as soon as possible. I did not have anything to talk about with my old friends, and I also did not know how to preach to them.

In one sentence, I was struggling without Krishna and His devotees. The devotees had given me some tapes and pictures, which became my life and daily meditation. Although I was absorbed in Krishna and guru meditation, at the same time I could not give up drugs and smoking habits. From time to time, I would visit my friends and have some so-called fun, but I was always thinking of Krishna and was never satisfied with them or their company. I called the temple sometimes and once spoke to Sako, who was very happy and inspired. He asked me when I was planning to come back. By then it had been about a month since I had left him with the devotees.

The next time I called him, he said, "Please just cut all your attachments and come stay here with us. It is so nice here! This life is temporary. Please come and let's serve Krishna together. We have been always together! What are you searching for in this lifetime? Whatever benefits you desire to achieve are right here!"

I asked him how he is feeling without drugs for such a long time. He replied, "O my God, I had completely forgotten about it until you said something! Krishna is amazing, and He can make wonderful changes in our lives! Come and stay with us if it is possible! It is so nice with the devotees' association. Hare Krishna." That was the end of the conversation.

I did not want to hang up the phone, but at the same time I had nothing more to tell him. I can never forget his words, so sweet, so serious and so warm! They made me think a lot about the direction my life was taking. I knew that I had to make some very serious decisions as soon as possible.

It did not take a long time for me to decide what to do; everything was working towards Krishna's direction. All the roads were leading to Krishna only. After some more days, I wrote a long letter to my parents, packed my bag for the last time, and left my home to go to the temple, to the devotees of Krishna. I did not give any notice to my office.

This time, moving in with the devotees was even better because I already knew many of them. Everybody was very happy to see me back there. They gave me some prasadam to eat and asked me how I had been doing in the past weeks. Sako was not there, because he had gone for the day to distribute the sacred books to the public.

"We just printed thousands of new flyers about a Srila Harikesa Swami lecture which we are distributing all over. It is in the Russian language so we can distribute it all over Soviet territory as well." They told me that Sako was doing great and progressing a lot in his Krishna consciousness. I was very happy to hear that.

I asked them if it was okay to stay with them, and they said that they would be very happy to have me there. I asked if I could do some service for Krishna, and they gave me a pile of flyers to fold. As I sat on the floor in the temple room, collating and folding the papers, I was intensely remembering everything I knew about Srila Prabhupada bringing Krishna consciousness to Russia.

[Please see the appendix for a summary of Prabhupada's activities in Russia.]

# CHAPTER FIVE

# My New Lifestyle

*Whatever action a great man performs, common men follow.*
*And whatever standards he sets by exemplary acts,*
*all the world pursues.*

*–Bhagavad-gita, 3.21*

When Sako came back from book distribution, he was extremely happy to see me there and embraced me, calling out, "Haribol! Haribol! Finally, you came back to home, my brother! So, this time we won't let you leave. You already know what maya is and what Krishna is! Now, find out what is reality!" I was thinking I would have a long discussion with my best friend, but he told me that it would be better if we went to bed early, so we could wake up on time for mangala aratika. I could see a lot of changes in him and his behavior right away, and I was amazed to see how well he was relating with the devotees. He was so natural and happy. I felt happy for him, too.

The next day, after doing some different services, such as washing pots in the kitchen and mopping the temple room floor, he packed his bag with the flyers I had folded the day before and was about to go out. He looked at me, smiling, and asked if I would go out with him for distribution. I was already thinking of somehow going out to smoke a cigarette anyways, and did not know what to tell the devotees or how to find some reason for going out. So this was a good opportunity, and I agreed to it right away.

As soon as we went out I started to smoke a cigarette. But I felt ashamed to smoke in front of my friend with whom I have smoked all my life, and who just a month ago was smoking with me and never even thinking of giving it up.

I expected him to say something to me about it, but to my surprise he pretended that he did not notice. Of course I was also trying very hard to blow the smoke to the opposite direction towards the wind so it wouldn't touch his nose. After we got on the bus, he took some papers out of his bag and offered them to a young man. The man agreed to take them. He then told me about some basics of distribution and gave me some of the flyers. One of the small books, or flyers, that we had was the transcript of Srila Prabhupada's talk with Professor Kotovsky in 1975. That little text was immensely popular in the then Soviet Union, and it greatly enhanced our credibility as well as improving Professor Kotovsky's reputation.

"It is very easy!" Sako said. "Just pray to Krishna, and He will give you some intelligence to distribute His literature and glory!"

So, I tried it and it worked. The first time in my life I offered a book to a young university student, he took it happily. But the second man read a little bit and then threw it in my face. He told me the Hare Krishnas are crazy and one of his relatives had taken to Krishna consciousness. He shouted, "And he is a totally crazy man—he is not eating meat, eggs, and fish, not even alcohol! What kind of madness is that? God created everything for us to enjoy, and this stupid guy is saying that he cannot eat with his friends!" I felt miffed but did not lose my enthusiasm from the first man, and I continued to distribute more. After some time, Sako came to see how I was doing and told me that it is better if we go to the large buildings and fill up all the mailboxes with flyers. We would meet later.

It took me several weeks to completely stop smoking cigarettes and using drugs, and become a regular devotee, if I can call it that. I would wash my hands well after a cigarette so the devotees would not know about it. But, no matter what I did, they knew but somehow tolerated me for a while. I was happy to be there and was slowly progressing, which according to them was very pleasing to guru and Krishna.

I started to like devotional life and service. The 3:30 am alarm was no longer annoying, and I started to wake up on time and take a cold shower every day with pleasure. I could never have imagined that life could be so simple and blissful. Sleeping on the floor was also no problem for me. I felt so much better than before. Sitting on the floor to study or eat was also kind of fun, too.

Almost everyday we used to do some flyer distribution in a nearby city and then have a wonderful meal. What I mostly appreciated there was that devotees were extremely clean and humble. After finishing each small task on a kitchen table, they would clean it right away and wash their hands. They would also clean the floor after eating or any work. They would wash their clothes every day. So I quickly adopted all these good habits. They became part of my life, part of my nature. Soon this way of life became so natural that I could not imagine how previously I could have lived without a bath every day.

The only problem I had now was that I did not want the police to disturb my parents, but it was practically impossible because my name and address were already on the black list. Two or three months after I moved into the temple, I heard that police were starting to arrest devotees and put them in jail in Russia. We were told by Sannyasa and Kamalamala that we had to be extra careful and pray every day for our brothers and sisters who were in trouble. We were informed that among the arrested members was the first Russian devotee who took initiation from Srila Prabhupada, Ananta Shanti dasa. Also arrested were some of the first initiated disciples of Harikesa Swami, such as Japa dasa, Sucharu dasa, Vrindavan dasa, Premavati devi dasi, who was pregnant at that time, and many others.

At the same time, I could see that instead of the devotees becoming like turtles that hide in pools, everyone became tigers starting to print and distribute even more flyers and books. One day after distribution, all the devotees were very happy. There was lots of prasadam. Everybody looked as if they were celebrating something. We asked Atmananda what was going on and he happily told us that we had to go to the temple room and see what was on the altar. We quickly went inside and saw two beautiful books in front of the pictures of present and past gurus. One was the Russian Bhagavad-gita and another one Coming Back in Armenian. We looked at them and started to call out loudly "Hare Krishnaaaaaa!" I asked Sannyasa dasa if I could look at them, but he told me that these were the only copies and we must be very careful with them. He said, "We just got these from Harikesa Swami and they should be used as originals from which to print more. So it is better if we do not touch them and possibly leave any fingerprints on the pages or pictures."

I was a little bit sad, but he looked at me and said, "Do not worry, Gago, soon we will have hundreds of thousands of these books, and instead of flyers we will distribute Srila Prabhupada's books all over the Soviet Union!" I then thought about the incident with yogi Karen who wouldn't let me touch his copy of the very first Gita in English. This time I was forbidden for practical reasons, not because I was too sinful to touch it.

"When will we have them?" I asked him.

"Soon," he replied. "Very soon."

Every day Sannyasa das would go out with his briefcase and return back late afternoon or evening. I could clearly see his anxiety and desire to print Srila Prabhupada's books for distribution. Sometimes he would not speak much but we could see that he was working very hard and mentally was very much disturbed. I guess he was always praying to Krishna so that He would make all the necessary arrangements and remove all the obstacles from his path for printing and distributing books. In a few weeks, Sannyasa brought us the first printed pages of the Gita. We tried to see if everything had been done properly. After that he taught us how to fold, and we all sat down to fold all the pages in order to make a book. We applied glue to the side of the set of pages, pressed it into the cover, and placed it under some heavy suitcases next to the heater so that it would dry quickly. After some time, it was dried, and Sannyasa marked it with a pencil cutting line. He then started to cut the extra papers with a razor blade and metal ruler.

Soon our first hand-made book was ready. Armen wanted to open and read from it, but Atmananda grabbed it from his hand and told him that we have to first offer it to guru and Krishna, then only could we see it ourselves. So after placing it on the altar, we started a nice kirtana. It was an ecstatic and unusual kirtana. At that time I didn't realize the full significance of what was going on in that little room on the ninth floor and what a very special sacrifice I was participating in. After many years, I understood that we were actually founding a powerful mission in the USSR. I did not know at that time that these books would make a revolution and that after only ten to fifteen years there would be hundreds of temples and thousands of Krishna devotees in the Soviet Union just because of these small handmade books.

After the kirtana, Sannyasa took the book from the altar, opened it, and started to examine the quality with a large smile. We all took turns looking at it and reading a little bit from it. Afterward, he told us that this was just the beginning. He promised that in the future he would make better quality books with the help of certain hand operated equipment he would bring.

In the process of making the books, we noticed that one of the most interesting qualities of Sako was that he would utilize anything and everything for Krishna's service. He was very careful with all kinds of waste and would check out everything before throwing it into the trash can. For example, one day he started to collect paper dust from the books. When we cut the pages with a hacksaw before binding and threading to keep the book pages together, bits of paper dust, very much like sawdust, were produced. Everyone was curious about how he could possibly use this dust or shavings from the pages and covers. Sometimes devotees would talk about him when he wasn't present, and made jokes about him. So now, everyone wanted to know what he was doing with the paper dust, but for a long time no one was successful. It was not so easy to figure out what was in Sako's mind.

But one day, finally, Ivan (Haridas Thakur das) caught him in the kitchen while he was putting the dust in his dahl soup bowl. Ivan laughed loudly, joking with Sako. "Hey, everybody, I caught him! I caught him! Now, I know what he is doing with the dust! Ha ha ha!" Everyone was curious to know about the news. Vardan (Nityananda Ram das) and I went to the kitchen to see what was going on there. Sako was standing there, hanging his head with embarrassment and holding a plastic bag full of dust from the books on his hand. Everyone started to make a joke and was teasing him. Sako just took his bowl, sat in a corner of the room, and started to eat his meal.

Ivan asked him why he was doing that, and Sako simply replied, "All this dust is coming from the Bhagavad-gita and some other of Srila Prabhupada's books, so if the books are holy, then the dust produced from the books is holy, too. So I decided that it would be better if we utilized it somehow or other."

Everyone was laughing and teasing him. Kamalamala told him, "I hope you aren't regularly mixing the holy dust in a big pot and feeding all of us!" Sannyasa was curious to know if he was mixing it in the food before offering it to Krishna.

This was a time in the Soviet devotees' history that one could expect anything and everything from new devotees. It was common for members to come up with some strange idea such as putting book dust in one's meal. As we were all new devotees, we just had to trust that "Krishna will rectify our mistakes in time." Sako humbly tolerated all the teasing of the devotees and continued his wonderful service to Krishna every day.

I remember even a worse case happened during Harikesa Swami's first visit to Russia. One devotee raised his hand and asked him what to do if after offering some fruits there were found to be some worms inside. Since we had already offered it, that means it has become prasadam, so shall we eat them or throw away?

I remember Harikesha Swami was holding his head and didn't know what to answer for several minutes and laughing and laughing. Then he screamed loudly "No, please do not eat them; just throw them away. We are vegetarians, and we don't eat worms."

Once, there was a period when all the devotees were staying in the apartment of a devotee named Yura. He was a lawyer who had fancy furniture as well as very expensive and rare books on his book shelf.

Every day after breakfast, when Sachisuta, would pack his shoulder bag and go out for distribution, we noticed that he was taking some of Yura's books from the bookshelf with him. We asked him what he was doing with the books and he told us that he was taking them to the black market, where they are buying and selling all kinds of books. He was giving the money he got for them, along with the money he made from the distribution of Srila Prabhupada's books, to Sannyasa dasa for the printing of more books. He told us that he would prefer that Yura didn't know about it, because Yura was still attached to material things and might feel bad about it. He said, "But, since I am selling his books and using the money for Krishna's service, Yura will progress in his spiritual life automatically! By the time he comes to know about it, I'll have sold a lot of his books and he will be very happy for it!"

Soon Yura noticed that the top shelf appeared to be a little barer every day. He looked at it carefully and found out that there were a lot of important books that were missing. He asked all the devotees if anyone knew anything about it. We all knew about it, but no one told him, because we figured out that it would be better if Sako would explain it himself. When Sachisuta came back from book distribution, Yura called him to the balcony and started to question him about the books. Sachisuta told him the truth and apologized many times. He asked Yura to forgive him for selling his books without his permission. We were all watching the scene from behind the curtains and, honestly speaking, we all were expecting Yura to get very angry. We all knew his nature. He would even complain about a small thing that we would do wrong in his apartment. But to our surprise, he hung his head and said something soft to Sachisuta that we could not hear. After some time, Yura stood up and embraced Sachisuta, patting his back in a friendly way. He just told Sachisuta to stop doing it and ask before taking anything from his apartment. We were happy that he did not chastise Sachisuta heavily since we all loved him very much for his simplicity.

After a while, Yura came in, shaking his head. Smiling, he told everyone, "Oh my God, that Sako (Sachisuta) is trying to make me a pure devotee of Krishna!" Everyone was laughing and making jokes about him and Sachisuta, and suggesting that Yura should check Sachisuta's bags before he goes out for book distribution.

Every day we started to read directly Lord Krishna's words and get more enthusiasm for distributing Srila Prabhupada's books. One day we saw a strange sight. "What is that commotion over there, Sachisuta? There's a crowd of excited people outside the church."

"That's the Communist Party. They are recruiting everywhere. Srila Prabhupada spoke about this when he was here. He said the Communists say to the poor, 'So, Comrade, good morning, I see you have been to the church. Did you pray to God for your daily bread? And did you get bread? I have a truck full of bread! Take as much as you want! Now, who is better—God or the Communist Party?' Of course, the poor, hungry man says, 'Oh, you are, O Communist brother!' "

"This is incredible!" I said. "Such nerve!"

"Yes, Srila Prabhupada said that the people should ask, 'You rascal! Where did you get this bread? Can you produce wheat? No, without rain and the soil you cannot produce grains. So, actually, Krishna is supplying bread for everyone and therefore the Communist Party is a group of thieves!' "

"We cannot speak boldly; what can we do?"

"Srila Prabhupada gave us a program; it is the same program that is used in temples around the world—we rise early and concentrate on our spiritual strength through classes, meditation, and association. Then we open our association to everyone. They may join us or practice Krishna consciousness in their homes. To attract them, Srila Prabhupada has shown us how to distribute wonderful Krishna prasadam, foodstuffs offered to Krishna, and how to purify the cities by sweetly singing the holy names in the town square, and he has written many scholarly books for us to study and distribute.

"We have strong public support, but the Communist Party is trying to stop us from preaching. Sometimes, they say that we are disturbing the peace or that we are crazy. They say that we do not have proper permits and do not represent a bona-fide religion, and on and on. The obstacles to our establishing a far-reaching organization here are seemingly insurmountable, but I'm not worried about it! Srila Prabhupada told us that it is Lord Caitanya's desire that this chanting will be heard in every town and village in the whole world.

"Srila Bhaktivinode Thakur, one of the past spiritual masters, envisioned Krishna consciousness being spread worldwide. He even said that there would come a day when the high court judges of the Supreme Court would wear the clay tilak markings, which symbolize dedication of the body to Krishna, on their forehead. He predicted that devotees from all parts of the world would converge on Lord Caitanya's birthplace, Sri Mayapur Dhama, and chant Hare Krishna together. His son, Srila Bhaktisiddhanta Saraswati, inspired our spiritual master Srila A. C. Bhaktivedanta Prabhupada to fulfill that vision. Srila Prabhupada acquired land in Mayapur and built a temple, and his disciples come every year to Sri Mayapur to chant together! 'Success is inevitable,' Srila Prabhupada said, adding 'If you like, you can take the credit.' "

"All glories to Srila Prabhupada!" I shouted.

# CHAPTER SIX

# My First Arrest

*After many births and deaths, he who is actually in knowledge*
*surrenders unto Me, knowing Me to be the cause of all causes*
*and all that is. Such a great soul is very rare.*
*–Bhagavad-gita, 7.19*

"**B**ooks are the basis," Prabhupada had said. Every day, morning and evening, we used to hear in the classes that book distribution is our most important business. Any new devotee would figure out within seconds that book distribution was the only issue he really had to think about.

Soon, Sannyasa filled a room full of printed pages of Bhagavad- gita, and everybody was busy folding them and turning them into hundreds of bound copies of Srila Prabhupada's teachings. It was ecstatic to see how our first book came out of that room and was sold right across the street. It was a hard but lovely job. We were all trying our best and creating new techniques to do it faster, easier, and better. We had a line of people, and each one was doing one operation. Sannyasa was telling us that we should all learn each step of the operation perfectly so that if one devotee was not there, the others could do his part.

We could understand his mind well. He meant that if one devotee got arrested, then the others could carry on. We were trying not to speak too much about this subject, but at the same time, it was impossible to avoid it. Almost every day the police would catch some devotees, beat them up, take all the books, and then free them after hours or days.

No one said it, but everyone was thinking that he or she might be the next one to be arrested. I was thinking in that way also. "What if they catch me? What am I going to do? What will I tell them?"

After a while, we created stories that we had to be ready to tell to the police in case they happened to catch us during book distribution. One of the stories was that we found these books in the railway station. Someone dropped them there, we found them, saw that they were nice books, and so started to give them away. We were not supposed to tell them that we were selling them, or they would be able to arrest us for illegal sales on the street.

We were going through a kind of training. Day by day, it was becoming more intense. Therefore some devotees started to go home and hardly ever come to the temple. No one really wanted to be arrested, but at the same time, we had lots of books to produce and sell.

We also seriously needed money, so different devotees started to give donations for book production. Some of the girls, such as Armine (Damayanti devi dasi) and Gayane (Gaganeshi devi dasi) donated their gold jewelry and some savings they had. I had sold all my personal books and also earned some money for printing books and our living. Others sold valuables and gave the money to Sannyasa dasa. He was the one who was taking care of the money and spending it strictly only for books.

After some time, we celebrated the production of the first Armenian translation of Srila Prabhupada's book called Coming Back. It was sensational news for all of us. We were all so happy that Armenia was the second of fifteen republics, after Russia, who had Prabhupada's books translated and printed in their own language.

It was a small book and was not as difficult as Bhagavad-gita to fold and bind, so we were moving faster. We were selling them faster as well, since they were less expensive. Sannyasa found a way to make a beautiful photo cover for it, and Sashik (Shyamakunda dasa) was the one who was expertly printing the covers at home and supplying them to us. Because of the beautiful cover and attractive inside picture, in addition to it being in the local language, it was much easier than the Russian Gita to distribute in Armenia.

We had good-natured competitions to see who could distribute the most books for the day. Sometimes we would go out with our bags full of books, come back with lots of money, eat, and go back out to the field again. It was interesting and blissful to meet people on the street who really were waiting for those books. Soon we became so expert that just by a glance we would know who would take a book and who would not.

When I first started distributing books, I would sometimes be brought to meet people who were re-typing the books out with carbon paper to make four copies. They would be doing this in a secret room because in Armenia you could not own a typewriter or a photocopier openly unless you had a special permit, which was not easy to obtain. And they were typing very slowly with one or two fingers. When I asked them what they were doing, they would say, "So many people asked me if they could borrow this book, but I didn't want to lend it out because who knows when I would get it back. So, I am making four copies."

I would say, "Why didn't you just ask for more?"

Their jaw would drop, and they would say, "There's more?!" as if they never thought that there would be more!

Another time, a man came up to me and gave me some money. One said, "We heard that in the future you will be publishing Sri Isopanisad in Russian. So when you do, you make sure that we get a copy."

"But ..." I said, "Who knows when that will be. It may be years!"

"So," they said, "we have waited for so long already for the Gita, and we will wait little more for the other one. You just make sure that when you do, we get a copy." They then left after giving me an address and phone number.

Soon, some Russian devotees came to us—Mamu Thakur, Bharadvaja, Yamaraja, Sanaka and others. The association of advanced older devotees would encourage us to try to become more spiritually serious. They were so happy to see that in this little country of Armenia we were able to print those important books successfully. They brought lots of money and encouraged Suren (Sannyasa das) to print more and more in order to send some books to them. They would regularly come and stay with us for a day or two and go back with lots of books. They would bring some new letters from Harikesa Swami or Kirtiraja das, tapes and records of lectures or devotional singing, some new tapes or records of Srila Prabhupada, and so on. Even their bringing incense was a huge encouragement at that time for us, since it was not so easy to find it in the former USSR.

Soon after that, we started to send books to Russia by post. For some time it worked out well, until the KGB found out about it. They made a new rule that a package of more than a certain size and weight was subject to inspection.

Then we started to smuggle books out of Armenia in trucks. We contacted people who brought goods to Armenia and took other materials back to Russia. We were able to contact them in their parking garage and pay them some cash to transport many boxes of books out of Armenia. It was a risk for them. But money was talking, so they knew how to hide our boxes in the front of the truck behind other goods. Sometimes they would give us boxes that were the same as those used for their cargo so we would fill them up with books and no one would know what was in there. Sometimes we would give books to the drivers too, and explain the philosophy to them so they would know what a valuable service they were doing for Lord Krishna.

One morning after breakfast, I went out for book distribution and did not return until the next day. I did not spend the night at some friend's home or anything such as that; I just accidentally offered a book to one man on the street who happened to be a KGB agent. He took the book and started to look at it, asking how much I was selling it for, and so on. He started to ask many more questions, which made me start to feel that something was fishy, but I did not know what to do. I was thinking it would be better if I ran away, but what about the book? I did not want to let the book go for free, so I started to answer all his questions with some tricks. But he wasn't satisfied. He wanted to know where we were printing the books and so on. It was very clear that I had met the wrong person early in the morning. Unfortunately he took out his police identification and asked me to follow him. Then I decided to run away, but he expertly caught my hand and warned me not to run, showing me his gun. At that point, I had no choice but to follow him to the nearest police station.

As soon as we entered the building, he handed me over to two men who were standing there as if they had been waiting for us. He told them to check me out and search me before he came back. So they took me to a room and asked me to take out everything I had on me, which I did. One of them started to take out all the books and money I had in my bag.

"Why are you here?" one asked.

"I do not know," I replied.

"Oh, you don't know? What are these books about?"

"They are about God," I told him. "They are nice books. You can have one if you want to."

"What will I do with them?"

"You can read them," I replied. "They are so nice and important."

"What they will give me?

"Knowledge," I said.

"Ha! What do I need knowledge for? All I need is money!"

"No, that is not enough!" I exclaimed." You should know about your relationship with God as well!"

"How much are you selling them for?"

"I am not selling them," I told him. "I am just giving them away. Whoever wants them, takes and reads them. It is wonderful isn't it?"

"Where, then, did you get this much money?"

"That is my money, "I told him. " I was planning to go to the market and do some shopping."

"Okay, that is enough for now. Let's go."

"Where?" I asked, very surprised.

"We do not have time, you know. Place your hands behind your back and follow me."

This was the first time that I was made to walk with my hands behind my back. I had only seen this kind of imposition in the movies, and just a year ago I would never have believed that one day I would be treated in that way, too!

"O Krishna," I was thinking, "please help me to get out of this situation! What am I doing here? Please help me!"

I started to chant the maha-mantra in my mind while walking. I could hear someone screaming and crying loudly from some room. It was clear that some police officer was beating up someone for some crime. I was worried and was praying, "O Krishna, where am I? Why did you bring me to this hell? Please help me get out of here as soon as possible! Please!"

They took me to a room that was as narrow as a telephone booth and locked me up. I was trying to ask what would happen next, and how long would I have to stay there, but they just pushed me in and locked the door. It was dark there, and damp too. At first, I was standing, but after some time I got tired and sat down on the wet floor. I kept chanting and praying constantly, and because they took my watch, I did not know what time it was or how long I had spent sitting in that room.

Anyhow, my mind was working very fast. Sometimes I thought of going home to my parents, sometimes to the devotees. Sometimes I thought I smelled wonderful prasadam. I also thought about my sleeping bag, and I wished that I had it now. After such intense thinking, I fell asleep and did not know how long it was before someone opened the door and said extremely loudly, "Buniatyan Gagik! Now it is your turn to come out!"

My eyes were hurting from the bright light from the room so it took me some time to realize where I was and who was in front of me. "Come out, priest. Someone is waiting for you."

So I started to move slowly while thinking, "What will happen now?" I was walking through a long corridor and chanting in my mind. Soon, the officer opened one door, pushed me in, told two other policemen in that room that I was to do what they asked me to do, and closed the door. One of the men was very fat and ugly; another one was skinny and smiling at me. That is usually the tactic of the police; later on I became very familiar with it. One is beating you up, and another one is gently asking questions. They asked me to sit and tell them what I was doing there.

I told them that I really do not know why I was there and would like to know why it is wrong if I have a book and offer it to others, when the book is not about anything but God. We had a long conversation, and I answered hundreds of different questions. They recorded everything on paper, having me sign each page. I was trying as much as possible to give them false information, so they could not figure out where the books actually came from.

Suddenly the fat man got very angry and stood up. He kicked over my chair and I fell on the floor and hurt myself badly. He started to kick me several times while pulling me up by my hair.

"Okay, all you told and wrote is okay. Now tell me where you got these books from and you are free to go home, "he said.

"I told you everything, sir," I replied to him.

"No, no, no, that is a joke! Now we are not joking any more, as you see."

He hit me once more and I felt my mouth filling up with blood. My face was burning hot. I was sitting on the floor shaking and wondering what to do now and what would be next. The soft-spoken man came to me and started to ask me how I was feeling, and so on. The other man came and wanted to kick me more, but he held him back and asked him to get out of the room, which he did, cursing me with his last words and offending me any way he could.

"Would you like to wash yourself?" he asked me.

"Yes, of course," I replied.

"Go ahead," he said. "The bathroom is there." He pointed to the door. I staggered into the bathroom and started to wash my face, looking around to see if there was any chance to run away, but it was not at all possible. All the windows had iron bars. So I came back to him again after some time.

"I know," he said, "you do not want to tell us where the books are coming from but you see this man? He will beat you to death! Please consider carefully. It is always better to tell the truth and go home."

"I told you that I have told everything I know and there is nothing more to tell!" I declared as firmly as I could.

After some time he told me, "This time I am going to tell them to set you free, but the next time you are brought here I won't be able to do anything for you, okay? My advice is that if you don't give these books to others, then you can do whatever you want in your home. Sing and get as mad as you want at your home, but do not do that anywhere else, and no one else should know about it." He asked me to sign some other papers, then told me that I was free and could go.

I asked him if I could get my money and books, but he replied that since I had committed a crime, anything I had with me is connected to it and I couldn't get anything back, not even my watch. I asked for some change for the bus to go home, and he gave me some change from his own pocket. It was around 9:30 pm when they let me free. It was a relief to be outside after such an experience; I was so happy and thankful for that.

I was looking around, breathing deep, and enjoying my freedom, while looking at people who were rushing left and right. I wanted to scream to them to tell them that they do not know how fortunate they are to be free. If anyone was looking at me more than two seconds I was thinking that he knew exactly where I was just a few minutes ago, and I tried to tell them with my eyes that I was totally innocent.

I did not want to go straight to the temple, thinking that those men might be following me to see where I was going. So it took me a long time to reach there, since I changed buses and walked some distance, and even hid for a while. Sometimes I went through a big building and walked out again from a different door so anyone behind me would surely lose me. Once I got to the temple, I knocked on the door as I was taught. Sachisuta quickly came and opened the door for me. He was very happy to see me, but sad to see what those men had done to me. He embraced me and was about to cry. Whoever was not sleeping came to see me and asked me to tell them everything that had happened.

After I told them all that happened to me, devotees asked me to take a shower and take some prasadam. It was so nice to be back in the temple again; I was taking a shower and thinking, "What demons, what demons!"

I could hear devotees were talking in the room, "What did they do to Gago, huh, such demons?"

Everyone was sad. They were trying to tell me that this was happening for a reason. The mood was to somehow fight against these demons. "We will win the war no matter what, because that is Lord Chaitanya's prediction—that this chanting of the holy name will be spread all over the world, in every town and village!"

Sachisuta brought me my clean clothes, which he had washed while I was not there, and while I was eating he went to the bathroom and started to wash the clothes I was wearing when arrested. I tried to stop him, but he did not open the door. Instead he was singing and telling me to eat nicely and rest. I had no choice but to surrender to my brother. Oh it was nice to breathe the beautiful aroma of our small temple again.

## CHAPTER SEVEN

# In Every Town and Village

*Every endeavor is covered by some fault,*
*just as fire is covered by smoke.*
*Therefore one should not give up the work born of his nature,*
*O son of Kunti, even if such work is full of fault.*

*–Bhagavad-gita, 18.48*

Soon, this type of short arrest became a common event. Many of the devotees had been arrested several times and went through what they had to. The regretful part of it was that we were losing our books and devotees because of this. In terms of books, in each arrest the KGB confiscated books which we were spending so much time and effort to make, plus the cash collected from the books. As far as devotees were concerned, many were leaving the temple, or not coming to the temple, because they did not want to be arrested. Of course, no one liked to be arrested, but it seemed to be becoming part of our preaching mission for those who stayed dedicated to book distribution.

Day by day, the devotees' lives became somewhat hectic, and tension was in everyone's heart. We started to think about different ways to distribute books without provoking as many arrests, or possibly not being arrested at all, a goal which was, practically speaking, impossible. Soon, anywhere we went people would recognize us, saying, "Oh, you are Hare Krishna devotees!"

In the newspapers from time to time negative articles about Hare Krishnas would appear. Some long, bad articles were printed in one very popular magazine at that time called Nauka i Religiya or Science and Religion. The main point in these articles was that Hare Krishnas are brainwashed people, be careful not to take any books from them, and so forth.

One day, Sannyasa came up with a fine idea. The main focus, he decided, should be to keep the book printing headquarters in Armenia secure. Therefore, we should stop distributing books around our temple in Yerevan, so that the KGB wouldn't be likely to stop the production. His idea was to print and bind books in full speed only in the Russian language and ship them to all territories of the Soviet Union. Everyone was happy with the idea, and we worked out some plan to practice it.

First, we made groups of two devotees for each city. Then, each group got some money for the tickets and started to pack many boxes of books and flyers. They then mailed the boxes to their own names with addresses in the different cities where they were planning to go. Agvan (Adwaita das) suggested including some dry prasadam such as the milk powder sweet, burfi, so that after distributing all the books we could have some of our favorite sweets to eat. Sannyasa dasa agreed to make some sweets for all of us. He was always enthusiastic about cooking, and we all loved how he cooked. He was the best cook, and one of the best devotees in Armenia. We all loved him because he was so special—he risked his life by printing Srila Prabhupada's books. Additionally, he was always very smart, knowing what to do in critical situations when no one could figure out solutions. We did not allow him to go out for anything that we could do, so that he would not risk being arrested. We wanted to protect him by any means because we knew he was rendering important service to Lord Krishna and was very dear to our guru. It was impossible to imagine the mission without him. He was the main bearing that was turning all other small bearings at that time.

Soon our devotional "army" was ready to attack Russia with Prabhupada's books. After a sweet kirtana, we all wished each other all the best and left. Sannyasa, Kamalamala, Atmananda, and others who were staying there for book production, embraced us and gave us their last suggestions in an encouraging mood. We had our airplane tickets, and we called a taxi, loaded all the luggage, and left. A few hours later, we were in Russia, a new field with new people and a new language in which to preach.

After checking into the least expensive hotel, we were out distributing the small amount of books that we had carried with us on the airplane. Sachisuta and I were very happy to be together. We went in two different directions and agreed to see each other in the evening for dinner at the hotel room. We did not stay together so if the KGB caught one of us, the other one could still go on with the mission.

It was quickly obvious that it was much easier to distribute books in Russia than in Armenia. Peoples' reactions were different. Even if they did not buy a book, at least they would not ask all kinds of rude questions and waste our time. We both had a positive experience and distributed almost all the books we had with us for that day. During our simple dinner we shared our first experiences, and both of us were sure that in Russia we would have both much more success and fun than in Armenia. We were also glorifying Sannyasa for his idea. Russians love reading, which meant we were dealing with intellectual people. The next day we went to the post office and received our first books and sweets. It was nice to see that our plan was working out well, by Krishna's mercy, and in ten days we had no more books left. We called the center in Yerevan to inform them that we needed them to send more books, but no one answered the phone.

We were a little bit disturbed and did not know what to think. We tried again, but finally we had no choice but to return to Yerevan. Not even one single flier was left. We felt sad and peculiar to walk without books or preaching materials. The next day we reached Yerevan by train, but the door of the temple was locked and no one was there. We were standing downstairs and debating about what to do and where to go when we saw Atmananda coming towards us.

"Hey, Haribol, boys! What are you doing here? When did you return?"

"We just came," we said. "The door is locked so we did not know where to go and what to do."

"Yes, I know," he said, "we had some indication that the KGB might come to this place, so we moved everything out. No one stays here any more. Sometimes just Kamalamala or I are coming and going. But don't worry; we have a better place now! Armen just got his new apartment on the other side of the town. It has bigger rooms and it is in a nice location. You will like it there, so let's go."

He took us to the other house, on the way showering us with many questions about our experience in Russia. We saw that there were some new devotees sitting and folding books along with the devotees we already knew. Everyone was happy to see us back and asked about our success. We enjoyed telling everything we experienced there, ending with our eagerness to go back again.

Sannyasa das and Kamalamala were very happy and called us to the next room where we gave them all the money we brought with us, as well as a list of our expenses, including food and hotel. They told us that they were glad to have us with the group of devotees, and that we were undoubtedly going to get the full blessings of guru, Srila Prabhupada, and Lord Krishna.

Sannyasa das asked me, "Would you like to go to Russia again, since there are a lot of books ready to go out immediately and there is no one, so far, to take them? It is very important to take out books from this place after binding them, so that if the KGB comes, at least they will not confiscate so much of our hard work."

We had no objection to go out again, so we started to prepare for our next trip right away. The day we were supposed to leave, Atmananda told us that we would have a phone conversation with Harikesa Swami. We happily waited for the call. By the time he called, Atmananda, the scientist, had all the necessary equipment ready to record the conversation.

Everyone was trying to get as close as possible to the phone, but we could hardly hear anything. Atmananda reported everything needed and translated for us. He said that our spiritual master was happy that everything was going on nicely, and he was especially happy to hear all the good news from our end. However, no one could mention anyone's name or location, or specify anything that could be used against us by the KGB, since we had no doubt that they were hearing and recording each and every phone conversation.

We were very happy to hear our dear guru's voice for the first time ever, though at that time, hardly anyone spoke or understood English. Mainly he was encouraging all of us to distribute more and more books and preach to people in our country. He thanked us for our dedicated service to Srila Prabhupada and Krishna. He repeated several times that we should never stop book distribution, since that is the only way to win the war against illusion, or maya. This conversation encouraged us even more. We were ready for our next trip to Russia after two days.

On this trip we ventured beyond our base, going to the nearest cities and towns as well, so police would not figure out where we would be the next day. It was fun to do this wonderful service for Krishna. This time, we already had some experience, so events were transpiring smoothly. Then one day when I was waiting for Sachisuta at the hotel, he did not return back from book distribution. I could not sleep all night. I was praying and praying to Krishna to protect my good friend, chanting all night in the hotel room. I felt lonely and worried, but I did not know what else I could do.

In the morning, after finishing chanting Hare Krishna on my beads, I ate a little breakfast and left my room. I did not take any books with me, and I asked someone directions to the nearest police station. I walked towards that direction, thinking that I might see him coming out of there, but considered that going there was not such a good idea.

I sat down under a tree and chanted the Narasimha prayers of protection for him, waiting for some miracle to happen. I wanted to cry and ask for help, but I did not know whom to ask or what to say. I spent quite some time there and then returned back to my room. On the way, while walking through a green park path, I could hear hundreds of birds singing, freely flying anywhere they liked. I was thinking how bad my friend must be feeling in a police station, where he could not do anything, even walk freely and hear the singing of birds.

Since I was not in the mood to go out and distribute books without knowing what actually happened to my friend, I started to read the Bhagavad-gita in my room. I soon fell asleep, since I had not slept all night. It was nice to find some time to read as well, because sometimes, when we were speaking to people on the street, they would ask us questions about our philosophy but we were unable to give them satisfactory answers. Reading Prabhupada's books enlivened me a lot and gave me courage to go out again, no matter what, and distribute books to everyone I saw.

In the evening, after I woke up about 6 pm, I decided to go out again and distribute some books. I was already sure that the police had arrested Sachisuta. It was a little bit different to be alone in the battlefield than back in Armenia. Together, we were encouraging each other and feeling strong. I missed my friend so much that three days seemed to be three months!

On the fourth day, I was very sure that I wouldn't see him again there. Therefore I wanted to move from that place as soon as possible, but I had a lot of books with me. I did not want to have to take them back with me to Yerevan, or even travel with them to another city since it was risky. I then promised myself that I would not leave that city until the last book was sold! So the next day, I went out again with about fifty books. I figured out that one of the best places to sell books was near the large bookstores and libraries since many intellectual people came to those places. I was standing outside a bookstore to offer books to people, when I saw a pleasant looking gentleman with a full beard walking towards me. Just by looking at him, I could see that he was a spiritual person, but I did not want to offer a book because I thought that he might be a Christian and would start an argument with me, as Christians often did, and of which I was not terribly fond. He was almost next to me and smiling at me. I do not know why, but I took out the Bhagavad-gita almost against my will and offered it to him.

He looked at me, took the book, and started to examine it very carefully, page by page. He had a shopping bag in his hand that was disturbing him while he was looking at the book. After some time, he gave his bag to me and asked me to hold it for him. I was holding his bag and looking around to see if any police were nearby, while thinking that hopefully there was no meat in his bag since it was quite heavy and I didn't want to be holding dead bodies.

"Wow! Where did you get this book?" he asked me. "How many do you have?"

"Not so many. How many do you need?" I asked him.

"Five, ten, or more," he replied. "I have good friends who I am sure will be keen to have these wonderful books! They are very much interested in Eastern philosophy."

I did not know what to tell him. Usually this type of question was asked by KGB and police, no one else.

I thought that I should say, "I have some more at home and if you wish, I can bring them to you another time." I had never sold more then one book at a time, so this was a new situation for me with someone asking for more than one book on the street. I was trying to listen to my heart, what to do, give him the books or not? I had very little time to think, so I told him that I had with me as many as he wanted. I could give them to him right now.

"Okay, give me ten of them."

I was trying to take them out of my bag, but then I realized that it is not wise to show them to everyone and I put them back again.

"Do you have any extra bags?" I asked him.

**Sarvabhavana Das** (Gagik Buniatyan)

Sarvabhavana das with his son Sachisuta in Radhakund, India

**Three children of Sarvabhavana das. From left to right: Rasa-Lila, Sachisuta (Sarkis) and Balaram (Narek).**

# Salted Bread

By Sachisuta Buniatyan

**Cover of the first single printed "Salted Bread" in USA**

Dayanvisha devi dasi offers a flower garland to Sachisuta prabhu's newly installed Murti (statue)

Hare Krishna devotees during "Free the Soviet Hare Krishnas" demonstration

Their Lordship Sri Sri Gaura Nitai, which were the first
marble Deities smuggled to former USSR, were worshipped by
Sarvabhavana das and his wife Dayanvisha devi dasi (Dustrik
Buniatyan) for several years.

Sachisuta Prabhu's (Sarkis Ohanjanian) Murti (statue) in Sarvabhavana's home. Sarvabhavana fulfilled Sachisuta's last desire which was to see, hold and distribute the first Armenian Bhagavad-gitas.

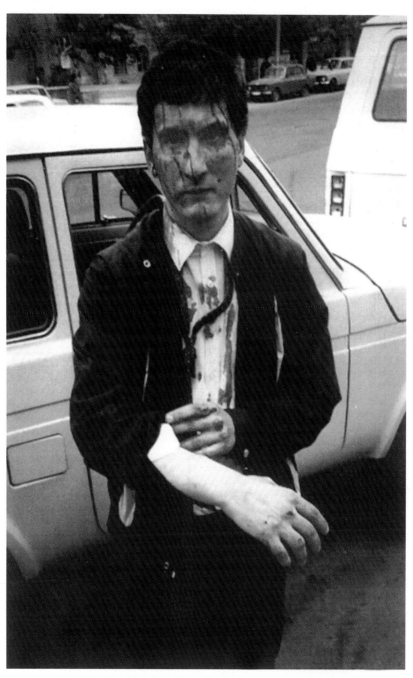

**Amsu das after the attack, all covered with blood**

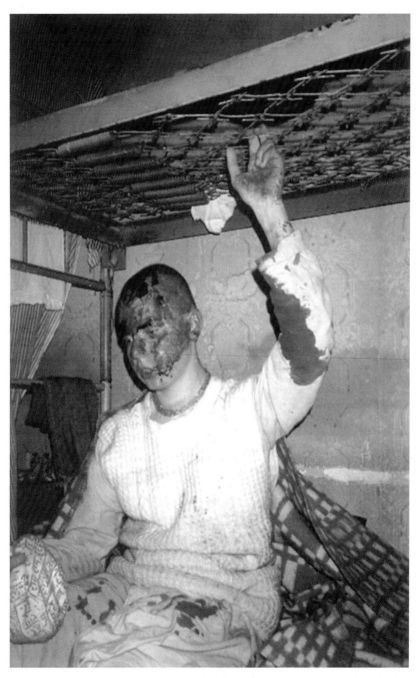

**Dhanesvar das all covered with blood in Yerevan temple after heartless beating**

Sarvabhavana das and Tridandi das (Tadevos Manukyan) in the
Kolkata International Airport in 1989 on their first visit to India.

**The wife of Vedavyasa Das (Valentin Yurov) during a demonstration to free her husband from the psychiatric hospital in Moscow.**

**Sarvabhavana das leading ecstatic kirtana with Armenian devotees**

**Shyamasundar das shares his memories with Sarvabhavana das about Srila Prabhupada's visit to Moscow.**

Krishnadas Kaviraja das with three devotees from Sukhumi,
Abkhazia who were arrested by KGB in the late eighties.
From left to right: Ambarish das, Krishnadas Kaviraja das,
Mayuradhvaj das and Vakreshvara Pandit das.

The Armenian sculptor working on Sachisuta
prabhu's murti (statue)

**Armenian devotees cooking for the victims of the earthquake in Gyumri (Leninakan)**

Most of the following devotees have been officially adopted by Amnesty International as:

# Prisoners Of Conscience

Yamaraja dasa
(Jacov Dzidzhevadze)
A thirty-year-old musicion, Yamaraja is serving two and a half years at a labor camp in Sukhumi.

Anatoli Samollov
Anatoli is serving three years in a labor camp.

Sannyasa dasa
(Suren Karapetyan)
Sannyasa dasa, twenty-nine years old, graduated in cybernetics from Yerevan State University. He is confined indefinitely in a Soviet psychiatric hospital.

Japa dasa
(Yuri Fedchenko)
A graduate in biology from Moscow State University, thirty-one-year-old Japa dasa is serving a four year sentence in a labor camp in the Stavropol Territory.

Amala-Bhakta dasa
(Yevgeny Lyubinsky)
Amala-Bhakta is serving a four-year sentence in a labor camp. He has a wife and three small children.

Nugzar Chargaziya
Nugzar is serving two years in a labor camp.

Sanatana-Kumara dasa
(Sergei Priborov)
A music instructor, Sanata na-Kumara is now serving a four-year sentence in a labor camp in the Stavropol Territory.

Kamalamala dasa
(Karen Saakyan)
A twenty-nine-year-old radio technition, he is confined indefinitely in a Soviet psychiatric hospital.

Sachisuta dasa
(Sarkis Ohanjanyan)
Sachisuta is serving two years in a labor camp.

Sarvabhavana dasa
(Gagik Buniatyan)
Gagik Buniatyan is serving a two-year sentence in a labor camp.

Advaita Acharya dasa
(Agvan Arutyunyan)
Agvan is serving a three-year sentence in a labor camp.

Visvamitra dasa
(Vladimir Kritski)
Visvamitra is a computer scientist serving eight years in a strict regimen labor camp near Perm and is thirty-six years old.

Vakresvara Pandita dasa
(Ashot Shaglamdzyan)
Vakresvara Pandita is serving two and a half years in a labor camp.

Atmananda dasa
(Armen Saakyan)
Formerly a scientist at the Yerevan House of Scientists, thirty-two-year-old Atmananda dasa is confined indefinitely in a Soviet psychiatric hospital.

Asutosa dasa
(Aleksei Musatov)
At twenty-eight years of age, Asutosa is indefinitely confined to the Special Psychiatric Hospital in Smolensk. He previously worked as a kindergarten guard.

Alexander Levin
Alexander is currently serving four and a half years of compulsory labor in Udmurtskaya A.S.S.R. He is a twenty-six-year old journalist.

**Page from the Back to Godhead magazine**

First page of Sarvabhavana's prison diary.

Sarvabhavana das with Dharmendra.

**Sarvabhavana das with Hema Malini.**

Sarvabhavana das and his wife Dayanvisha devi dasi with Amitabh Bachchan.

Sarvabhavana das and his wife Dayanvisha devi dasi with Hema Malini.

"No, but my car is parked nearby we can go put the books in there. Let's go."

I found some courage to walk with him towards the car and give him all the books he needed. On the way I asked if he knew anything about these books. He replied that actually he has a friend who has been practicing yoga for about ten years and who told him about the Gita, encouraging him to read or buy the book if he ever sees it. Then he opened his thick wallet and handed over five hundred new Russian rubles. This was my first bulk book sale ever. I was very happy, and honestly speaking, even a little bit proud. Or to be even more honest, I was very proud. After he closed his trunk, he introduced me to the elderly lady who was sitting in the car waiting for him, "This is my mother. Her name is Mariya, and I am Grigori."

"And I am Thomas." I gave a wrong name to start with, since I wasn't that sure with whom I was dealing.

"We are very happy to meet you!" they told me and sat in his car ready to go. After starting his engine, he asked me if I would be inclined to go to his house for a lunch. I told him that I am a strict vegetarian and do not like to eat anything that is cooked by anyone else, especially strangers. We both laughed and understood each other.

"I have vegetarian friends, so I know how to treat them. C'mon, let's go have a lunch together, and we will have some time to chat. You can tell me, perhaps, more about your philosophy."

"The thing is, I eat only what I cook, so it's better if I do not offend your family traditions." I replied.

"No problem," he said. "You can cook whatever you wish, and it will be my pleasure to taste food cooked by you. Please sit down in the car."

I was very scared and did not know what to do. But since he was both serious and peaceful, and especially since my book bag had become a little lighter, I agreed to join him. On the way, he was playing beautiful organ music on his tape player and asked me if I liked it.

"Yes," I said, "it is really a beautiful composition! From my childhood, I have enjoyed organ music very much." From the music I decided that he must be a religious person, a Christian who had a lot to do with church.

Soon, we reached his house. He asked me if I could help him to carry some groceries so that he could help his mother into the house.

A young lady opened the door and quickly came to help his mother walk to her room.

To my surprise, the rooms were very large and full of light. There were many fine antique Christian icons displayed here and there on the walls. In the middle of the living room was a long table with fresh flowers and fruits. There was a beautiful hardwood floor decorated with exquisite carpets. It was not difficult to understand that he was a very wealthy man. He offered me a seat and asked me if I would like to have a drink before he took a shower.

"No thanks," I replied.

"If you would like to take a shower, you are welcome," he said as he pointed to a guest room, "and you can use a bathroom there. Please feel at home!"

I started to walk towards the guest room while looking all around. I liked his taste in decorating his rooms. I then heard some strange sounds of a man from one of the rooms. One man then started to walk in by the help of the young lady. It was obvious that he was very sick maybe from birth; he was walking towards me with a wide smile, holding a toy in his hand. He was almost screaming, "Who is this, who is this?" Grigori came near me and slowly told me that this is his brother, and although he is forty-two, he still acts like about a seven or eight-year-old boy. He had some mental incurable disease from childhood, which later on started to destroy his general health.

Grigori then went to shower. After some time he came out of the bathroom in his robe and handed me a bag and a new towel. "This is for you to change into after you shower. Please try it on. If it does not fit, let me know and I will give you another one." I was trying to refuse, but before I opened my mouth he dismissed my objection with a wave of his hand and left, leaving me alone in the room.

I went into the fancy bathroom and took a shower. In the bag was a finely crafted shirt and beautiful pants with socks. They fit as if they were made just for me. After I came out, Grigori came to the guest room, and while smiling, told me, "Okay, now you are ready for cooking! Come on; let us see what you would like to cook for us! I am anxious to taste vegetarian food cooked by a Krishna devotee! Anything you need, you can ask Olga here; she will help you out. At this time, I have some affairs to do in my room while you cook, but if you need me, feel free to call me. Is this okay with you?"

"Yes," I replied and started to relax a bit and find out what to do. I asked for some new pots and started to cook something simple with vegetables and rice. I also prepared a large salad. After I finished, Grigori came to the kitchen and told me that his house had never smelled so wonderful.

"What did you do to make this wonderful smell?"

"I just cooked for Krishna," I said. "Probably that's why it smells so pleasant!" But at the same time I was thinking, "All glories to Sannyasa das!" because all that I knew about cooking was mainly, or really only, from him.

I told Grigori that usually we offer our food to the Lord, so if he didn't mind, I could offer it quickly.

"Go ahead! That is fine! We do the same as Christians; we say a prayer before eating. I am a priest in this town and am inclined to following rules and regulations." I then asked him if he could give me a small bell for offering the food.

"I do not think I have a small one, but there are many bells available here. Let me see," he said and went to one of the rooms.

After a while I could hear some bell sounds, and he came out with a huge bell in his hand. With a large smile, he handed it over to me, telling me he was sorry, but this was the smallest one he had.

The large bell felt strange in my hands. I left the kitchen and started to offer the food at my little traveling altar, which I had with me always. After fifteen or twenty minutes his servant started to serve the prasadam. We were ready to start eating when he said, "If you do not mind, I would like to say a prayer first."

"I don't mind," I said. "I appreciate that, as we must remember and glorify God before each meal."

He then stood up and chanted some very beautiful prayers in Russian, followed by "The Lord's Prayer," and then we started our lunch. He was in a blissful mood and ate a lot.

"I have never eaten such tasty food!" he told me. "Can you cook for me every day? Then, I would not need to eat any meat!"

"Yes," I told him, "I wish I could, but I have more important activities."

"What are the important activities that you have to do?" he asked me.

"Book distribution!" I said, "I like to give this knowledge to everyone in this world. This is the most important business to do since there are so many innocent souls waiting for these books. Then everyone will cook and eat tasty food like this!" I finished, smiling.

"How can I help you in your mission?" he asked me.

"I do not know. All I want to do is sell all these books and go back to Armenia. You are already helping me by purchasing ten books, anyways."

"How many books do you have altogether?"

"Many."

"How many?"

"I have more than one hundred," I replied.

"What if I buy all of the books from you; will that help you?"

"Yes, a lot, why not? But, what will you do with them? I am not interested in making money only; I want people to read them and apply this knowledge in their daily life. I do not want you to buy them and keep them here for the rest of your life; I am not here for that. "

"I am not going to keep them here. I am going to give them away to all my friends and people I know."

"Then, that is okay! In that case, I can sell them to you."

"Fine, bring them tomorrow morning and I will pay you."

"But, you did not even read them. I do not understand why you would want to do this, especially since you have told me that you are a priest in this town, and usually Christians are very much against our philosophy."

"But I have heard about this long ago from my friend, Igor, who is a yogi. I am very inclined toward Indian philosophy. You can meet him also, if you wish to."

"Okay, that will be a great pleasure for me."

"Now we can go to the next room and read your book, if you wish."

"This is not my book; this is Krishna's book!"

"Okay, let us read Krishna's book," he replied. We sat down on the parlor floor, and he started to read verses from Bhagavad-gita to me. I was amazed by his excellent reading. I was especially enamored by his careful pronunciation of each and every word of Srila Prabhupada. We stayed there until late at night, discussing anything and everything, from life in general to religion, and from Christianity to Hinduism. We agreed to meet again the next day. He told me that he had graduated from the highest spiritual academy in Russia, where he had obtained a very broad education in many subjects. In addition, he had been a right-hand man to the Russian monarchy for some years. He then showed me pictures of the patriarch with him. I was further astonished at his talent in singing beautiful Christian songs.

He turned out to be a very sweet man, a spiritually advanced personality. I was so happy with this visit and impressed with my new friend that from happiness I could not sleep all night. I could not believe how a Christian priest who was an aide of the Russian patriarch accepted almost everything the Bhagavad-gita said. He was sure that meat eating is wrong and that somehow he would have to give it up sooner or later. It was interesting to think that this influential person actually wanted to distribute more than a hundred copies of Srila Prabhupada's books.

We met in his house again on the next day, and after breakfast he asked me how to sing the maha-mantra that Srila Prabhupada always mentions in his book. I therefore gave him a tape of Harikesa Swami to play. He appreciated it very much and started to sing along.

Then he asked me to go with him to the next room where there was a concert piano. As soon as he sat down in front of it, he started to sing the maha-mantra while expertly playing the tune just as he had heard a minute before from the tape. I corrected him a bit, singing with him. It was great fun to be with this expert musician and singer. I grabbed an empty flower pot which was on top of the piano and started to bang it as if it was a drum. Soon we were in ecstasy, starting to sing more and more loudly.

Sometimes he varied the tune with such amazing melodies that I thought I was in heaven. For a while we could not stop singing. From time to time it was I who changed the tunes, and a second later he would be playing exactly what I was singing.

He paid me for all the books. Then he asked if he could give me a large, expensive Japanese-made tape recorder for Krishna. I agreed to take it with me to Armenia. This was the first time I received a donation for Krishna's service other than money for books.

After a long conversation and some philosophical arguments as before, I became convinced that I was dealing with a very gentle and delicate person, and was very careful to treat him well so he would continue with his Krishna consciousness. I explained how wonderful it would it be if there were many devotees in this world, and how fast changes could and would soon appear on the planet if that were to happen.

He was one hundred percent in agreement that what God has said in the sixth commandment was also applicable to animals as well and not only for people. It made me very happy that finally I had found a Christian who was in agreement on this point, which had caused me to think so much and which I found so very difficult to explain to others.

He offered me a gracefully carved seat covered with maroon velvet, opened his safe, which was full of shiny objects, and pulled out something covered with soft velvet. He delicately took off the cloth as he walked towards me—it was an incredible crown with many kinds of precious stones, golden leaves, and other decorations. I have only seen such artifacts in the museum or the movies. He was trying to place it on my head, though I refused to wear it. But somehow or other, he put it on my head and told me, "Oh, this is wonderful. You are the one who has to wear it, not the meat eater. One who follows the ten commandments is considered to be a real Christian but not someone who was just baptized and goes to the church every Sunday!" I gathered that he was referring to himself. I took it off and started to examine it very closely. It was something that I can never describe; it was a fine piece of art, a rare piece of Russian handiwork.

We spent the rest of the day together, and then he ordered my airline ticket to Yerevan. The last request he made was, "As soon as you print any new books, please make sure that you bring or send some for me."

I came back to Armenia in an unusual, mixed mood. I was very happy from my meetings with Grigori, which allowed me to return with empty hands. Yet I was very unhappy about not having any news from my friend Sako (Sachisuta das). After a few hours I was already in Yerevan, feeling a little bit proud that I had sold all the books and was bringing the money for Krishna. It was very hard for me not to be proud, since this was the first time I had sold so many books so quickly and maybe even no one else had yet done so. To my surprise, when the temple door opened, there was Sachisuta! We were both so ecstatic to see each other again. As soon as he saw me, he ran to embrace me tightly and laughed loudly. He started to ask how everything was with me. Everyone was happy to see me coming back without any books; all I had was one bag with my clothes and the donated tape recorder.

As I told all my experiences to the devotees, everyone was so happy to know there were some Christians who were ready to accept our philosophy or think well of us. After that, I gave all the money I brought to Sannyasa das and asked Sachisuta how he had suddenly disappeared and was now in Yerevan.

He then told me an amazing story. He was distributing books in one of the buildings in the city when a lady closed the downstairs main door and called the police so he could not escape from the building. They took him to the police station, took all the books, and made a lengthy report on him. Then, they took him to the county jail after some days of keeping him in the police station.

After three days they were supposed to take him to prison along with ten other criminals, but on the way to the truck one of the criminals ran away, with one of the two police officers starting to run behind him. Now only one policeman was left there with nine criminals. One of the criminals said in Sachisuta's ear, "If you want to go home, this is the best time to do it, since it is obvious that the policeman will not leave the other eight criminals here and run after you!"

Sachisuta replied, "If you run, I will run, too." They agreed, and one ran left while the other one ran right. The police did not know what to do except to scream and curse.

Sachisuta knew that I was in the hotel waiting for him but did not want to lead the police to me in case they followed him. After a while, he ran to the woods and stayed there all night under a big tree. He did not have any money and decided that there was no other option but to try to return to Yerevan.

He went to the railway station and jumped onto the Yerevan train while it was moving. He was standing in the corridor for a while before one of the conductors came out and asked him for the ticket.

The conductor was an Armenian man and was easy to talk to. Sachisuta told the conductor that someone had stolen his bag and he did not have any money or document with him, but had to go home somehow. He requested humbly whether or not the conductor could make some arrangement for his travel. At first the conductor was very angry and suspicious and wanted to call the police so they could take him off the train. Then Sachisuta started to speak about Krishna consciousness. Gradually, the conductor admired his attitude and gave him a place to sleep in his own room. "But," Sachisuta said, "as soon as we reach Yerevan, I will give you the money along with a really grand present, a present that is so valuable that no one can purchase it. It has no price. It is priceless!" The conductor then gave him some food and took good care of him.

After they arrived, Sachisuta asked the conductor what time would be best for him to come back to repay his kindness. The conductor laughed and replied, "Better you go home and that's it! I have seen many such as you—they go and never come back to see me! I have never seen any of them in my life again, and no one ever came and gave me money! If they give something before they go, then I'll take it, but I do not expect anyone to return and pay me a penny. I just helped you out because you are a humble boy with good qualities. I don't want anything in return. You can go and God be with you."

Sachisuta insisted on getting the conductor's address and left after thanking him a lot. The next day, he took money and two books from the devotees and went to the conductor's home. The conductor was happily surprised to see Sachisuta and invited him in. After giving the books to the conductor with some explanation, the conductor accepted only the books and refused any money from him. They felt they had become friends and promised to help each other whenever and however they could in the future. I was happy and proud to hear my friend's adventure story.

More and more, many devotees came to Armenia from different parts of the USSR to get Srila Prabhupada's books and flyers. It was welcome to see those wonderful souls and spend time with them, even if it was just one day. Every devotee was very unique in some way, and there was so much to learn from each and every one. As Sachisuta used to say, "We had better be like the honeybee, taking nectar from each and every person, not like the fly who goes to only dirty places and finds only fault."

Some of these visitors were already initiated by Harikesa Swami and were working hard to spread Lord Chaitanya's mercy. I will never forget my brief association with devotees such as Mamu Thakur das, Bharadvaja das, Yamaraja das, Mayuradwaj dasa, Yagya devi dasi, Vakreshvar Pandita das, Vrindavan dasa, Japa das, Ambarish das, and many other great souls who were ready to give their lives for this most important mission of Sri Caitanya Mahaprabhu. Everyone had some inspiring story to tell us.

They used to tell us regularly how important the service of the Armenian devotees was in the distribution of Srila Prabhupada's books. One devotee said, "It would be wise if you Armenian devotees did not go out and distribute books at all. Just print and bind good quality books for us, and we will come here, take them from you, and distribute them for you as well! So many people are out there waiting for those books you are making, and if they arrest you then where will we get the books from?"

"Yes," another devotee said, "Imagine how some devotees cannot wait any longer. They are making photocopies of the Bhagavad-gita and binding and distributing them from home! Some of the devotees do not have the original books so what they produce is a fifth or sixth photocopy, which is hardly readable. You can barely see the pictures. The only way to know what the pictures are is if you already had an understanding of the philosophy, or saw the original pictures. Sometimes the pages are mixed up and one cannot find the right page. But people still buy them from devotees because they thirst for those books!"

A very sad point in the devotees' lives was when we came to know that the then General Secretary of the Communist Party of the Soviet Union, Mikhail Gorbachev, made a resolution wherein it was clearly stated that all the active members of the Hare Krishna Movement should be arrested immediately without any excuse. This, of course, wasn't good news. But hardly any of the devotees made any practical changes. We just did what we were doing before the resolution. Since we were already prepared and informed that we could go to jail at any moment, it made little difference. The threat became part of our life, as we felt we couldn't do anything about it. We could not avoid being persecuted and arrested if we were to continue our dedication to our mission. Despite all these difficulties, we were finding many different ways to do our service better and better. Every day someone would come up with a new idea for a project that would please Krishna and Srila Prabhupada.

Shyamakunda das started to make some extraordinary covers for the Bhagavad-gitas at home, which he brought to us to bind. Some of the covers were so beautifully made that we did not want to sell them, wanting him to let us keep them for ourselves!

Sachisuta das started to visit the libraries often to assist with book binding. For example, he found some books by Karl Marx, Maxim Gorky, and Lenin that were exactly the same size as the Gita. He would then throw away the pages and keep only the cover, glue the pages of the Gita into the cover, glue the jacket on top of that hard cover, and the book was ready. Soon he had taken out books from all the libraries in Yerevan.

Sometimes, when he did not have time to put on the jacket cover, he would go out and distribute books which had "Lenin" on the cover but were actually the Bhagavad-gita within. He told us that doing this was a good idea. No one would be suspicious of what is inside, and it would be easy to explain to people the reason why it was made that way. This is just one example of the experimenting the devotees attempted in order to fulfill the mission of:

"DISTRIBUTE BOOKS, DISTRIBUTE BOOKS, DISTIBUTE BOOKS"

Sometimes we were joking and telling that Sachisuta had became a communist nowadays and was distributing Lenin's philosophy instead of Bhagavad-gita.

One time I decided to go to the Urals for book distribution. I knew this area well, since I lived there for two years when serving in the Russian Army. The place I stayed when in the military was Sverdlovsk, also called Ekatirenburg. It is an extremely big city, and I got to know many people there. On my book distribution mission, I first came to Perm city, where I received my parcel full of books and flyers. I distributed them all within a very short time without any problem. My next stop was Chelyabinsk, where I waited two or three days for the parcels of books to arrive. I had no other option but to rest and chant all day long, and also plan my service for the next days. As soon as I received the books, I went out for distribution. Books were going slowly but without problems. I stayed there about seven days. I had a few books left, but on the way to my next and last destination of Ekatirenburg, I sold them on the bus. It was nice to be in that city again without an army uniform. I went to see some of my former officers to give them Srila Prabhupada's books. I got a room in Uctusskie Gora, which was very near to the main areas I chose for book distribution. No one ever went to this city before me, and that was a big advantage since the police were not yet on alert in that area and I was able to be little bit relaxed.

One evening I decided to go distribute a lot of flyers. I therefore went to the other end of the city, where I proceeded to put a flyer in each of the post boxes in several large buildings. Usually all the mail boxes in this city were on the second floor, which allowed me to hear people coming upstairs and then quickly close my bag and go either up or down so they wouldn't notice what I was doing. Some buildings were very difficult to enter since they had electronic number locks. I used to wait for someone else to enter and then walk right behind them. In one building, some people noticed me and looked at me suspiciously, since mostly they knew the other residents and workers, but no one said anything. I quickly filled up the boxes and left there. As I was about to finish my flyers that night, I decided that I would enter one more building before going back to the hotel. The next day I would start book distribution again. It would have been better if I had not done so.

I entered the building, quickly went up to the second floor, and started my job. As soon as I came in I heard someone enter behind me, but I did not hear anyone walking upstairs or towards the elevator. I felt a little strange, like someone was spying on me, but I had no option with nowhere to run. I was effectively in a trap. I started to fill up all the boxes with flyers and got ready to go out. My feeling was so sharp that I was one hundred percent sure that someone would arrest me now or something was fishy. I turned and started to walk downstairs. I didn't even make four steps when it felt as if someone had pushed me back, although no one was visible. I then turned towards the mailboxes and started to fill them up with Sri Isopanishads. I thought that if the police were going to catch me, then at least I'll save the books from being confiscated and give people the chance to read them. There were still some flyers left, too, so I filled up some boxes with ten to fifteen of them just to avoid having anything on me.

After doing this I had about three Bhagavad-gitas left which would not fit in any mailbox, so I decided to get out of that place as soon as possible. I was ready for anything and very carefully started to walk towards the first of a set of double doors. As soon as I had opened the first door, I noticed two people standing there. I wanted to walk between them without paying any attention to either of them, and I tried to smile. One of them asked me if I could give a match for lighting a cigarette. I replied that I didn't smoke and tried to pass through. I didn't even make one step when both of them kicked my stomach, and I fell on the floor in great pain. They started kicking me everywhere without saying a single word. It took them no more then two minutes to make me bawl, and then they left the building, maybe thinking I was dead. I was holding my bag very tightly so they wouldn't take it away, but they weren't even interested.

I do not know how long it took me to come back to normal, but as soon as I stood up and cleaned myself off I went out of the building and started to walk somehow towards the main road to catch a taxi. I needed to pass through a small tunnel under a huge building where there wasn't any light.

As soon as I reached the middle of the tunnel, I noticed these same men walking towards me. One of them said, in Russian, "Are you still alive?" Then they started to beat me up again. This time I threw my bag in the corner of the tunnel and started to fight with them. I started boxing them and cursing while asking what they wanted from me and why they were beating me. No one answered, and the fight was becoming more intense. At one point I became unable to protect myself and fell down on the ground again. Both became very angry and started to kick me everywhere, including my face. One lady who was walking nearby noticed what was going on and started to scream, "Police, police, hurry up, hurry up! They killed this poor boy! Hey, people, quickly help, help!"

The men then stopped while saying, "You know, guy, why we are beating you up, don't you?" The men started to run away from me. The lady was screaming behind them, asking why they had beaten me, and they had screamed while running "He deserved that, aunty."

She then came over to me and started to help me out, cleaning my face with her handkerchief. She started to cry and curse them, remarking on what a hellish thing they did to me. Finally she helped me stand up and walk towards the bus stop, where I then took a taxi to the hotel. The hotel manager was horrified to see me in that condition and asked me what had happened. I explained how two unknown guys were trying to steal my money and then went to my room. He wanted to call the police, but I requested him not to do so, explaining that it wasn't going to help me anyway. Actually I was afraid that if the police came to my room, they would find many illegal books there. He sent someone to help me out, and after taking a shower, I was in my bed for the next couple of days trying to recover from my injuries. The third day I felt all right again, and so distributed all the remaining books in Sverdlovsk city within a short period of time. I left that city promising that I would never ever go there again. I took a flight to Yerevan and was again with my friends. I felt certain that the incident was a KGB arrangement, and so I was relieved that I was able to distribute all the books and return without being arrested.

# CHAPTER EIGHT

# Preaching is the Essence

*In all activities just depend on Me
and work always under My protection.
In such devotional service, be fully conscious of Me.*

*–Bhagavad-gita, 18.57*

Sometimes, there were aspects of the book production that only some devotees would understand or be able to perform expertly. Some information on book production was top secret, and everyone knew that certain information could be dangerous for some of our most important devotees, such as Sannyasa das, Kamalamala das, and later on, Brahmananda das. Brahmananada, for example, started to print books with a stolen printing machine. After I married and had my son Sachisuta, we stayed in the same house he used for printing. The machine was stolen with the help of the man who used to print books for us secretly. When the company the printer worked for received a new printing machine, Brahmananda brought a truck and took the old one, bribing the man with a large amount of money. That machine is still there today, a symbol of the money and risk given to print Prabhupada's books.

It was amazing how in one night three or four people broke through a brick wall of the ground floor of the printers, brought the heavy machine inside the house, and built the wall again by morning so that the neighbors could not tell what had happened. Later on, part of the upstairs floor of the house where we kept the printing machine was cut to make a kind of entrance. Then, by removing a part of the floor one could easily enter the room that held the printing machine. Usually, when Brahmananda was printing books, someone stayed outside and played some loud music to cover the noisy sound of the machine.

Many years after the printing machine was installed in that house, and after the legal registration of ISKCON, several leading Hare Krishna devotees and friends visited Armenia and were very happy to see the printing machine so they could have a clear picture of how the books were printed. They asked Brahmananda dasa to turn the machine on and print some pages of Gita. When Brahmananda turned it on for them, they took a little ink from the machine and made a dot on their foreheads just as one would do with ashes from a sacred fire sacrifice. They also paid obeisances to the machine after printing some pages.

One day, Sannyasa called me and asked me if I would do an important task for Krishna. He said that the printer had proposed that he would take university diplomas instead of money for printing books. A devotee in Aphasia was so dedicated to book publication that he was eager to part with his diploma so the printer could sell it on the black market. Since the diploma was worth a lot to the printer and money was scarce for us devotees, we decided to go through with the deal. Our whole book publishing and distribution program was illegal, anyway. Sannyasa wanted me to get the diploma from the devotee in Aphasia.

I obtained an airplane ticket and went there to meet Vakreshvar Pandit dasa, who offered his diploma to Sannyas as an exchange for printing books. He and some other devotees took me outside of the city so no one would find me or discover our operation. Devotees there were telling me amazing, encouraging stories about people taking up Krishna consciousness in their country. The atmosphere was friendly, and I was happy to spend time with them. They had two cows and a little farm. The next day I returned to Yerevan with the diploma.

Another time, I was fortunate to visit Ambarish Prabhu's house in Sukhumi when I was trying to collect funds for book printing. He was the first devotee that I knew whose parents also became devotees. They were a wonderful family; father, mother, and son were very serious devotees of Lord Krishna. It was so refreshing to visit a house where everyone was a devotee. They used to secretly stock books in their house and gradually give them to the devotees for distribution.

They invited me to visit them again sometime and stay with them for a while to distribute books in their city. So I went there a few weeks later, after Gorbachev's resolution to arrest all Hare Krishna members. Many devotees had been arrested there, but I didn't know about it. As soon as I came close to the house, two police officers arrested me and took me to the police station. While they were taking me upstairs, I heard some familiar voices. The police pushed me inside the room where Ambarish Prabhu was sitting. He had been beaten up already. As soon as I saw him, I wanted to tell him "Hare Krishna," but he winked and turned away from me, so I understood that there was no need to show the police that we knew each other.

After many questions and curses, the police took me out and sent me to the temporary jail, where I heard Ambarish and some other devotees singing Hare Krishna. The police beat me and made two large dogs bark at me threateningly. The dogs appeared as if they wanted to bite me. They were jumping, sometimes getting right next to my face. Their wide open mouths and loud barking was very frightening. It was terrible to see the white teeth of the huge dogs with their saliva sometimes spattering on my face. I just closed my eyes and started to chant the Hare Krishna mantra as loud as I could. Five or six policemen were laughing and laughing at me and making nasty comments. After a while, they took me to one of the rooms and threw me in like a piece of cloth.

Some other men were there, too, and they immediately started asking me why I was arrested. After answering all their questions, I collapsed on the nearby wooden bench.

In the morning, I joined in the singing of devotees from the nearby rooms. It was comforting to be part of a special kirtana in the jail. Some criminals started to sing with us too, but others were somewhat offensive and complained or criticized us. One of the criminals asked me if I could take some important message to his wife and brother. He explained to me exactly how to reach his home. I was supposed to keep everything in my mind since they were not allowed to have pen or paper there. After I was released the morning of the third day, I followed his instructions exactly, and his family was very happy for the information I gave them. They told me that they would take nice care of any Hare Krishnas if the government placed them in labor camps since they had a good friend there.

When the police let me out, they gave me just enough of my money to buy a train ticket to Yerevan. They told me that they didn't want to see my face there again, or they would keep me in jail for sure.

It was nice to be outside again and see the blue sky above my head. Since I was very hungry, before I took a train to Yerevan I ran to the nearest store to find something to eat. Then I went to the Black Sea to swim and rest a little bit on the shore.

At the temple in Yerevan, everyone was busy preparing for the celebration for Janmastami, the appearance anniversary of Lord Krishna. It was so comforting to be in the temple again with the devotees. Although the police had taken my chanting beads, I did not have to take the trouble to make new ones because Sachisuta had made ten sets specifically for devotees coming out of police stations. In addition, Sannyasa das somehow found someone to make thousands of sets of wooden beads for all new devotees. We used to send the beads to Russia as well.

At first, we decided to have the festival ceremony in our rented house where we kept only a few books. Then, if the KGB came, they would not be able to confiscate as many books as in other places. Each time they arrested us, the police took everything we had and never returned anything. Once, in the central police station, I was shown a cavernous room where half the space was filled up with our books, papers, mrdanga drums sent by Harikesa Swami, japa beads, book binding tools, suitcases, and so forth.

Sannyasa suggested that we celebrate the festival not in our rented house but somewhere in a nearby village, without any sacred fire ceremony or anything of that nature. Everyone was happy with this idea. We started to do all the necessary shopping and arrangements for that auspicious event. This is one of the most holy days in the ISKCON movement— celebrating Krishna's coming to this world. The date is calculated by the lunar calendar; it usually takes place around the end of August. We secretly told all our members of the festival's location without using the phone, since the KGB was recording each call. Then, gathering the supplies, we started our journey.

The neighborhood where we had our Janmastami celebration was in a lovely rural area. The large house we used for the festival was that of a beginner devotee, one boy Sannyasa knew who appreciated Krishna consciousness and who lived with his mother only. We all decided that the location was a good choice for the festival. We also had a visiting devotee from the Moscow temple, Mamu Thakur, who was a good kirtana leader. He also played the mrdanga drum expertly, which we all enjoyed. I remember that this was the first time I had seen a devotee wearing the traditional devotee clothes of a dhoti and kurta. Manu Thakur was a monk, or brahmacari, and looked wonderful in the saffron color of a celibate.

We started the Janmastami program at noon, with everyone supposed to fast until midnight. Around thirty devotees were gathered, all busy with some devotional activities. The atmosphere was unbelievably different. We were all feeling a little freedom there, happy that finally we could sing kirtana as loud as we wanted without any complaints from the neighbors. But unfortunately, at around 7 pm we heard Damayanti and Rukmini devi screaming at someone outside. We ran out of the front room and saw about fifteen police officers trying to come in. Damayanti and the homeowner were trying to keep them out, asking them for their reason for coming and to show proper papers from a higher authority allowing them to enter. The police said that since this town was very close to the border of Turkey, they were allowed from time to time to come and visit any houses where there were gatherings. For fifteen minutes the ladies detained the police at the door. During that time, many of the devotees went out the back door, jumped over the fence, and ran away. Sannyasa tried to convince Mamu Thakur to run as well, but he said that he would rather stay with us. Plus he was wearing traditional Vaisnava clothes, which he didn't have time to change and which would have both made him an easy mark as well as possibly identifying others as Hare Krishna members.

The police finally came in and immediately looked everywhere in every room like dogs on a hunt. Because of his dress, they especially singled out Mamu Thakur and started to check his documents. It became obvious that they thought Mamu Thakur was Harikesa Swami, whom they knew was our main leader. Somehow they got wrong information that the devotee with the saffron robe was our main leader from Sweden. After a long time they brought us all to the police station. About fifteen devotees were arrested, including the elderly homeowner and her son. After some time, the police let those two go home, but the devotees who had come to their house for the festival all stayed in the police station until eight o'clock the next morning. We decided to perform loud kirtana in celebration of Janmastami through the whole night. No matter how hard the police tried to stop us, we did not comply. We were very hungry, but the kirtana was very sweet. Everyone was released in the morning, after signing many papers, except poor Mamu Thakur. After two days, they took him to the airport or railway station and told him never again to come to Armenia, or he would end up staying in jail.

In the morning after we were released, we went back to the temple in Yerevan to see if anyone was there and if there was any prasadam we could eat to break our long fast. It was good to see devotees waiting for us such as Sachisuta, Haridas, and Nityananda. They were relieved to see us back, and we swapped stories about our adventures. After they ran away from the house it was too late to catch a bus back to the city, so after one hour they slowly came back to the same house from behind with the idea of sneaking in to see if it was safe to sleep there. While they were looking in from the bathroom window to see if there were any police left, they saw Sachisuta sitting all alone, singing sweetly while crying. Welcoming them, he regretted that most of the devotees would not be able to take part in the planned festivities.

Haridas suggested that the devotees should eat prasadam and go to sleep, but Sachisuta said he would not eat until all the devotees came back from the police station. He then sang all night kirtana, and early the next morning all those devotees took all the feast prasadam to the city temple. After both groups of devotees came together we had a feast and slept the rest of the day. Unfortunately, this problem with the KGB became a pattern at festivals. For several months, the KGB came to almost each and every gathering we had and spoiled everything in a similar way. It seems that their greatest fear was our gathering in a relatively large group.

One day, Kamalamala suggested that it might work better if we celebrated our festivals in the forest or mountains, so no one would disturb us any more by any means. It turned out to be a good experience for all of us to have festivals in nature. For each festival, we would stay two or three days in a mountain area, enjoying lectures and leisurely talks with the devotees and then return to the city again fresh and full of enthusiasm.

After some months, we were all busy preparing for the feast and activities to celebrate the birthday of our beloved spiritual master, Harikesa Swami. Sachisuta decided to distribute books all day long until the feast. The rest of us were cooking or decorating the room where the festival program was supposed to take place. At that point, we did not have so many devotees left in Armenia. Many devotees left because they did not want to have any more trouble from the KGB. Probably there were no more than ten devotees who were still actively carrying out Srila Prabhupada's mission.

That festival was the first time Tigran (Prana das) was with us. Nityananda Ram had brought him; they were next door neighbors and knew each other for a long period of time. He was interested in yoga and Indian philosophy. He was about twenty-eight to thirty years old. I had a long talk with him and found out that he was ready to start chanting the holy names and follow the four regulative principles. He seemed to me to possess humility and other good qualities.

Sachisuta das returned from book distribution and was happy that he had sold everything he took with him. As soon as he came in, he started to glue some books and pack some of the Russian books in a box to be sent out to Russia. The atmosphere was peaceful, with some devotees singing a sweet kirtana. Nityananda and Haridas were talking about Krishna consciousness to Tigran. Sannyasa, Armen, and some others were still cooking in the kitchen. Then, all of a sudden someone started to scream, "The KGB is here!"

In a moment, it was as if there had been an explosion in the house. Everyone ran out except Sachisuta, Sannyasa, Kamalamala, Atmananda, and Armen. Sachisuta quietly and deliberately quickly put some glue all over the box he was packing and placed another box over it so if the KGB investigated, they wouldn't be able to read the outgoing address of devotees in Russia.

All the devotees started to run left and right and jump through the fence. Tigran was the shortest so Nityananda helped him to jump over the neighbor's fence. Five or six police could not catch all of us, so some were able to escape. The next day, Nityananda told us how one of the police officers was running behind him with a gun in his hand and screaming, "Stop running or else I am going to shoot you!"

Tigran left in a hurry and could not take his shoes, so he ran away barefoot. We were thinking, "Oh, we have just gotten such a nice man who was ready to be a devotee and here the police came and spoiled everything! Probably we won't see him any more because of this stupid KGB!" But to everyone's surprise, he came back the very next day. Actually, he stayed with us and became one of the most active book distributor devotees in Armenia.

The police took the captured devotees to the police station. The next day they released some of them, but unfortunately not Sannyasa dasa, Kamalamala dasa, Atmananda dasa, and Armen. We were in great anxiety—we didn't want to think that these important devotees would stay in jail. It was depressing and difficult to be without them even for one day, since they were our senior devotees and leaders upon whom everything was depending. The next day, Damayanti Mataji came and told us that the police had already told Sannyasa's mother that they were not going to release them, no matter what. She offered to go to the police station and at least bring some prasadam for them. We all agreed with her, but at the same time no one liked to have any dealings with the KGB. We didn't know what to do.

So in the evening, Nityananda, Haridas, Damayanti, Prana, and I went there and asked the police to let us give some food to our friends. As soon as we came in, they asked us to explain what we were doing there. We started to explain that our friends are vegetarians and could not eat prison food. But they refused our request to bring them food.

Damayanti was very upset and started to argue with them. She said, "First of all they are innocent! Second, they should not starve there just because they are vegetarians," and so on, but nothing worked. Instead, they told her that she will be the next to go there. We did not realize that actually this was their last arrest, and we would not see them for a long time.

After the fourth day, it was clear to all of us that they had already taken these devotees to the jail from the police station. We were trying to do something useful for them but did not know how. We often saw Sachisuta crying and saying, "It would be better if they had taken me to jail instead of them. I am a useless man here. They were doing so much for Krishna; what are we going to do now?"

Whenever Sannyasa had made money from book sales, every three or four days he would give it to Haridas so that it would be safe. He also had purchased a new hand-made book cutting machine, which was of first-rate quality and helped our book production a lot.

We came to know that Sannyasa had told some of his book publishing secrets to Haridas and they had agreed that in case they arrested him, Haridas would t ake care of our little BBT (Bhaktivedanta Book Trust) publishing arm. So, a new life started for us for a while without the devotees who had been our key leaders.

The media was trying everything they could to show that Hare Krishnas were crazy and brainwashed, and they were writing all kinds of false articles and TV shows. Once they had made a show on TV and invited one lady to speak as if she were Kamalamala's mother. She was crying on the TV screen and telling how bad was this Krishna cult, how her two educated sons were involved in their activities, and warning all parents to be extremely careful with their children.

In general, though, we were discouraged, always wondering who would be next to go to jail. The pattern continued that some devotees were afraid of the whole situation and finally gave up coming to even see us in the temple, gradually giving up chanting and following the rules and regulations.

Having our leaders in jail was so depressing that sometimes we would not go out for days, only chanting, eating, and sleeping. We had no mood for anything else. Sometimes we would sleep even during the daytime. The only person who was doing some active work was Sachisuta—he was making more and more books ready for distribution and hardly ever talking with us. He was serious, and it was as if he was in a different world. He would do anything and everything we were not willing to do. He was working in such a humble way that we often wouldn't notice how busy he was. For example, he was often the only one who would clean the floor, do the shopping, wash the pots after cooking, and so on.

One day, he called for a meeting and told us his own opinion about the situation. He said, "Dear brothers, I know it is a very difficult time for all of us. We are going through a very bad period, but we have to see everything as the mercy of the Lord, and try to do something wonderful no matter what the situation is that we are in. Believe it or not, this is illusion's trick and Krishna's test. We have to pass this test by any means. Otherwise, all that we have accomplished so far will soon be forgotten. What we did in the past will be zero."

"Now, we have to prove to the KGB that Sannyasa dasa and others are not our leaders, and by arresting them they cannot stop the book distribution. Harikesa Swami and Krishna are our leaders. We are all doing whatever they are telling us to do, and Sannyasa is just one of us. If we stop book distribution, then the KGB will understand that they have indeed arrested our leaders. So I am thinking that we must go out by any means and distribute books, with even more enthusiasm than before! If anyone does not agree, they may go home and rest. Whoever wants to carry on the mission of Srila Prabhupada can stay here with me and go through all these difficulties."

"Just try to remember," he said, "each and every time we got any letter or call from our guru, he was telling us to never stop book production and distribution, so we must follow his order, and Krishna will take care of the rest."

It was a very heavy statement, and for a long time no one else spoke. We were looking at each other and revealing our hearts to each other without any single word. Silently we all admitted that he was actually right. But, we did not know what to do, at all.

Some of the devotees chose to go home, and only Adwaita, Prana, Sachisuta, and I stayed at what we called our "temple." Haridas and Nityananda decided to live at their home but often came to help. During this time, a devotee couple, Tulasi dasa and Madonna, visited us from Sukhumi. They explained their strong desire to be devotees, and the difficulty they experienced practicing Krishna consciousness in her parents' home. Madonna's father was very upset about his daughter's involvement with ISKCON. He had tried several times to take her to a psychiatric hospital, and once he had also called the police. So she and her husband had run away from home with almost no possessions. For some time, they had stayed in Moscow where they met with devotees, and then they decided to come to Yerevan to help with book production. He had brought with him one new cutting machine that was specifically made for home book production.

This machine made the whole process more convenient because it enabled us to perform one more operation at home, rather than taking so many books out to the cutter and bringing them back again. With this new machine we could cut five books at a time, and it did a better job than the cutter where we used to go. It had a metallic press and a sharp disk mounted on the handle which went back and forth in a groove just like a train wheel. After each cut we turned the tread of the disk a little bit, and slid it again and again, so that it cut, slice by slice, and one by one, the uneven parts of the pages.

The day I went to bring Tulasi das to our newly rented place he had the machine in his big bag. He firmly decided that he wanted to go on the metro underground train. I had suggested that it would be much safer for us to take a bus, but somehow or other he chose to go by metro. Since he was an initiated and senior devotee I did not argue with him. But while he was passing through the narrow gate it accidentally made a loud sound when the gate hit the machine's corner.

A police officer who was standing nearby looked at Tulasi suspiciously and then stopped him immediately. Tulasi waved to me to keep going so the policeman wouldn't know we were together. After some questions the officer took Tulasi das to the police room. I felt very bad and started to pray intensely for help. I stood on the platform for a while, but then left since I did not know what to do.

I was trying to imagine the situation of his wife, who had just somehow run away from her father, and now her husband got arrested. "Poor lady," I was thinking while walking home.

After thinking for a long time I decided that it would be better if I went back to the temple a little late. That way if the police released Tulasi, then I'd get there after him and wouldn't have to bring bad news to his wife and all the devotees.

I started to sell some books to take up time. When I returned I saw that Tulasi was indeed there before me, by Krishna's mercy. I asked him how he was freed. He said that he explained to the police that he is an engineer who had come to Yerevan for only three days to show to some Armenian scientists his invention. He told them he had just been on his way to show it to one of the most important scientists visiting Yerevan. Believing him, the policeman asked Tulasi to show him how the machine worked, which he did. Tulasi was then released and even got a handshake from the police officer.

The temple president of Moscow had asked Tulasi to send him a list of the names of all the active devotees in Yerevan so they could be formally initiated in the Hare Krishna Movement by Srila Harikesa Swami. All of our names, including Sachisuta's and mine, were sent to them. In the initiation ceremony, a devotee promises to the spiritual master that he will always chant sixteen rounds of the Hare Krishna mantra on his beads every day and follow the four regulative principles of no meat-eating, no intoxication, no illicit sex, and no gambling. The spiritual master gives the candidate a new spiritual name and agrees to personally guide him in his spiritual life for the rest of his or her life.

# CHAPTER NINE

# My Last Arrest

*Engage your mind always in thinking of Me,*
*become My devotee, offer obeisances to Me and worship Me.*
*Being completely absorbed in Me, surely you will come to Me.*

*–Bhagavad-gita, 9.34*

**W**e were trying our best to continue with book production and distribution in the long term absence of our leaders. I had forgotten how many times they had arrested and released me, but at the time of Sannyasa and Kamalamala's arrest, I thought that because the police were now convinced they had the leaders of our movement in Armenia, they wouldn't be arresting the rest of us anymore. But I was wrong. The police arrested me and some other devotees many times after Sannyasa and the others were kept in jail. Each time we were again released, somehow or other. During this time, we rented another house to store books and important items, and we would go there perhaps once a week. One day, for reasons we still don't know, the house owner used her second key to open the house door when we weren't there. Naturally, she saw all the books, as well as equipment and paraphernalia, which looked suspicious to her. So she informed the police. We were unaware that the police had been contacted. At about eight o'clock one evening, Sachisuta and I were going to that house, bringing some missing Gita pages to complete the books. At that time I had a strange premonition while riding on the bus. I asked Sachisuta if he had the same feeling. He said that he also felt that there was some danger and strange faces were staring at us, but we did not know what to do and which way to go, forward or backward.

It was a very cold and dark evening, the 24th of January, 1986. I remember that day very well, since that was my last day outside for a very long time. It was even snowing a little bit that night. How could we know that this would be our last day outside of jail?

Both of us had such strong feelings of danger that we decided to go back without taking any further pages for the books. I do not remember any other incident of Sachisuta stepping back from any situation, ever. Everything was strange. He told me that we should go back to the new temple as soon as we could, and so we immediately turned around and started to walk away from the house we were renting. It was cold, and hardly anyone was on the streets. After we walked about a hundred meters, we noticed a white car coming towards us very slowly. Since we had already become expert at reading and remembering license plates, we kept the number in our mind. After a while the same car came behind us slowly and again got lost in the winter night. We looked at each other and understood our predicament without saying anything.

We had hardly walked more than five more minutes when two cars started to slow down behind us. Before they completely stopped, Sachisuta pushed me towards the park and screamed, "Run!" Both of us started to run as fast as we could down a little hill through the knee-deep snow. We did not even know where we were running. Before the police stopped and got out of the cars to follow us, we were already pretty far from them. They started to scream loudly and told us to stop or they would shoot, but we did not care and kept running and running through the park.

I stopped for a moment to breathe, at which point I looked behind to see whether or not the police were still coming. I saw that two of them were running like mad, cursing us badly.

We came to the end of the park where there was a high fence. Fortunately, someone had already broken part of it so it was not so difficult to jump over, but the problem was that we did not see that on the other side of the fence was a ditch with water at least a half meter deep, covered with ice and snow. We both broke through the ice and fell in. We were completely wet and cold, but there was no time to think. We looked at each other for a second and started to run again, finally hiding behind some bushes. Fortunately no one followed us over the fence for which we felt great relief.

Our throats were burning after running for about fifteen minutes; we could not say a single word to each other. Sachisuta started to eat some fresh snow and made a sign to me that it was okay to eat. After a while, we started to freeze in our wet clothes, so we decided to go to the former temple at least to change our clothes. As we walked, our frozen pants made a clattering sound in the wooded park. Soon we were in front of our door, where we very carefully entered the house. Fortunately, we found some of our clothes and quickly changed. Not even ten minutes had passed when we heard someone trying to open our door from outside. We guessed that since the owners had an extra key, they were trying to open it without even knocking on the door. After they had realized that we had locked it from the inside and they could not open it from the outside, they started knocking. Sachisuta asked, "Who is there?"

All they said was, "Open the door."

Sachisuta said, "I cannot open the door for a stranger, so please leave us in peace."

They started to kick the door, shouting, "This is the police department! Open the door, or we will break it down!"

"Okay," he replied, "do whatever you wish."

So they started to break down the door with some tools. We looked at each other and embraced tightly. He looked at the clock on the wall and said to me, "So, Gago, our turn has come as well!"

We felt that if they were so intent on getting in that they would break the door down, then definitely they would arrest both of us. To prepare for the inevitable, Sachisuta started to make a hole in his clothes and put small pictures of Pancha Tattva and Srila Harikesa Maharaja in between layers of fabric. He asked me to do the same as well, which I quickly did. As soon as we were done, the KGB was done too. The tiny entranceway filled with scowling faces. They entered like tigers attacking two deer.

As soon as they came in, one of them came and kicked my chest and knocked me down, while another one started to kick Sachisuta. They were cursing us and beating us with batons without any compassion. Sachisuta was calling out loudly, "Krishna! Krishna!" They kicked us like this for about ten to fifteen minutes as we both lay on the floor in great pain.

Then they put one of our spiritual books in Sako's hands, placing him next to the altar. They took a picture of him there and then took us out of the room by kicking and pushing us. They placed handcuffs on us and put us into a car. The owner of the house was standing there and watching the whole scene, maybe wondering whether or not he had done a good thing telling the police about us. They took us to the central police station. It was one of the worst days in both of our lives. They seemed so angry at us that we felt even our death would not have pacified them.

They took my fingerprints and, as usual, three or four pictures from the side, front and so on. They then took us to different rooms where they beat us up. I could hear both Sako's prayers and the policemen screaming loudly at him, which was so horrible for me. One fat policeman hurt me the most, even stomping on my toes with his boots, giving me excruciating pain.

"So," he said while hurting me, "Now I think you can tell us where your books are printed and where you are storing them."

"I do not know, sir. I do not know where they were printed. I only distribute them and nothing else."

At this point the policeman resorted to lies, a common tactic even in modern democracies. "No," he said. "Sannyasa told me that you know everything. Before he died, he told us all the secrets, so today tell us—where is your main book storage?"

"I do not know, sir." I replied, "If Sannyasa already told you, then why are you asking me the same questions?"

At that point, three large, muscular men started to kick me as if I was a ball. My nose was bleeding until I could not feel it any more. Then they asked me to stand up, which I did. One of them took hold of my ear and took me close to the metal door and asked me to place my fingers between the door hinges. I refused to do so. He then asked help from the other man, who placed my eight fingers there and started to close the door slowly while screaming into my ear, "Where are the books hidden, who is printing them, and where?" I do not remember what exactly happened after that, but after I came back to consciousness, I noticed that all my fingers were cracked and bleeding.

While I was lying down there one of them took the electric heater and brought it close to my face and screamed at me, "So now we will cook you, man! Let's see who is who, we will eat you up okay?!" My face and nose were burning. I closed my eyes so they would not be burned. Then another man came and asked the first man to take the heater away. I was screaming and trying to tolerate the pain. Two men took hold of my arms and took me to the bathroom and asked me to wash myself quickly. I looked at myself in the mirror and closed my eyes immediately. I was all bloody and swollen and bruised. I had seen a face resembling that in the movies, but not in real life, especially not my own!

Somehow, I started to wash my bleeding hands and face without looking at the mirror any more. While I was washing my mouth, one of my teeth fell out. Then I noticed that I had lost two of them, one from each side, and a couple others were very loose, ready to come out as soon as I ate something. After some time, one man came and called me out. He told me that I was going to jail, and for some reason I took it very seriously, unlike during my other arrests. After all, they had lied to us many times about going to jail, just to scare us. I had been arrested and released many times within two years, in different cities all over the USSR. Each time I had been held no more then three days just in the police station, and then released. Each time they kept all my books, money, and personal belongings. The law was that they could hold us without there being a specific criminal charge for three days only, but if they wanted to hold us longer they would have to get permission from the higher authority to take us to prison.

By the time I finished washing my face the short policeman, who appeared to be the angriest of all, walked into the bathroom and kicked my back very heavily so that I collapsed again Then, pulling my belt, he brought me to the first room again and threw me on the floor. I was covering my face with my hands so as to try and protect at least some part of my body, but at the same time being prepared for a kick anywhere.

He was kicking as he screamed, "You are not this body; right, you are not this body?"

I started to hold my stomach with both hands when the same short man came from behind and hit me on my spine with both hands. I fell down without making hardly any sound or movements. I looked in his eyes and said, "You are not born from a human being. How can you do this to an almost half-conscious innocent person and strongly curse him as well?"

"What, what did you say, innocent?" he laughed. The others just looked and showed no reaction.

"You are one of the most dangerous criminals I have ever seen, who is spoiling his own nation by distributing all kinds of nonsense literature and garbage. You are preaching this useless philosophy to Armenians, who are actually Christians from 301 AD. We were the first who accepted Christianity as an official religion in our country, you know that?

"We Armenians have been Christians, are Christians, and will be Christians all the time. We do not want to become Hindus and worship one hundred gods and demigods. You are an Armenian. Go and preach Christianity, not Hinduism, to our nation. We are not Indians and do not know any Krishna. We have lost so much blood and innocent people in order to be a Christian country, and neither Muslims nor any others could change our religion for many centuries. Now you stupid guys want to damage what we have earned from centuries?"

I looked at him and slowly said, "But Jesus was also not born an Armenian, so why have you decided to follow him?"

"Shad upppppp!" he screamed at me. "You do not know what serious damage you are bringing to our nation by distributing all this trash." He took one Bhagavad-gita and tried to cut it into half, but he couldn't. Then with both hands he hit me on my head and cursed me.

He came close to me and started to speak very loudly in my ears, "That's why I want to know who is the guy who is printing these books for you, so I can kill him right away so you guys won't continue this nonsense, okayyyyyy? So now, tell me who is giving you these papers to fold and where are you keeping the main stock?"

"I really do not know. I told you that many times already," I said.

"Okay, after I prepare a nice seat, then you will tell us everything immediately."

He waved his hand to the policeman next to him and asked him to bring one beer bottle. Then he came close to me and with his whole strength stepped on the tip of my toes with his big boots. "O God," I thought, "This is one of the worst things I have ever experienced." Then a policeman came in with a glass bottle in his hand and placed it in the middle of the room.

"So now for the last time I am asking you, and that's it. Either you will tell me or you are going to sit on this bottle."

I hung my head and started to chant loudly, "Namaste Narasimhaya," and prayed for help.

Then he came and twisted my hands while another one held my legs, and they pulled me up. The third one came and tried to take off my belt. I had started to jump and shake my whole body so they wouldn't be able to take my pants off. So then he hit me, probably with his full power, on my belly, and I thought that maybe now I'll be cut into two pieces. But still I didn't give up shaking.

I started to kick them and scratch as much as I could. I tore the shirt of the policeman who was holding my hands, which made him even angrier. Somehow, even after so much beating, I got some enormous amount of power and started to move in such way that they could not take my pants down. I started to scream more loudly than I had never screamed in my whole life, like a tiger, non-stop for a long time. I started to think how loudly Nrsimhadeva screamed when He appeared to kill the demon Hiranyakasipu. As soon as they brought me close to the bottle I moved fast and it fell on its side. After several times of trying, they finally dropped me down and left the room.

Soon a woman came in, handing something to the one policeman who had remained in the room. Looking at me in a way that reminded me of a snake, she quickly left. The policeman then helped me to get up off the floor and gave me a chair to sit on. After a while he started to look at me with bloodshot eyes that seemed especially ugly and round. He pushed some papers at me, asking me to tell him what I thought about them. I was breathing very fast and could not calm down for a while, and the room filled up with my screaming. My ears were hurting from my own screaming, but it seemed to be keeping the police away from me.

I took the papers with my cracked and pained fingers, and started to read slowly. It was all about the Hare Krishna movement and me, a confession that I felt very sorry to follow this path and how bad it is to be a devotee and so on. I put the paper down without finishing it, stretched, and asked him what he wanted from me now.

"All you have to do is," he said, "just sign these papers, and then you can go home peacefully and chant Hare Krishna as much as you want without any problem. But if the next time we catch you printing or distributing your books, then there will be no more chances and you'll go to jail for sure. Now you know how bad we are and can clearly see that Krishna is not at all protecting you guys in these most important circumstances. Now I am your God, and if I want I can send you to the jail. And if I want to, I can send you to your home. So choose which one will be better for you at this time and let me know now. Remember we do not have much time at all, so make your decision as soon as you can."

I told him that I would never sign such lies and that I am ready to go to jail. He took the papers and pushed a button under his desk. Soon one other policeman came there to take care of me.

They took me downstairs and locked me up in one of many rooms. It had heavy iron doors and no chair, bed, or windows. At first I couldn't see in the dark, but after some time I became used to it. Also, there were small light bulbs right above the door, which gave some very dim light to the chamber. Some criminals were in the room, too, and they started to ask me many questions about the reason I was there. Some of them had already heard about Krishna, and one had even read theBhagavad-gita a little bit. So we had a long talk. It was refreshing in the sense that all day long they were reminding me about Krishna, not giving me time to remember my body and its pain. The main problem I felt was extreme hunger. The only food in the room was fish and bread.

After some time, some policemen took me out to sign some papers and introduce me to my prosecutor, whose name was Armen Sardaryan. He was going to start investigations in our case, which was different from the cases that he usually handled. He was a friendly man about my age. He told me that he was not inclined to take our case, but because he was graduating, his law school gave him our case as one of his first jobs. He had no choice but to take it.

In order to investigate our case, he was supposed to know about our philosophy, so he had to study all our available literature. We sometimes had long discussions. He acquired a decent understanding of our philosophy and agreed with many points, but argued about a lot of it as well.

Once I asked him why he was willing to prosecute us if he understood that he would get some bad karma through doing so. He replied that he is a ksatriya and was just following the orders of his authority, just as Arjuna was following Krishna's instruction. Thus he actually believed that he would not get any karma. We had a defense attorney appointed to us also, but he was useless. He also worked for the KGB, and he disliked us so much that he never met with us more than for a brief introduction.

One evening, the police opened my door and took me to a room upstairs to sign some last papers. Sitting there were two young and attractive women, whom I supposed were there to provide enjoyment to the policemen on the night shift. The policemen decided to have some fun and introduced me to them, saying that I am from Hare Krishna and strictly following strange rules that prohibit me from having relationships with beautiful girls. After I signed the papers, a policeman looked at me and said, "What kind of gentleman are you that you do not want to associate with these ladies, ah? Shame on you, shame! They are two of the loveliest ladies we have ever seen in this town! So, now we will leave you alone with them and give you an opportunity to enjoy a little bit before going to the jail. I hope you will be very thankful for that. See what you can do and remember this might be the last chance for you." With that, the policemen left the room.

One of the ladies started to ask me why I do not intimately associate with ladies. I started to explain to her, "It says in our scripture, 'A wise man sees all women except his wife as equal to his own mother or sister.'" I started to tell them the story of Haridas Thakur and the prostitute, which I don't think was so interesting for them, but at least one of them was listening. But the other one was taking off her upper clothes slowly and coming towards me while saying, "Now, for a moment you can think that I am your wife. What's wrong with that?" She came and sat right next to me and started to touch my hair. I took her hand away and asked her to not touch me, or I might feel like hitting her. I started to tell her how serious it is if she offends someone like me, who is trying to be Krishna's devotee. I told her that no matter what I do, she will get a bad karmic reaction. But she did not care and continued to try and seduce me. I finally got so frustrated that I stood up and told her that if she touched me once more I was going to beat her up and have that criminal offense on my record as well. She then opened the door and told a policeman that I was just a fool for not even touching her before going to jail. She turned to me and said, "God knows how long you are going to be there! You'd better take your last chance. Who knows how long it will be until you see such a fine lady again?"

At that point, I thanked her for her good offer, and said, "Hare Krishna."

Whereupon both teasingly replied, "Hare Krishna to you!" They then left while showing me their long tongues. The policemen then took me downstairs again, teasing me on the way by saying that I am a useless guy and have no brain for not accepting such a good offer.

The very next evening a policeman called my name loudly from behind the door, and while opening the door, asked me if I am prepared to go to jail, scratching my name from the paper he was holding in his hand. Several policemen then took me upstairs where two hefty guards were already waiting for me, ready to put me in their ugly truck and take me to jail. One policeman who was always more or less kind to me those days, was standing there looking at me compassionately and shaking his head as if he wanted to tell me that he felt very sorry that I was going to jail for nothing.

I quickly asked him softly, hoping that others wouldn't hear, whether or not I was actually going to jail. During all my previous arrests I had only been kept in the police station. He nodded his head, again looking at me sadly as he said, "You are a young and healthy boy; why don't you cooperate so you can go home, huh?"

I said doing that would be exactly the opposite of what Krishna wants me to do. I think it is better to suffer out of obedience Krishna.

The lawyer Armen signed all the necessary papers, told me he would visit me once a week in jail to ask more questions if necessary, and then left. The police officers asked me if there was anything I would like to request before they took me to jail. I asked them if I could play the mrdanga drum. It was my guru's drum, and therefore we were all so attached to it. So they gave it to me. I started to play a little bit on it with my very painful fingers while sing Hare Krishna slowly. One of the policemen was laughing; the others were telling me to sing loudly. So I started to sing and sing. Soon all the policemen were in my room watching me. Some police officers had brought criminals with them, too.

Some of the on-lookers started to tease me, some clapped, and some made funny movements, but all responses of any kind encouraged me a lot. So I started to sing with great enthusiasm for almost thirty minutes without paying much attention to them. Then one guard came with a hefty ring of keys in his hand, and by shaking his hand, indicated that I had to stop the kirtana and walk out of the room. Understanding that my time had come, I started to walk while still singing and playing mrdanga. Both sides of the drum were covered with blood. While I was walking through the corridor, the mrdanga sound was even better, so I started playing and singing the Narasimha Pranama prayers for protection very loudly. At the end of the corridor, one policeman came and opened handcuffs to put on me, but another one said that they were unnecessary in my case because I was not a criminal, just a mullah, or Muslim priest. The guards waited for me to finish my kirtana. Then one took the mrdanga from me and wished me "Good luck." They pushed me into a car and started driving towards the jail, which was hardly twenty minutes from the station.

That day I entered hell. It was an experience that I can never possibly forget. I can remember even the smallest details about that hellish, cold, and unfortunate day.

# CHAPTER TEN

# Entering into Hell

*Always think of Me, become My devotee, worship Me and
offer your homage unto Me. Thus you will come to Me without fail.
I promise you this because you are My very dear friend.*

*–Bhagavad-gita, 18.65*

The car entered the prison courtyard through a massive electric gate, stopping right in front of a door inscribed with the modest title, "Reception."

"So we are at home, my friend," one policeman told me.

As soon as we entered through that door, one fat man was sitting there as if waiting to receive his next customer. He threw away the newspaper he was reading and called out, "Welcome home, boy!" While looking at the policeman who brought me he asked, "Which article?"

"244 part 2," was the reply, delivered as if memorized from a codebook.

"What the hell is that? Is this something new? So far, I have never heard of that one!"

"It is a special case. Have fun! Yes, by the way, he sings very sweetly!"

"Oh, that means that he is our next 'Krishna?' "

"Yes, exactly."

"How many more do you have there in the police station?"

"I do not know. We think all these seven guys are the most active ones, and hopefully there are no more to bring to you."

"There are already four of them dying here! I guess he wants to die too."

After this exchange, the policeman who had brought me asked the other one to sign his paper, wished me good luck, and left.

"So tell me about yourself a little bit," the "receptionist" started, offering me a seat that was fastened to the floor with nuts and bolts so no one could lift it and hit his head with it. I sat down and told him the whole story. He was laughing and cursing me while saying, "Shame on you men! People are coming here for serious crimes, and you are here for nothing! If one has to come here, it is better if one comes for a good reason. You men are fools!"

After filling out my papers, he asked me to take off all my clothes, and he started to check everything everywhere. My heart was beating fast, and I was praying to Krishna that he wouldn't find the small pictures hidden in my clothes. Fortunately, he did not. I guess he didn't think that I would carry anything with me, since I was not at all looking like a criminal.

Next, he took my shoes, and by expertly bending them, he took out with pliers the iron that's embedded in some types of shoes. I did not even know it was there. Later I came to know that prisoners were making high-quality knives with this and killing each other or police officers. I was freezing cold standing there in front of him completely naked. He asked me to sit and stand several times and then asked me to put my clothes back on. After all this was over, he asked me to walk before him with my hands behind my back. He had a large ring of keys in his hand; I had never seen such a collection of keys in my life! Soon, he stopped in front of a huge, heavy black door and, without even looking at it, placed the key right inside the hole and opened it very expertly.

I was thinking, "O my God, how many thousands of times has he opened this door that now he doesn't even have to look at it to place the key in it, even in a dark corridor?"

"Welcome to hell!" he said as he pushed me in and quickly closed the heavy door. It was a vast room, full of people sleeping on metal beds. There was a large wooden table in the middle. Some people were sleeping on it, too. I said hello to whoever was awake and sat next to the table. For a while, no one spoke. I was looking around and trying to become familiar with my new home, trying to understand who was who there.

One man looked at me for a long time with half-sleeping eyes and then asked me my name and what I was there for. We started to talk about everything we could possibly think of. I had often been asked about Krishna consciousness so I often knew exactly what would be his next question. I asked him if this room would be the place where we would stay all the time, and he said, "No, tomorrow they will take all of us to different rooms according to what kind of crime you have committed. That's it until they sentence you and then take you to the labour camp. But how long this will take only God knows."

When I was about to fall asleep a bit later, I noticed something bulky under my feet. I looked down to see what it was and saw a scruffy rat right next to my leg!

After a while in that room, it became usual to see the rats around me. At midnight, there were about eight of them going here and there as if we were the guests and they the hosts, which may have been the truth of the situation. Each rat was at least five to six kilograms. I could not sleep all night and started to watch them carefully. There was a sizeable hole in a corner of the room from which they all came.

One man left his shoe on the floor while he was sleeping on the metal bed and snoring very loudly. A rat came and started to smell it and play around with it. Although the room was dark, I could clearly see how he started to eat this shoe and made a lot of trash all over. The next moment, another rat came, and they started to fight for the shoe. The first one took the shoe and pulled it to the corner to take it into his hole, but it was too large. I watched as he chewed the shoe into two pieces and took them into the hole. It didn't take long for him to do so. They were making some sounds that sometimes sounded as if they were talking or fighting with each other. Some kind of awful smell was in the room, and I was trying not to breathe too deeply, a technique I learned from my many times in police stations.

The next morning, that man woke up and started to search for his shoe, but he found only some pieces of it, whereupon he started to curse like anything at the rats. Everyone was laughing at him, and one of the men, who said he was in this same jail for the third time, told us how once those rats ate half of his shoe while he was wearing it during his sleep. He said that rats have some kind of a liquid in their mouth that they apply to peoples' flesh, and after that the people do not feel anything, so they can do whatever they want. This was quite an experience for me, and I was wondering what was left to come in my jail experience.

In the morning a guard came, knocked three times on the door with his heavy keys, and screamed, "Stand up!" When he opened the door, everyone stood up slowly and placed their hands behind their back. He came in and started to count all of us. He read our names, we replied, and then he left.

One of the men said, "O my God, every morning and evening we have to do this same thing again and again!"

Then another guard came and opened the tiny food door on the main door with a tumultuous noise and called out, "Breakfast!" But instead of the prisoners, all the rats started to run towards the door, waiting for their food! Those men who had been there the longest came forward and held their aluminum pots in front of the door. Each man was given a piece of bread and one large spoonful of some horrible substance that was very stinky. The first man who took the food shared it with the rats right there, and so did the next man, and so on. The rats fought over every scrap of it and soon finished it off. This was one of the most amazing sights that I had ever experienced.

I did not take anything. I told them that I do not want to eat then. One man told me that I must take it and give it to someone else or to the rats, so I had no choice but to obey the new rules in the new place. The same phenomenon happened at lunch time. After that, they started to call us one by one and took us to the rooms where we would stay until our court day.

Soon, my turn came as well. They called my name and took me to the second floor. It was a very unusual building constructed in such a way that you always felt a heavy pressure. Since it was round you tended to lose your sense of direction. It had thick black painted iron doors and windows. After I got my mattress, pillow, cup, pot, and spoon they took me to the fourth floor, chamber number 73. The guard opened the door and pushed me in, saying, "Here, I brought a priest for you men; he is going to pray for all you guys, and you have to confess!" and closed the door.

There were eight criminals sitting and looking at me with a question mark on their faces. I looked around and said hello to all of them and asked the man nearest to me, "Which one could be my bed?"

He replied, "Find your own place. We have three empty beds." So I chose to be as far as I could from the toilet. That was the first lesson I had learned from being arrested so many times—that you always try to be as far away as you possibly can from the toilet, which is in the same room and almost always open.

After placing my mattress and utensils there, one of the criminals, Khatsik, asked me to sit and tell him about myself. He was also from Armenia, and he was the so-called boss in that room. I briefly described my case. He was interested to know more about it. Some others started to ask me questions as well, and soon I was bombarded with all kinds of questions and challenges.

It looked as if it would not be so bad in this place. Slowly I came to know why and how each of them came to this hell. They had nothing else to do so they questioned me a lot every day. Some of the inmates started to take me very seriously while others were against me and hardly talked to me. This was beneficial for me because otherwise I would not have enough time for my own chanting.

I used to wake up very early every morning and walk around the table to chant my sixteen rounds peacefully on my fingers. Sometimes a guard would look through the little hole on the door and ask me to go to bed. I usually chanted on my fingers—many thanks to Atmananda das who taught devotees that technique in case we did not have japa beads with us.

Here's how to chant sixteen rounds of japa on your fingers:

Start with your right thumb at the base of your smallest finger of your right hand. Chant the sixteen-word mantra. And then move your thumb up to the next line on your finger and repeat. Move up, repeat. Move up to the next finger and work down this finger, up the next finger and down the index finger for a total of twelve mantras chanted.

Now, mark the set of twelve mantras chanted by touching your left thumb to the base of your small finger on your left hand. When you have chanted twelve more mantras on your right hand, move your left thumb up one line and repeat. But, on your left hand we only count to nine. Nine sets of twelve equals one 'round' of one hundred and eight mantras. Then, one takes a little stone or bread, whatever one can find, and sets that to the side. When you have moved sixteen counters to the side, you have finished your sixteen rounds. Srila Prabhupada asked that every ISKCON devotee promise at initiation to chant sixteen rounds of the Hare Krishna maha mantra every day without fail. This will ensure our success.

Khatsik turned out to be a nice person. He was the only one with whom I could speak deeply about our philosophy, life in general, and share my opinions with him. Even his arguments were respectful and made some kind of sense, so it was a pleasure talking to him. I felt that I at least I wasn't wasting my time. The days passed slowly and I was getting more and more into a different lifestyle. I learned some tricks and interesting stuff from people there, and I was trying to remember Krishna as much as possible and never forget Him.

Three times a day, they were providing us some meal, but it was horrible and non-vegetarian. Usually it was fish soup, pork, or wheat mixed with some meat. I used to take only a piece of bread and one spoonful of sugar in the morning. The bread was of a very substandard quality. It was black and wet, and if you pressed it hard, water would drip out of it. So, I kept the bread on the window for three or four days until it was dried and crunchy, and then ate it. So I had different stacks of bread for each day because I was eating the bread three or four days after I got it.

It was more difficult to save sugar because the ants would try to get in it all the time. In jail, even the ants use their brains to the last extent to figure out all the angles of their survival. First, I was told to put the container with the sugar in the middle of a plate of water so that the ants could not get in it. But the ants would build a bridge of drowned ants and cross over their bodies. I even tried to suspend it from the ceiling but soon I saw a perfectly straight trail of ants going up the wall and across the ceiling. The ants were so ingenious that they would release their hold on the ceiling just above the sugar, and you could see them drop down into it and start to enjoy for a while. But the problem was that they could not come out after they were full, because they couldn't cross the water around the cup! Their situation reminded me of the material world in general, where we go to a lot of trouble to enjoy something only to become trapped and suffer.

I became slowly familiar with the new lifestyle and even more, I learned a lot as well. For example, since the inmates were expertly making all kinds of beautiful objects out of bread, I learned the technique and made my first japa beads out of it by saving my daily bread.

This is how you make something out of bread:

First, you take a soft piece of bread and knead it in your hand for as long as you can. Then you place it in a plastic bag and close it tightly so no air will get in. Store it for a couple of days. Then open it, mix the bread with some sugar, and keep it for about three days more. The bread becomes stinky and either black or brownish. Then, you open the bag and push the bread through some old cloth such as your shirt or handkerchief. We placed cloths on top of the aluminum cups we had there. Tightly and slowly with your fingertips, push the bread through the cloth. After this long and hard procedure, your material is ready for making anything you wish, just like play dough. Prisoners made all kinds of amazing items out of that bad quality bread, and after it dries, it becomes hard as rock.

Here's the story of japa beads and the Hare Krishna maha mantra:

Krishna incarnated in this world just 500 years ago in order to spread the chanting of the Hare Krishna maha mantra. This prayer means simply, "My dear Lord, please engage me in Your devotional service." It is pleasing to Lord Krishna and may be sung loudly or it may be chanted softly on beads as a meditation. Members of the International Society for Krishna Consciousness vow to chant at least sixteen times around a string of 108 beads (called a "round") every day.

Japa beads consist of 108 beads tightly strung in a circle and meeting at a larger bead called the Krishna bead. Traditionally, japa beads are made from the wood of the sacred Tulasi plant and are carried in a cloth bag that can be hung around the neck. The bag also serves to keep the beads clean.

I used the thread from a new sock to string my 108 bread "beads." I loved chanting on them, but unfortunately I only kept them for one week or so. One morning, a guard noticed that I was chanting on them, so he took them from me and arranged for me to receive punishment. Without explanation, he suddenly became very angry and used my beads to strike my face and body until he was exhausted. I felt so sad. Those japa beads were my only possession there, for which I had saved so many pieces of bread. But the bitter reality was that there was nothing I could do.

Soon I had become an expert and started to make all kinds of Krishna conscious items, even a small bell for my offerings. It worked amazingly well and had a very sweet sound.

One day, I received my first letter from Sachisuta Prabhu, who was on the fifth floor, one floor above me. It came through a secret "postal service." I was surprised at how letters, illegal drugs, money, and various items were going through this system. In any case, he came to know which room I was in and sent me a letter with a set of japa beads made out of bread, but instead of 108 beads there were 54. He told me that the shorter strings of beads are easier to hide and if I chanted two times around, it would be one round. In his letter, he asked me how I was doing in general and how I was getting along with the criminals in my cell. He encouraged me to always keep up with chanting my rounds, to do whatever I could to always remember Krishna and never forget Him, and utilize everything for His service. I was happy to hear that he was doing well. Soon I received regular letters from Sannyasa dasa and Adwaita as well. We were encouraging each other and preaching to whomever we met.

After a while, everyone in the jail knew about Krishna. Some people from the other cells started to ask me and the other devotees questions, which we answered as soon as we could. We used to write answers on tiny pieces of papers from cigarette packages and similar insignificant items. It was dangerous to attempt communication in such ways. The guards caught others and myself on several occasions and beat us up badly for it.

The jail was set up as is sometimes seen in movies with the bars of the cells open to a central lobby with cells stacked on top of each other along the four sides. Anytime we heard someone beating on the floor or ceiling three times that meant they wanted to send something to us. We then sent out our "post box." This was a long "string" made of strips of bed sheets with a sock connected to the end that had a smashed bread ball at the bottom to give it some weight. The other party would catch it, putting in whatever they had for us and taking whatever was for them. It was not a simple operation because we had to somehow put our hands through the corner of the bars and throw the sock down to the other person while holding the end of the string. The other man was waiting with his hand out the same way and as soon as the string touched his hand, he needed to catch it and bring it into his cell. Since everything was done by touch alone, sometimes it took many tries until the operation was successful.

Some inmates were so expert that they would throw the "post box" from the fifth floor to the second or third floor directly rather than having the package go one floor at a time. We called that the "speed post." Sometimes we tangled two "post boxes" together so that they would go continually up, around and down like a clothesline.

Soon, we were preaching about Krishna to many prisoners. Sannyasa designed a flyer and sent one to each cell where each of the seven devotees was imprisoned. This flyer gave a summary of the history of the Hare Krishna movement and explained our devotional principles. Each of us copied the same wording and sent one flyer to each of the cells. Soon people stopped asking the same basic questions again and again, and only those prisoners who had more serious questions asked them and discussed the answers with us through this postal system.

One day, one of the guards came to me and said, "Mkan wants to see you." I knew that Mkan was a well-known personality in the Armenian criminal world. He had the reputation of almost going from one jail to another, hardly coming out. Even the police were sometimes afraid of such people.

I said, "Okay, I am ready to see him." So they opened his cell door, and he came to my room to see me. He was under the influence of drugs, probably illegally brought into the prison. He asked me all kinds of questions. He was challenging me from different angles, and we had a bit of an argument. I was extra careful with him, and he was satisfied. After I told him about Lord Caitanya and Srila Prabhupada, showing him my small pictures, he asked me to sing the maha mantra. When I finished, he told the guard not to bother me whenever I am singing. Then he left.

I was very happy that he had asked the guards to allow me to sing; it seemed the guards respected his authority. I then started to sing Hare Krishna while sitting next to the bars so my voice would go out and reach many people in their cells. Soon Sachisuta, Adwaita, and some girls from the fifth floor joined the kirtana too. Some of them were drumming on the tables, others were banging on pots with spoons, and some were clapping their hands. Wow! It was such a nice effect that I could not stop singing. I had not sung for a long time! This was such a good spiritual opportunity for all of us. In this way, we inaugurated the sankirtana movement in Sovetashens Jail, or "hell."

Soon everyone came to know that I had pictures, and they insisted on seeing them. I felt compelled to pass them through the whole jail. It took at least a couple weeks until they came back to me. In this way, everyone got the divine view of my most merciful Pancha Tattva and guru.

Sachisuta sent me another gift—it was a very unusual looking pen made out of synthetic sock thread. He made two or three of them every day, writing on them a colorful message such as Hare Krishna, Jaya Gurudeva, and so on by using the same threads. He then gave them out. Some policemen would ask us to make japa beads for them. Soon we realized that even fifty-four beads were too risky to keep, so we started to make twenty-seven bead strings. Being smaller, they were easier to hide from antagonistic persons. The difference was just that we had to chant four times in order to make 108, or one round. Sometimes, I even used a nine-bead set, keeping it almost all the time in my hand.

Some of these days were better than others, or I should say some days were different and perhaps less painful. Some of the prisoners, after some time, started to become more or less Krishna conscious and liked to hear more from me and the other devotees about Krishna. Some started to chant with us in the morning and to share with us whatever food their friends or relatives would bring.

It was nice to see how, after receiving their parcels from home, they would separate the vegetarian from the non-vegetarian food and place the vegetarian items on a table for me to start an offering. I would place the food in front of the small pictures of Pancha Tattva and my gurudeva, using my magic bell made from bread to offer whatever was there.

Soon, offering food before eating became a tradition in our cell. Everyone in the jail was taking prasadam from the devotees. Even people who were against Krishna consciousness ate something out of our offerings. Many of the inmates told me that they could actually tell the difference between offered and non-offered food.

Once a week, the guards took us all to the vast shower room. We would take off all our clothes and hang them on a long rack in a special oven-like room. While we showered, our clothes were heated to such a degree that it killed all the lice and germs. There were many large sinks where we could shave and wash out our socks and clothes. Only being able to take a bath once a week was really disgusting, so sometimes Khatsik or others in my room would bribe the guards to take us twice a week.

Anything that was used by the prisoners was all chipped and dented and twisted (and sometimes sharpened) practically beyond use. I never saw a new looking plate, cup, or anything that appeared smooth or shiny.

Everything had been used before by who knows how many people. In addition, the prisoners used anything that wasn't bolted down to fight with.

It was an unwritten law of the jail that all jail items stayed in the jail. When a man finished his sentence, he was given back the clothes that he came in with. He would change into them right there in the hall and hand his prison clothes to some friend waiting around the corner, or to a guard with instructions as to whom to give them. Sometimes a prisoner would have a sale, like a garage sale, where he would have used clothes for sale or trade along with small articles that had been mailed from the outside.

Money was everything there just like elsewhere; you could pay to obtain practically anything. One could get drugs and cigarettes, food and beverages, towels, color pens and paper—everything you could possibly need. The prisoners used to write a letter to their family members asking them to send any amount of money and whatever they needed. Then they would give the guards the family's address so the letter would be delivered. When the money arrived, a guard would act as broker, taking 100 rubles from each gift as a fee. It was my fondest dream to have one or two of Srila Prabhupada's books to study there, but I had no money to arrange for the guards to send a letter to the devotees. Another consideration was that I did not want to take a chance of getting other devotees into trouble. In addition to getting books, I also daydreamed about eating some prasadam made by devotees, but I could not imagine how that could be arranged either.

The other men in my cell liked to hear stories about Krishna, but unfortunately I had not studied the books well and could remember only a few stories. These stories I told again and again. I also explained philosophy, such as that Srila Prabhupada's guru had said that the whole material world was like a prison house. It is a place of suffering only, and therefore most people believe in the existence of a better place. I would make the point that everyone is forced to act, pushed and pulled by their senses. The prisoners and guards could immediately understand these points. In fact, the senses are actually less troublesome when one is confined in the jail. One knows that there is no use endeavoring to get more than just the bare necessities of life, because luxuries are impossible. The essence of spiritual knowledge, that I would repeat often, is that we are the soul, not the body. The soul is eternal, full of knowledge and bliss, or as Krishna says in theBhagavad-gita, "The soul cannot be moistened by water or burnt by fire. It is not slain when the body is slain."

When I told my cellmates that Krishna was born in a prison cell, they found that very interesting. I said, "Krishna always promises that whenever there is a rise in irreligion, He will come Himself to protect His devotees and annihilate the demons. Five thousand years ago was such a time—the world was overburdened by demoniac, godless warriors. So the devotees prayed for Krishna to come, and He said that He would. To accelerate Krishna's appearance, a demigod told the worst of these demons, King Kamsa, that the eighth child of his own sister, Devaki, would kill him. Kamsa immediately drew his sword to kill Devaki, but her husband appealed to Kamsa to reconsider. He argued, 'If you kill Devaki, a woman and your sister, then your reputation will be ruined. You don't have to fear Devaki, and we do not even have eight sons. I promise that when a child is born to us, we will immediately bring him to you.'

"Kamsa knew that his brother-in-law's word was as good as gold, but still he threw the newly married couple into his prison cell. Every year, Devaki would bear a child and her husband, Vasudeva, would bring the baby to Kamsa. Kamsa was so afraid for his life that he would dash these babies to the stone floor, killing them. But when Krishna was born with dazzling form and jewelry, His parents prayed that He would disguise Himself as a baby so He could be hidden away in the cowherd villages. Thus, Krishna grew up in a village of cowherds, giving His wonderful association to His devotees. Finally, he killed that powerful demon, King Kamsa."

Krishna consciousness philosophy was so appreciated there that sometimes I used to think that Lord Krishna brought me there just to preach His holy name and pastimes to these poor, suffering souls. Sometimes, I would be in real ecstasy while preaching to my cellmates. The most interesting point was that sometimes I was able to tell them stories or give them answers or use some examples that I had never in my life heard from anyone or read anywhere. It was as if I could hear and see myself from the outside, well at least I was trying to, and I was laughing and asking myself, "Where did you get this one from, man?" At such times the atmosphere would change so that everyone forgot his sufferings and problems, listening to me with great attention and agreeing with everything I, actually not I, but what Krishna was saying. This would sometimes go for hours until the guard would hit the door with his huge keys and scream that it is time for counting the prisoners, or lunch time or some such function. There were several artists in my cell who used to draw with color pens prison-related pictures or, mainly, girl pictures, on a handkerchief or clothes. They could do professional-level drawings of another prisoner's face, which that man could then send to his loved ones. We were all constantly thinking of how we could use their talent for Krishna's service. One day, I think Sannyasa or Kamalamala described Lord Krishna's beauty to one of these artists who then started to draw Krishna! Believe it or not, the picture resembled Lord Krishna perfectly! It was such a sweet drawing, with peacocks and a Surabhi cow in the background. I became very attached to this picture, but I do not know what happened to it afterwards.

One of the more interesting prisoners I got to know liked to gamble. He used to make a substantial amount of money. Sometimes his gambling was unusual. For example, one day at lunch time, a cellmate had a fly in a cup that was filled with water. He took it out and wanted to throw it on the floor, but the man who liked to gamble stopped him and asked him to place the fly on the table. He took a little stick and started to touch the fly to make sure it was dead. Then, he approached all of us and asked if everyone agreed that the fly was dead. Everyone was sure it was dead without a doubt, since there was not a single movement at all. Then he asked if anyone would believe that this fly could come back to life and fly from the table again. "No," everyone said. "No, of course not!"

The gambler declared, "I am willing to bet that I can give this fly life and it will fly away right in front of your eyes! If I do not do it, I will give you all 100 rubles, right now. But if I do, you men give me 100 rubles all together."

Everyone was astonished, and for a minute no one spoke. Then he asked us, one by one, who believed him and who did not. Some did not play at all, some said they did not believe it, and others were ready to give him or get from him 100 rubles. Then he approached me. "Hey, Hare Krishna, do you believe I can do it? You are always talking about the soul and I do not know what else, like life after death. What do you think about this soul?"

I said, "Yes, I do believe that you can do so."

So the money was collected, and believe it or not, the fly flew away in front of our eyes. It was simply amazing!

My son, who is writing this story of mine you are reading, couldn't believe that this prisoner had brought a fly "back to life." But once, in Houston, Texas (where we lived for a while), he asked me for ideas about a science project for school. The project had to be interesting, scientific, and demonstrated in front of the class. That was the first time I told my son the story of the fly.

I smiled when my son asked me to show the trick to him so that he could demonstrate it to his teacher and the students. The hardest part was to catch a fly and "kill" it in the water. Once you have a fly in water on your table, then you need a handful of salt only. Make a pyramid of salt over the fly. After a while, the salt will suck all the water out of the fly's soft body. It will slowly come out of the pyramid of salt, and after shaking its wings, it will fly away in front of your eyes! I do not know if the fly was truly dead or not, or answers to any similar questions. Often I was thinking also, what is actually happening to the fly? The soul is leaving the body then returns back? Or it was still there till the body of the fly dries up? Still I can't get it. I do know one thing only, that gambling is not a good thing to do.

# CHAPTER ELEVEN

# Who is Crazy

*There is no possibility of one's becoming a yogi,*
*O Arjuna, if one eats too much or eats too little,*
*sleeps too much or does not sleep enough.*

*–Bhagavad-gita, 6.16*

One day, my investigator came to talk to us. At the end of our conversation he mentioned that the KGB was planning to put us into a psychiatric hospital, so I had to be prepared for it.

"Your other friends are already there," he told me, meaning Sannyasa das, Kamalamala das, Atmananda das, and Bhakta Armen, "and you will go there soon, too."

I asked him the reason that they had to take us there and he replied, "Well, according to some Russian psychologists, most people who get involved in fanatic religious activities have some kind of mental disorder. So now they want to test all of you and see if everything is all right with you."

"Do I look like someone who has a mental disorder?" I asked him.

He started to smile and replied, "I do not know. They will let me know that after they examine you, and all I am here for is just to put into writing whatever they say."

I told him, "This is just another trick of the KGB! Now, they are trying to make people believe that we are a bunch of fools and fanatics!" He hung his head and said nothing.

So after that, I was just waiting, thinking, "When will they open the door, call my name, and take me to the psychiatric hospital to endure horrors that I have never even dreamt about?"

Some days later, the guards screamed my name, telling me to come out with all my luggage and be ready to go to an even worse place than the jail. As we had been warned, they took Adwaita, Sachisuta, and me to the Sovetashens Psychiatric Hospital.

I said goodbye and Hare Krishna to all the people in my cell and embraced them one by one. Everyone wished me good luck, saying they hoped that I would not have to return again to that hell. Usually if you say goodbye to someone, you add at the end, "Please come back again, or see you soon!" But the people in jails say to each other, "Never come back!" That is the most important blessing one can wish others.

Soon, I was walking down the stairs carrying a little plastic bag with a few belongings in it. In such situations, one gets very attached to every small article he has, and every event becomes important and sweet.

They put me in an ugly, black truck with Adwaita and Sachisuta. All three of us were very skinny and quite different than we remembered each other as being before our imprisonment. But despite all this, we were really happy to meet each other and share our feelings and experiences in that hell. We were so happy to see each other that we forgot completely about all the sufferings in there. It did not take a long time to reach the hospital, so we hardly had enough time to talk together.

We already knew from others in the jail who had already gone to this hospital, to expect a small place with only four cells available. We knew also that another group of arrested devotees had already been there for the last month or so. It was obvious that four of our friends were sitting in one cell, and we hoped that each of us would be meeting and staying there with one of our brothers.

Since I was very much attached to Sannyasa das from our first meeting, I was praying to Krishna to make some arrangement that I'd be with him in one cell. Later on, we had a conversation on the way to Russia by train, and Sachisuta was telling us that since he liked Atmananda das, he was praying to Krishna to be with him there, and Adwaita was praying to be with Kamalamala das. Krishna is in everyone's heart and knowing exactly what we were thinking, He fulfilled all of our desires just as we had prayed.

After a while, our truck stopped by the hospital, and someone opened the heavy gate for us to enter. First, they took us to a room where they gave us some very strange looking over-sized clothes to change into. Then they took all our belongings and put them in a box. They did not allow us to take anything else with us. It was absolutely prohibited there to possess anything, even pen and paper.

We did not like to wear those old stinky clothes, and we all looked very peculiar in them. God only knows how many people had been wearing these ugly clothes before us. Adwaita was smiling and looking at Sachisuta and me gently while he said, "This is our next exam, dear brothers. Let's be strong and with Krishna always, and He will surely help us no matter what." We both nodded our heads in agreement. A guard called us out right away and asked us to place our hands behind us while we followed him.

All kinds of unusual sounds were coming from upstairs, and we knew that we were just a minute away from seeing our old friends there. As we started to enter the corridor, we saw a tall man smiling and calling, "Hare Krishna, brothers! Haribol!" At first we did not recognize our own godbrother because he looked so thin and pale. They had given him so many injections of harsh chemicals that we could hardly believe that here was our dear friend Armen. He noticed that we did not recognize him and for that reason started to tell us, "Hey it's me, Armen! Brothers, how are you?!" He took his hand out of the bars and was waving to us. My heart was beating faster and faster, and I could not hold back my tears. Next we saw Kamalamala, who was also very different in appearance now, but strong and happy looking. His posture was bent down but he was smiling, asking how we were doing. They opened the cell and put Adwaita in with Kamalamala.

I was thinking Atmananda's cell was next, and Sannyasa had the last cell. Who will they ask to go in with what person? They opened Atmananda's door. He looked at us happily, while calling out "Haribol." I started to think, "Who do they have to throw in now?" I did not pay attention to my fear. I started to relax and chant the Hare Krishna mantra in my mind. They pulled Sachisuta's hand and closed the door behind him. "O my Krishna," I said in my mind, "I thank you so much for your kind arrangement! Thank you so much, that now was a 100% guarantee that I would soon be with my Sannyasa das after a long time!"

Sannyasa was waiting for me and happily embraced me. We sat on his bed where he asked me many questions about the past months. It was a big room with a high ceiling and one or two windows covered with metal bars. The windows were so high that we could not see outside. In order to look outside one needed to stand on top of another's shoulder and place the tip of one leg on a little cement ledge. There were about ten or twelve metal beds in the room, just like in some hospitals. The walls were painted white and looked like they had been renovated not long before. There was enough light from the windows to make artificial light unnecessary. It was somewhat stinky there. Sometimes when the criminals were walking across the room I could smell some sort of terrible medicine odor from their clothes.

I could not believe that the person in front of me was the same Sannyasa I knew before. He was so skinny! He moved slowly and slurred his speech. His chin had become sharp and his eyes sunk in. His beautiful face, which had some beard growth, was very white. I asked him what the matter was and how they were treating them. He told me that at first they took them to a Moscow psychiatric hospital and kept them there for about one month. Then about one month before my coming they had brought all four of them to Sovetashens Criminal Psychiatric Hospital and started to give them daily injections by force of a neuro-psychological drug called Galapiridol and some other drugs which I can't remember. These medicines make the inmates very weak and easily controlled.

Sometimes while he was talking, Sannyasa's mouth would become dry, and his eyes would roll like a drunk man. I could not stop my tears. Sometimes he would press me towards him while trying to smile and convince me that everything was okay with him. Somehow, I asked him through my tears, "What the hell are they doing to you, here? How can they do this to us? How?"

I had forgotten my pain completely, and his pain became mine. I felt so bad and at the same time helpless. I was constantly thinking, "What to do, how can I help this wonderful devotee of the Lord, who is doing such an important service for Him?"

Some crazy men were sitting on one of the beds, looking at me, and saying loudly, "Hey, just see! Now they bring us another Hare Krishna! Now they won't let us sleep all night; they will start to chant, 'Hare hare hare hare bol bol bol bol kis kis kis kis and so on'!"

Then one of the guards looked in at Sannyasa and me and laughed loudly. I could not tolerate this, and I stood up and started to scream at him, "What did you men do to my brother! What did you do? How can you do this to innocent people? You have made him a half person already!"

The next moment the guard stopped laughing. He called another guard and started to select the right key for our room with a lot of noise. "Looks as if someone here already needs an injection to calm down!" he said. He entered our room and asked me to come out with him. Sannyasa came and stood in front of me and did not let me go. He asked them to please not take me out and asked me to stop cursing the guard immediately. Otherwise they would give me the same dosage, and I would be just like him.

They came and twisted both my arms and were trying to take me out of the cell, but Sannyasa was pulling them back and, with tears in his eyes, requesting them, "Please do not do that to him, please!"

He kept telling them that I had just come, and I did not know the rules and regulations yet. He assured the guards that he was now going to explain them to me and that I would never do this again. After a while, they dropped me and left the cell while cursing me.

Then Sannyasa started to tell me everything they were doing to him and the others, and what the guards could tolerate and what they could not. He told me about the trip by special jail train to Moscow and back, which took one month, and about all the crazy medications that they were giving to all of them for the last two months.

His suffering was making me suffer day and night. Sometimes I could not sleep just seeing how he was suffering and tolerating the pain of the injections and medicine. All four of the devotees were having the same types of problems, but Armen was having the most difficulty. We all could see how, day by day, he would act and speak in a deranged way. This was hurting me terribly because I didn't know how I could help my friends. How could I help them if I myself was in a helpless situation?

Atmananda was the next to become severely affected by the drugs. He started to laugh and laugh every day, saying things that were different from his natural state. Sometimes the guards teased him, and sometimes they would ask him to sing and dance for them, which he would do. He would chant the "Hari Haraye Nama Krishna" song while dancing in a funny way due to his bodily weakness. When Atmananda would dance like this, I would come close to the bars of my cell and ask him to stop because the guards were simply having a laugh at his expense. He used to tell me that, even if by teasing, these people are participating in a kirtana, and that would change their life sufficiently in the future. He would then continue dancing and singing.

Kamalamala das was the strongest of all of us. No matter how many injections they gave him, he walked fine and controlled himself well. He gave all of us courage and a lot of enthusiastic power, shakti, to tolerate the situation. He used to preach all the time very philosophically in such a way that no one could argue with him. We were all happy to have him with us. He had very much faith in our guru, Harikesa Swami. He was always telling us that our guru would rescue us from this hell soon and take us to the spiritual world.

I think it was the forth or fifth day after I came that we heard Adwaita cursing the guards very loudly and telling them that they were opening their direct path to hell by giving these injections to our friends. So the guards opened his cell and took him out of there. All the prisoners were looking from their bars as much as was possible to see what was going on. They took him to the doctor's room and it became very quiet. After about ten minutes they brought him back to the cell, but he was not the same person any more. He was not speaking any more, his mouth was dried just like Sannyasa's, and he was walking like a drunk man a little bit. The next day we all could see that he was still suffering very much from the drugs, tolerating the pain somehow.

The next day when they took him to the bathroom, I asked him how he was feeling. He replied slowly, "If they do one more injection like that to me, I may give up chanting because the injection is very painful. The drugs make it difficult to control the tongue and mind, plus my mouth gets very dry." I couldn't believe my ears. He was such a strong devotee and personality and was speaking like a weak person. Then I started to pray, "O my God, please do not allow these demons to give me these crazy injections. If Adwaita can't tolerate that pain, then how am I going to tolerate it?" The next morning, they took all three of us, one by one, to see Doctor Armen, the head doctor. After filling out some papers, he ordered guards to take me to the next room for a blood test.

Then I returned to my cell, where I thought about life in the hospital. We could not see the devotees who were in a different cell, but we could speak to each other if the guard was not there for a moment. They fed us much better than in the jail. For our meals, we came out into the corridor, where there were some tables and chairs. They even gave us twenty grams of butter every morning with bread that was the same quality as I'd had in the Russian Army. There was only one bathroom at the end of the wide corridor. We used to go there only at limited times. If we wanted to go out of the scheduled times, it was difficult to persuade the guards unless at least three people wanted the guards to escort them at the same time. So we used to go to the bathroom each time they took us out for a meal.

It seemed they liked my blood because they started to call me many times for it, taking a lot of blood from me. I asked the doctors why they had to take so much blood from my veins, but all they told me was that they simply followed whatever Doctor Armen was telling them to do. We later learned that the only reason they collected our blood was to sell it to other hospitals.

They kept giving injections to the other devotees with terrible results and sometimes some tablets. Sannyasa was feeling very weak, and I did not know how to help him. Sometimes he would sit and look at one spot for a long time without making a movement or saying anything. After a while, he would stand up and shake as if he were cold. I would then put my blanket on him, but after some time he would tell me it was too hot and would lie down in pain. I would then go under my blanket, tears pouring from my eyes, while I prayed to Krishna to kindly help His wonderful devotee, Sannyasa das. Sannyasa is a very strong personality, and no matter what happened and in which condition he was in, he would every day complete chanting his sixteen rounds of the Hare Krishna maha-mantra—a determination that surprised me and inspired me with more energy to go on.

One day they called me, placed me in handcuffs, and asked me to follow the guard out of the building. I think that was the first time in six or seven months that I walked on grass instead of concrete floors. It was a sunny day, which made my eyes hurt very acutely. I looked around as if I were a child, glad to see some trees and people who were walking or sitting on the bench under the trees. Everyone was looking at me, since I was in handcuffs and strange clothes. I felt ashamed. I wanted to scream and tell all of them that I am not a criminal but an innocent man, but who would have cared?

I was so happy to hear the birds singing, and the beautiful breeze was like nectar for me. When my nose started to itch, I scratched it with my shoulder. I wanted to scream and tell all the people how fortunate and blessed they were to be outside and free. Sometimes we do not appreciate being happy outside and free, and we complain about this and that situation, or we are unhappy that someone is creating some small problems for us and so on. I promise you that if once, even for a short time, you have to stay behind iron doors where there is nothing except dirty and dark walls, then as soon as you come out you will appreciate wherever you live, even if it is an old apartment or an uncomfortable environment. You will surely appreciate the open sky and the singing of the birds, your broken chair and rusted bicycle, the old car and the job that pays less than you want.

Sometimes in the many years since I have been free from jail, I have noticed that even devotees of Krishna can start to get attached to material things, which actually bring us only a little happiness and lots of troubles. Humans always want more and more from this material world than we actually need. It is impossible to satisfy our heart's desires or the senses, which are more powerful than a fire, ready to burn all surroundings just to satisfy the tiny, temporary, and actually useless desires. When we complain about the situation we are in, Krishna teaches us a good lesson by placing us temporarily in a worse situation so that we will appreciate the gift we had just a week or month ago. Then we understand the most important thing in life, which I think is that this material world is a place for miseries and that the only solution to our problems is fully surrendering to Krishna.

So I really appreciated what I had and paid my obeisances again and again to Lord Krishna for teaching me in a very short time what many people would have to spend many years, or perhaps lifetimes, to learn. The most important lesson is to appreciate all the devotees of the Lord and never commit any offenses to any of them. I learned that each and every devotee who is seriously chanting the holy name is a very unique personality, dear to Krishna. If perhaps they make some mistakes, then Krishna Himself will take care of him or her in a better way then we can imagine. It also might be that we do not like what a devotee is doing, but Krishna may like it. My friends, please be very appreciative for everything you have today; just continue with your devotional service to Krishna and love all the parts and parcels of the Lord as yourself.

After walking through the grounds of the psychiatric hospital, they took me to the next building, where they locked me in one room where three or four doctors were waiting for me. One of them appeared strange, like a mad scientist. He started to tease and offend me by making unusual faces. I tolerated that as Sannyasa had told me to do, and I answered some questions so they wouldn't beat me up again. The doctor seemed to be completely mentally ill, making ugly faces and sticking out his tongue to the point that I felt like kicking the table into his face. One fat lady was writing some notes on a big piece of paper very fast, and from time to time looking at me strangely. After some time, they took me to the next room, removed my handcuffs, and asked me to get into a huge machine and sit there.

Two male nurses started to clean some spots on my body and head with rubbing alcohol, where they then placed forty to fifty sticky contact pads with some wires that were connected to the computer next to the machine. Then they asked me to close my eyes and relax. They closed the door, turned off the light, and asked me to try not to think of anything. I did exactly the opposite, keeping my eyes open and making my body and muscles tight because I was afraid to follow what they had told me to do. A loud sound came from the machine, and the pads on my body started to tickle me and sometimes even poke me. When I heard the printer outside starting to print something, I started to chant Hare Krishna in my mind as fast as I could. We had learned that sometimes in situations like that, when you do not know really what to do or what is going on, it is better to chant Hare Krishna and only think of Krishna.

It took them about ten minutes to do I do not know what. They did not tell me anything about what they were doing or what was going on. Then they opened the door to release me from there and took me back to my cell. Sannyasa and I spent hours trying to figure out what they were doing to me. The strange thing was that they had done this only to me and no one else.

One afternoon we heard someone softly calling our names from outside. It was Damayanti devi dasi (Armine), asking how we are doing there. I brought Sannyasa up to the window, and he started to slowly speak to her. Some other criminals were standing next to the door and watching so in case the guard was coming we would bring down Sannyasa. Sannyasa was speaking by hand movements mainly; otherwise, the guard would come and catch us and punish us badly for speaking to outsiders. After speaking a little bit Sannyasa somehow could make her understand that it would be best if we could speak to her directly so she could tell the world what was actually going on with all of us.

He called the guard and asked how much he would charge us to talk to Damayanti. I do not remember exactly how much Sannyasa agreed to pay, but it was a lot of money for us. The guard said that she must come with the money in the evening, when all the so-called doctors were gone and only guards remained. He took Sannyasa downstairs to a separate room for about forty-five minutes to speak with Damayanti.

When Sannyasa met with her, we were all very happy that we finally had gotten a chance to send out the real picture of what was going on with us there to the devotees all over the world. Sannyasa related everything those demons were doing to us, and Damayanti sent the information to Moscow, where it reached our guru and Kirtiraja Prabhu, who were very actively organizing meetings and demonstrations all over the world in front of Russian embassies. They organized a "Free the Soviet Hare Krishna" program committee and collected thousands of signatures to send to Mikhail Gorbachev.

In Australia, devotees organized a program where a young devotee named Prahlad sang a sweet song written by him about the Soviet devotees. (This video is on hkussr.com.) The song soon became very popular all over the world, and sometimes it could be heard on the radio. The devotees used to hold banners and our available pictures as they sang and asked help from everyone. Prahlad, along with other children of the Hare Krishna devotees, used to sing "Mister Gorbachev, let our friends free!" with tears in their eyes in the streets. The devotees somehow managed to give the video of that program to the Prime Minister of Australia, who was at that time going to Russia to meet Mikhail Gorbachev. He promised to give the video to Mr. Gorbachev there, which he did.

There was a positive effect to the effort of all these devotees. We quickly heard that directly because of the devotees' propaganda the police demanded that the Russian psychiatric hospital administrator talk to the devotees personally before signing any paper stating that all Hare Krishna devotees are crazy and cult victims.

After some time, the Russian psychiatric hospital administrator did indeed come from Moscow to Armenia for several days and talked to each and every one of us separately. She was an interesting and good looking lady, about forty-five years old. I think her name was Lyudmila. She spoke to us kindly. She seemed to sincerely try to understand Krishna consciousness, what each of us devotees were like, and the real situation for us in prison.

First, they called Sannyasa and Kamalamala to meet her, then Atmananda and Armen, then Agvan and Sako. I was last. Everyone was preaching to this lady according to his ability, and she was very happy to hear all of us separately. It was up to her to decide what to write about us, as to whether we were insane or normal.

She asked me how I was chanting nowadays without my japa beads; so I showed her my new beads made out of a thick blanket thread. We used to pull out one of the threads somehow and make a knot several times in one spot and after a little distance make another one and so on, making a circle of twenty-seven or fifty-four knots and chanting on it. She was very impressed with that idea and asked me if she could have my japa "beads." I gave them to her, and for a long time she was looking and looking at them, turning them in her hand. She told me that my papers indicated that I used to take drugs before I joined the Hare Krishna movement. She wanted to know which kind of drugs I used to take. She was very surprised that I had given them up so easily, opium and hashish, and now refused them forever.

She spent three or four days with us, and since we all glorified Krishna prasadam, she said that she wanted to actually taste prasadam at least once to see for herself what it tastes like. Sannyasa told her that if she could arrange to bring some new pots and all the necessary ingredients and vegetables, we could cook lunch for everyone at the hospital, and she could taste it as well. She asked the chief doctor to arrange everything for us. The chief doctor was very surprised that such an important lady, who was at that time the chief of all the psychiatric hospitals in the Soviet Union, would eat food cooked by, according to his understanding, crazy people. Sannyasa made a detailed list, and by the next morning everything was there waiting for us.

The doctors did not allow all of us to participate in the cooking; Sannyasa was supposed to do everything alone. They only allowed me to cut some vegetables. Soon the hospital was full of the fragrance of the cooking, and everyone was talking about it, waiting to taste a little bit of food offered to Krishna.

He made several different preparations and offered them to Krishna in the kitchen. We took that opportunity to have a kirtana for Krishna too, saying that was the other half of our religious practices and without the kirtana the food would not be complete. I was leading the singing, with everyone repeating after me, and we could hear all the prisoners in the cells actively participating in the kirtana. All the guards were teasing us and making crazy faces, but they had no choice but to listen to the kirtana, since the chief doctor allowed us to sing. This was the only day they could not say anything to us; the chief doctor had told them to allow us to do whatever we wanted for that day.

After some time, wonderful prasadam was ready to serve. First, Sannyasa made up plates for all the doctors downstairs, and after that they allowed everyone, one cell at a time, to come out and eat on tables in the corridor. It was without a doubt the tastiest food I have ever eaten in my life, before or after my arrest! We had three sweets, five or six salty preparations, and two different juices. Everyone was in ecstasy! We were feeling just like Vasudeva celebrating Lord Krishna's appearance in Kamsa's prison; it was something extraordinary for all of us.

Only one crazy man did not eat prasadam. He was a fifty-something-year-old man who had been a butcher for all his life and was imprisoned for raping an eight or ten year old girl. He probably hated us more than anyone else there. Some of the people in our room were plain crazy, but this man was especially so. Some had committed crimes and were in the hospital to go through various procedures to see if they were insane when they committed the crime or not. But that man is one we can never forget!

He was trying to show that he was crazy so the police wouldn't take him to jail but would instead stay in the psychiatric hospital for the rest of his life. He knew well that if they took him to the jail the criminals would make his life miserable. Whenever the doctors would come, he would fall on the ground, shaking and vomiting, sticking out his tongue and other crazy antics. He was a tall, skinny man with a very animalistic face. He was very aggressive towards devotees. He would always tease me and Sannyasa and would harass me. Sometimes in the morning, when we sat and chanted, he would come and attack us screaming, "I am God! I am God! You have to worship me, not Krishna! Who is Krishna? There is no Krishna!" And then he would scream very loudly, "What kind of Armenians are you that you are doing Krishna Krishna?"

Whenever we would complain to the guards, they wouldn't do anything but laugh. Sometimes he would come down and sit with us and ask us what

Harivilas das, GBC of Armenia, who translated and published first Armenian books and current GBC of the CIS countries, Bhaktivignan Goswami Maharaja.

**Sachisuta das in the Russian Army in 1982**

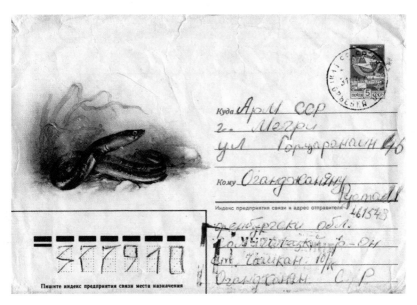

Sachisuta's Russian Army document

The envelope in which Sachisuta prabhu
sent his last letter to his parents.

# PETITION

I, the undersigned, present the following statement to Mr. Mikhail Gorbachev, general secretary of the Communist Party of the Soviet Union, and to Mr. Eduard Shevarnadze, the foreign minister:

I deeply deplore the inhuman treatment and conditions that members of the Hare Kṛṣṇa movement in the USSR are being subjected to. They are being denied the basic human rights to which they are entitled under the provisions of the Soviet Constitution, as well as all the international agreements and treaties that the Soviet Union has endorsed.

I request the Soviet government to allow the members of the Hare Kṛṣṇa movement to register their religion as an official state religion. I also implore the authorities to arrange the immediate release of the following Hare Kṛṣṇa devotees, who are imprisoned in psychiatric hospitals, prisons, and labor camps, or have been sentenced to compulsory labor, and following their release, to permit their emigration from the Soviet Union along with their immediate family:

Agvan K. Arutyunan, Gagik S. Buniatyan, Nugzar A. Chargaziya, Jakov E. Dzhidzhevadze, Yuri A. Fedchenko, Rafael Janashviili, Suren G. Karapetyan, Olga Khamidovna Kiseleva, Vladimir G. Kritski, Vladimir A. Kustrya, Alexander V. Levin, Yevgeny N. Lyubinsky, Alexei A. Musatov, Armen V. Saakyan, Otari S. Nachhebiya, Sarkis R. Ohanjanyan, Anatoli F. Pinyayev, Sergei A. Priborov, Karen V. Saakyan, Anatoli I. Samotlov, Ashot S. Shaglomdzyan.

Name:_____

Address:_____

City:_____State:_____Zip:_____

Country:_____

**The petition for "Free the Soviet Hare Krishnas"**

This wooden press was hand made by the Armenian devotees for the production of Srila Prabhupada's first books

Japa beads hand made by the early Soviet devotees

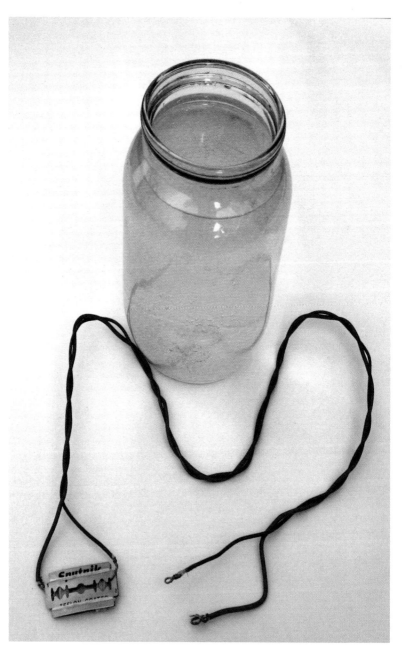

This simple yet magic device (made of two razor blades and a piece of wire) was used daily by sarvabhavana das in the prison camp to boil water before drinking to prevent disease.

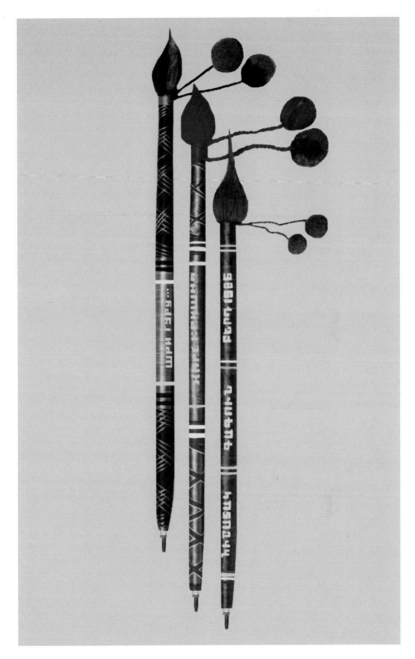

These beautiful pens were made by Sachisuta das using color sock threads and paper. He wrote Hare Krishna on them and kept preaching to the prisoners.

Sarvabhavana das in the Russian Army in 1982.

**Sarvabhavana das watching the test printing of the first pages from the Armenian Bhagavad-gita.**

Sarvabhavana's present family Deities, Their Lordships Most Merciful Sri Sri Radha Shyamasundara in Yerevan, Armenia

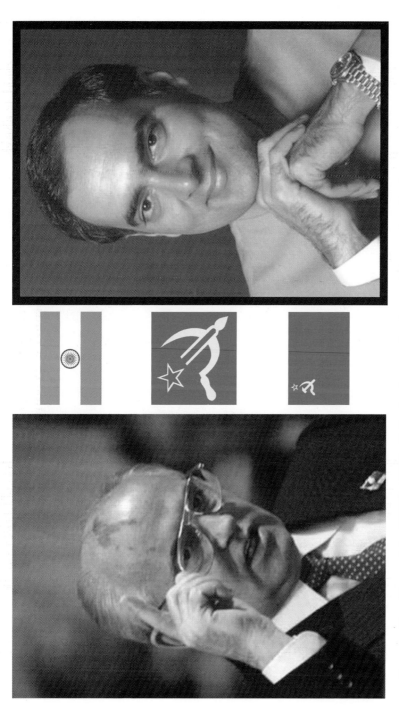

Former President of the USSR, Mikhail Gorbachev and Prime Minister of India, late Rajiv Gandhi. Two completely different views about Hare Krishna and religion.

Russian devotees during ecstatic Harinama

Armenian devotees after the attack on their temple, what a mess!

Sovietashens jail where seven Armenian devotees were hold for a long time. The red circle on the window indicates the cell where Sarvabhavana das spent six months.

Kirtiraj das with three famous Armenian devotees in Kolkata airport right after their historical arrival. Left to right: Atmananda das, Kirtiraj das, Kamalamala das and Sannyasa das.

Sarvabhavana's son with a Bhagavad Gita

The **Sovietashen** jail's psychiatric hospital where the Armenian devotees were tortured.

Sarvabhavana das during the historical first marriage ceremony in Vrindavan in 1989. Several Russian devotee couples were fortunate to participate in the fire sacrifice and had their Vedic wedding there.

Pages from Sarvabhavana's prison diary

Kindergarten picture of Sachisuta das

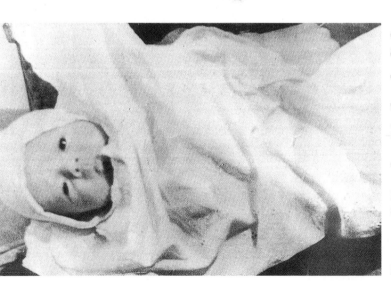

Premavati's Daughter Marika who died in the Russian prison

we thought about this or that. Sometimes he would glorify us and say, "Oh yes, that's right" and "great!" Whenever he saw something he didn't like, he would get angry at us and scream, and a couple of times he attacked Sannyasa and tried to choke him. Somehow we were able to push him off.

But one day he was probably in a good mood and started to tell us an amazing story from his life, which I can never ever forget. One day while he was working in a slaughterhouse, killing animals with his axe, he happened to see something very unusual that made him scared and astonished.

One day a huge bull was brought in a large truck to the slaughterhouse to be killed by him and his friends. The bull refused to come out of the truck, even after heavy beating with sticks by the butchers. This butcher felt the bull knew exactly what they were trying to do to him, and so was screaming and trying to hit them with his huge horns. They tried everything they could, and the bull still didn't move an inch. Then one of the butchers tied a chain around the bull's neck and the other end to a post next to the entrance. Then the truck was driven forward. In this way, the bull had no other option but to jump down from the truck. He hurt himself badly, which made him even angrier.

Somehow they pushed the bull inside the building, and brought him to the third floor, where they were supposed to give him an electric shock, kill him, and cut him into many pieces. But as soon as they opened the third floor door and pushed the bull in, he started to run around. With his huge horns he was breaking all the machinery and equipment that was used for killing thousands and thousands of innocent animals. Sparks and smoke flew everywhere from the burning electric cables. The metal hooks and equipment fell on the concrete floor, making an overwhelming noise. Everyone was so scared that they locked the iron bar door and started to watch the whole scene from there. The bull started to attack them through the door and was trying to smash the iron bars. He seemed ready to kill all of them right there, one by one. As blood was pouring from his horns and body, the bull was screaming from the pain and anger. He started to run around helplessly.

For a moment the bull stopped in front of the bars, looked straight into the eyes of the butchers, and then turned around and ran towards the window covered with steel bars. He jumped, pushing the whole window out of the wall. He then fell down from the third floor and practically speaking exploded, committing suicide right there in front of the eyes of the butchers. The prisoner told us that he believed that this animal had much intelligence. He remembered that when he was looking into the bull's eyes it seemed as if the bull was talking to him, cursing him for what he was doing to animals. He said that he could never forget that incident, the eyes, and the feeling of that bull.

We were really touched by this story, and we often told it to people whenever there was a discussion about animal killing. I think the day he told that story was the only day we ever saw him in a normal condition. Otherwise, he was always acting like a madman to prove to the doctors that he was crazy and thus avoid going to jail. In a jail, prisoners would beat him to death for the crime he committed. No one respects such people there. Usually he would walk across the room and speak to himself, cursing someone. He used to ask us to do something to hurt him so that the doctors would come and see how crazy he was.

The day after Sannyasa cooked lunch for everyone, the doctor called him to give her opinion about the prasadam, as well as to discuss what she was going to do about us and what kind of report she was going to write about us. We were all anxious to know the diagnosis of the doctor because her opinion could change our situation. After some time, when Sannyasa came back his smiling face told us that she told him something positive.

He was very happy to inform us that Lyudmila was pleased with all of us and our answers to her questions. She decided we were all nice, normal people, and she would not sign a false document that would be against her better judgment. She liked what all the prisoners were telling her about us as well. She said that she submitted a very thorough and positive report about us, and that's all she could do. The rest was up to the KGB, whatever they wanted to decide. She also said that the prasadam was very remarkable, and she wrote down some recipes from Sannyasa's notes. She left the next day, and I never saw her again.

Some years later, Sannyasa met her in Moscow. She was very happy to see him. She eventually became a very good friend of the devotees and started to regularly visit the Moscow temple. She would chant Hare Krishna sometimes and became a vegetarian. She told Sannyasa that since she did not sign the false paper for the KGB, she was fired, but never felt sorry about it.

Since her report was ready and there was nothing else to do with us, they took Sachisuta, Adwaita, and me back to the jail where we were supposed to wait for our trial. That's how the law was, and if a criminal was not mentally ill, then they had to be sentenced and sent to a labor camp. We came back to the same cell where we had already spent a lot of time and stayed there until the court day. Some of the criminals were not there anymore, and some who were there we already knew, which made our lives a little easier. We were told not to start preaching again.

# CHAPTER TWELVE

# Unwanted Days

*For him who has conquered the mind,*
*the mind is the best of friends;*
*but for one who has failed to do so,*
*his mind will remain the greatest enemy.*

*–Bhagavad-gita, 6.5*

N ot every day was interesting in Sovetashens, cell number 73. Some days were boring, some were scary, some were sad, and some crazy. No one could predict anything about the next day or even the next minute.

What was for sure was that each day was one more hole in our calendar. Every night before we went to bed we used to make a hole on that day's number with a pin or something sharp.

Slowly, Khatsik, the prisoner who was interested in philosophy, and I became good friends. We had much deeper discussions about life, religion, faith, and hope. We made up all kind of games to help our days pass a little faster. Many people came and many were getting sentenced and going to the other cells and afterwards to a labor camp. Whenever new criminals used to come in to our cell, we tried to guess what they did to get committed to this place. Almost every time we were right. Perhaps, under pressure our minds got so sharp that sometimes it seemed as if we could read others' minds just like you would read a newspaper. Many times, we knew exactly what people would do under certain situations and what would happen next.

Sometimes Khatsik's wife would come and bring him some food, and then he could see her from the corner of the bars on the window. He would pay ten rubles to talk to his wife from the window for fifteen minutes. He used to shout so that she could hear him. I thought, "Maybe one day some devotees will come to me as well, and I can talk to them and know what is actually happening outside of the walls and bars!"

One evening, everyone was in bed. I was walking and chanting when I heard some sound from outside, but I did not pay attention. After some time, one of the prisoners who was sleeping much nearer to the window told me that he had heard someone calling "Hare Krishna" from outside. I did not believe it and did nothing for a while. After some time, I really heard someone calling, "Hare Krishna, Sako. Hare Krishna, Gago. Hare Krishna, Agvan." And then after some time, again, "Sannyasa, Kamalamala, Atmananda, Armen" and so on. My tears started to run, and I jumped to the window and screamed "Haribol! Haribol!"

An answer came, "Haribol! Haribol!"

"Who is there?" I asked loudly.

"It's me, Armine (Damayanti devi dasi)!" She was there in the cold snowy yard with her two children, Sona and Tigran.

"Hey, Haribol! How are you? How is everything going outside?" I shouted.

"Everything is fine! We just got a letter from Sri Visnupad! He is organizing demonstrations for you men, and he wrote you a nice letter, which we will send you soon, somehow!"

We could only talk back and forth for five to ten minutes and then I could hear how she started to scream at the police, who caught her and took her away. I was very sad. All kinds of questions started to arise in my mind that I wanted to ask her, but it was too late and I was not prepared for it. After a few seconds, the guard opened the door and asked me to come out. As soon as I came out, he beat me and screamed, "What were you just doing?"

"Nothing," I replied.

"Who were you were talking to?"

"No one."

Using vulgar language, he said, "Who was that (blank) who came in this late night to the jail?"

"What do you mean?"

"I mean that you were just talking to some (blank)."

"No, I wasn't talking to anyone."

He kicked and beat me up mercilessly. He struck me in the stomach several times with his knee until I felt as if my stomach was about to come out of my mouth. I was thinking about Damayanti and hoped that they were not doing the same to her outside. He told me that the next time he noticed the same infraction he would take me downstairs, which meant the underground cell, where there is no window or natural light, a place four steps long and two steps wide. There, they only fed you once every second day. During the day time, they closed the wooden bed which hung from the wall; so you had to sit on the wet floor all day long.

After he threw me back in my cell, the other men cursed the guard until he went away. I was bleeding a little bit, but happy that at least I had a chance to know that affairs are going on well with the devotees on the outside. Now I knew that their situation was not at all as bad as the police had described to me—that all the devotees are in a jail or a psychiatric hospital. My cellmates helped me to clean myself and tried to pacify me with some sweet words. I was in pain for the next couple days, but then I was okay.

If someone was bored, he could sharpen the aluminum spoons in order to widen a hole in the wall that someone had started to cut many years back. The inmates used to hope that when they finally cut that piece of wall from the corner of the bars, they would be able to look outside.

Every morning and evening, and sometimes during the day, the inmates used to make tea in a pot. To make the fire last longer, they used to roll plastic bags and paper together into a kind of pipe, which made a terrible toxic smell, but was good enough to boil their cup of tea. It was usually more tea than water; they did not actually call it tea, but chefir. Smoke would stay in the room for a long time, and before the air cleared it was time to drink another cup. So there was hardly any time when the air was not full of toxic fumes. They told me that it gave them strength to be able to tolerate all the suffering in jail. They offered the tea to me as well, but I refused to take it. It is true that when someone is suffering, time seems to pass ten times slower. My only shelter was the holy name of Krishna, and I kept chanting all day long as much as I could, unless someone interrupted me to ask a question.

Sometimes we were allowed to walk on the roof of the building. According to law, they were supposed to take criminals to the roof every day for one hour, but they did not always give us such mercy. They asked a certain amount of money from each cell to take you there. If a cell was unable to collect the money, then everyone suffered, dreaming about the blue sky for a long time. Going on the roof was our only chance to see the sky! It was so refreshing and cleansing to my eyes and my mind to see the blue sky and sunshine, although from time to time the police walked above us on bars above the roof, as if on top of our heads. After constant meditation on the dirty black and bloody walls and almost black ceiling, it used to make a tremendous difference for me to see that sky. The others would smoke a cigarette there, and I could hardly get a breath of fresh air. But still it was far better than being in the dark cell, lit only by one stark and ugly dusty bulb.

In the fall, the flocks of white Siberian Cranes would fly all the way to India to "vacation," returning in April to nest in the harsh, barren tundra of the Siberian plains. Sometimes a bird would fly from somewhere else, sing briefly, and fly away. We were all thinking "Oh, if you could sing a little longer for us." I used to chant Hare Krishna, look up at the sky, and imagine that I was a Siberian Hawk soaring and swooping in the sky without restriction.

The swiftest and surest of all birds of prey is the white Siberian Hawk called the Goshawk or Tujhun. Its dive has been clocked at 187 miles per hour! Rarely domesticated, it is a mysterious figure in the grim legends of that sparse territory. It is said in the folklore that "the Gyrfalcon is the lord of all birds, the Peregrine is the killer of all birds, and the Goshawk is the villain of all birds."

Time passed slowly in that terrible, unclean place. The cell walls were covered with blood, either from fighting or from the mosquitoes and other bugs. Bugs constantly attacked us at night, sucking our blood with such a terrible pain, leaving ugly red spots on our bodies. It was practically impossible to sleep for more than ten minutes at a time. They used to come out mainly at night, walk on the walls, and slowly come to our bodies and bite. If anyone would see these guys on the walls they would immediately kill them right away with some paper or just their finger. The dead bugs would smell terrible and leave a bloody spot on the walls, so that where our metal beds were welded to the walls was all reddish black.

After some days, Damayanti came again and started to call us from the window. We had not even exchanged a few sentences before a guard started to knock on the door and scream, "Hey, Hare Krishna, get down from the window! Otherwise, I will come in and beat you up!" He was cursing us a lot. I jumped down and sat on my bed, feeling very sorry that again I was unable to talk to them.

After a while, one of the prisoners stationed himself to look under the door to see if the police were coming so I could talk to her again. I asked if she could give us a calendar of Ekadasi days, Gaura Purnima day, and other important holy days. She quickly told me the days while I wrote everything down so that I could tell all the devotees in the jail. She could only tell me some of them, and then I did not hear her anymore. I was so happy that at least I came to know the date of Gaura Purnima, Lord Chaitanya's appearance day, which would be only in about one week's time. We started to think of how we were going to celebrate that important event which was the 500th anniversary of Lord Chaitanya's appearance.

On March 25, 1986, I asked for a handkerchief from one of the prisoners and started to draw a picture with colored pens. Usually, I am not good at drawing, but I think by Krishna's mercy that day I drew something interesting from my heart. I drew an altar with candles on it, which we meditated on as a real altar. There were also handcuffs, my chanting beads, the Pancha Tattva mantra, and some other symbols in the picture.

In the morning, Adwaita called me up from the window and asked me to sing a little bit. I started to sing Sri Sri Gurvastaka (the eight prayers in honor of the spiritual master) beginning with:

> *samsara-davanala-lidha-loka-*
> *tranaya karunya-ghanaghanatvam*
> *praptasya kalyana-gunarnavasya*

And, at the end of each verse, all the prisoners were singing "Vande Guroh Sri-caranaravindam"

The ladies were singing loudly and participating very actively from the fifth floor, banging their spoons on the bars and pots. It was one of the most ecstatic kirtanas I have ever experienced in my life! Fortunately, no guard came to disturb us on that day because Khatsik gave some money to them in advance to leave us alone.

All the devotees observed fasting for Gaura Purnima. I collected some ingredients from the prisoners, and by kneading everything together, made my first cake out of black bread, margarine, and sugar. I then offered it to my Pancha Tattva picture altar on the handkerchief.

In the evening, we passed out the cake, and everybody was in bliss. I cut the cake with the handle of a spoon that I had sharpened for days on the wall. It was such a fine cake that some people asked for more. So I gave my piece to them as well, which left me with one little tiny piece. That was such nectar prasadam! I do not know how it happened, but it seemed to have a vanilla taste in it, and the topping tasted like ice cream! After that, we had a nice kirtana, and I told everything I knew about Lord Caitanya to them. That was one of the most blissful days I had there, but I had no idea at the time that on that day I was getting initiated by my Guru Maharaj! It actually would be more appropriate to say my Guru Maharaj was giving me initiation; I only came to know about it one and half years later. From this day on, Sako's name was Sachisuta, and my name Sarvabhavana das.

Soon it became a prison tradition to sing morning and evening prayers. When a devotee would lead, many prisoners responded. Everyone in the jail had a copy of the prayers. After showing my Pancha Tattva picture to many different people, one of the most influential prisoners became very attached to it and asked (Agvan) Adwaita for it. Adwaita wrote me a letter and asked me if I could give it to the prisoner as a gift. I did not want to give it to anyone, but it seemed that Adwaita was asking me to do so as if he was sure I would do anything that he asked of me. I wrote to him, "I cannot give this picture to someone who is eating meat and smoking. Please forgive me for not being able to give it to you, brother. I have decided to keep that picture until my last day of coming out of this hell, and that is my only attachment."

After about ten days, he wrote back to me, including a promissory note from the other inmate stating that he would immediately stop smoking and meat-eating and he would follow whatever Adwaita told him to do. So, I felt I had no choice but to give it to him. He was very happy and wrote me a letter of appreciation. Four years later, Adwaita dasa told me that he met that same man on the street, and he happily displayed the same picture of Pancha Tattva that I had given him! He had made a necklace and was wearing the Pancha Tattva picture around his neck. He also told Adwaita that by the mercy of Pancha Tattva he had felt very protected all those years and gave up drugs and many bad habits. It always amazes me when I realize how people have become so attached to Lord Krishna just by a little association with such fallen souls like me.

One day, when Khatsik received a parcel from home, he got an extra notebook and asked me if I needed one. I did not have any plan, but I accepted it and thought, "Maybe one day I can use it for Krishna's service." The same evening, I could not sleep and kept turning from left to right. Too many bugs were there, and I just kept scratching. At first, we devotees did not know what should be done with these pests, and we debated amongst ourselves by "mail," "Should we kill these creatures or not?" We were practicing ahimsa, nonviolence, and never killed even small creatures. We asked senior devotees about it, and finally Kamalamala wrote me a letter, "There is nothing wrong with killing living entities who are aggressors and attacking you. You have no choice but to kill them, and each time just chant Hare Krishna in order to benefit their soul." There are certain situations that you can kill aggressors, and you won't get any karmic reaction, such as when someone attacks you, your wife or children, burns your house, and so forth. This was some relief for me personally, and at least I was not letting them suck my blood as much.

The worst guard was a tall man from Leninakan. He was a very rough, sweaty man. He would regularly offend everyone and beat people up. I heard that he had been a prize-fight boxer before he became a guard. Everyone in the jail was afraid of him, and usually no one liked to talk to him. One morning as usual, he opened the door and came in. While he was counting and going around as we stood with our hands behind our back, he unexpectedly struck me very hard, and I fell on the table. Then he beat me again and again; most of the blows were taken by my arm, which I had raised to protect my face. I came to know from other devotees that he regularly did the same to them and that he often expressed his hatred for the devotees.

After this went on for some time, one of the prisoners asked him why he always beat me even though I neither looked at him nor said a word. He replied, "You know what my wife asks me every day? Every evening, she asks if I beat up Hare Krishna men today. Guess what? If I say no then she will not sleep with me! Ha ha ha ha ha!!.... So I have no choice but to beat these guys every single day!"

After he left, everyone discussed how demoniac this man was and the bad karma he would accrue by doing this to us. The pain in my arm developed into a bruise as long as a cucumber. It was red in the beginning and turned blue and then purple. It would take me a week to recover after each heavy beating such as that.

I sometimes told the inmates stories from Srila Prabhupada's books about tolerant devotees. My cellmates could relate to stories of persons being harassed and jailed for little reason or for what they believed in. They appreciated the story of Haridas Thakur being beaten in twenty-two marketplaces by the Muslim king in Navadwip, West Bengal, India. They could relate to Haridas Thakur and did not doubt the potency of the holy name. I told his story very briefly to them. (Please see Appendix II for a narration of the story with commentary.)

The inmates so enjoyed the stories that they asked me to tell more, but unfortunately I did not know many of them at that time. Again, it was amazing to me that the details of these stories came out of my mouth, although I had never read them, and had only heard some parts from devotees. It was as if Lord Krishna Himself was telling me the stories from my heart. In this way, I could personally realize, "Yes, Krishna is there in my heart and always guiding me towards the right direction!"

Upon hearing these stories, one prisoner started to laugh and joke, "Hey guys, guess what? We are blessed to be here in Sovetashens Jail." Several of these men became serious about Krishna consciousness. The most serious one was Karen; he used to chant eight to ten rounds of japa with me every day. Karen used to give me his share of bread saying, "Here, you eat my bread and save your bread to make more beads!"

For many years Karen had driven a huge tanker truck full of fresh milk for the government-run dairy industry. He decided once that he had to take a bath in milk with his girlfriend. So, one day during his work shift, he brought the truck up to his bathroom window and hooked up a pipe to the tank to fill his tub. Then he replaced the milk with water and took his bath. Neighbors reported this to the police, and he received a sentence of four years. His father paid a lot of money to reduce his sentence to two years. After we were released from jail, in 1990, I met Karen. He came to my home to see me and discuss about Krishna consciousness.

One day I started a kirtana. We were singing in our cell only, with no plan to involve other cells. It was a sweet and mellow kirtana. Almost everyone was singing in my cell. Soon we heard a knock from the top and bottom, asking us to sing for all the prisoners so they could join as well. We had to sit at the window to sing for everyone. Soon it was a real congregational kirtana with many cells participating. Karen was sitting there with me and drumming with a spoon on a plate. After a while, the guard who was on duty outside started to scream at us, "Hey man, stop singing there right away."

Shortly afterwards, the rough guard opened the door and ran towards my friend and me. We could not even jump down from the window; he grabbed both of us and threw us down from there. He dragged us across the floor by the hair to his room. First, he was mad at my friend, angrily asking him why he was singing with me. Then he kicked him several times in the stomach and threw him on the floor. Then he came to me, looking straight into my eyes. His eyes were like burning red coals of hatred! He cursed me and screamed at me as loud as he could, "Today you will tell me exactly where you were printing your books and who was printing them for you! I know you did not tell it to anyone but, you will tell me today, only to me. Do you understand that?"

His terrible screaming sounded like a demon, and I could hardly stop laughing. He took his baton and beat me very severely on my forehead and temples. Then he hit me once with most probably his full energy. The blow sent me flying to the other end of the room, and fell down with heavy bleeding from my nose and mouth. Then he came close to me and started to kick my back and chest so hard that I lost consciousness and do not remember anything whatsoever after that. I opened my eyes after some time and saw him dragging my body on the floor. He was cursing me and stepping on my stomach and face mercilessly. In order to protect my face, I then turned. As soon as I had turned he kicked my spine and I went unconscious again. Everything became black in front of my eyes. My ears were blocked completely, and only some kind of a strange sound was constantly whistling in my ears. Then he threw me in my cell and closed the door with a curse.

Some of my cellmates came and started to help me lie down on my bed. They washed the blood off my face, as they told me a few days later. I do not remember how long I was in my bed, but when I opened my eyes everyone was sleeping already. I tried turning myself and going to the bathroom, but I felt no connection between my upper and lower part of my body. I screamed loudly and fell unconscious again.

I lost my feeling of time and place and started to talk to someone. I knew that everyone was sleeping and I was not supposed to speak loudly, but I could not control my tongue. It was as if I was someone else and had nothing to do with this body whatsoever. Some people were taking care of me in my dream, and it was so wonderful to have their association. I do not know who they were and why I was with them. The only point I was sure of was that everything was wonderful there, and I had a different, better body—a light, very light body. I was so happy and blissful that I forgot everything that had happened to me the day before, or however long ago it had been. Time seemed different. Some beautiful, indescribable creatures were singing and dancing around me, and the sky was so blue and clear that I could see each and every bird flying there. Hundreds of birds were singing, and peacocks and deer were around me. They took me to a shady riverbank and offered me hundreds of different kinds of food and drinks. I was just about to start enjoying the feast with them when I felt someone slapping my face and screaming at me, "Hey, are you there, or are you dead?"

I opened my eyes and looked at the guard with tears coming down my face. I nodded my head to indicate that I was still alive. A guard who was doing his morning counting of the prisoners was standing over me. I was crying, not so much from the pain, but from the disappointment of being returned to the same dirty cell, where everything was so black and ugly. I was tired of always looking at the heavy, black door every day and night. It was disgusting to look at the dirty bulb, coated with bugs, which shook every time the guard opened the heavy door below it and cast the reflection of the bars on the wall. I thought of myself as so unfortunate and sinful that even in my dream I did not deserve to eat Krishna prasadam! I was so hungry and thirsty! I asked for some water. Someone gave me a cup of water, and helped me to drink it. It was a difficult task because I could hardly move my spine.

Karen, the man who was with me the previous night, told everyone how heartlessly and mercilessly the guard had kicked me that day. My whole body was in pain such as I had never experienced before. My right eye was so swollen and painful that I could not even open it. It took me some time to understand where I was and what was actually going on.

My cellmates advised me to call the guard and ask him to take me to the prison hospital, which I did. The guards told me that I was in prison to die, not to be cured. I told them that I was going to fast if they didn't take me to the hospital, but I still didn't get any help. I started to fast and announced that if they didn't want to take me to the hospital, then I was going to die in the cell. I abstained from food and water for a long time. However, it did not improve my condition, and no one even thought to come and help me. I lay down all day long, chanting Hare Krishna as much as I could. I was not feeling well, but after some time I started to walk slowly to the bathroom myself without needing help. I was very worried about my health because for more than two weeks I would see blood in my urine. Many of the inmates were telling me that it is very dangerous to have such symptoms, and if I did not see a doctor then I might even die.

So I tried everything I could to get attention, but nothing worked out. I stopped fasting after nineteen days and slowly came back to normal. Surprisingly, I started to feel better and better, and soon I had only a pain in my back, which I have even nowadays. My right eye was also getting better and better, but unfortunately I could not see much. Everything was out of focus.

Some prisoners were telling me that I might not be able to have children because of those heavy injuries to my lower spine and groin. Certainly, I would never be able to run or play sports or do many of the activities that formerly I was doing. And it was all for the sake of that man's sense gratification with his wife! Many weeks later, the pain was there, always reminding me that the man who did that had probably no heart at all. For the first time in my life, I could not control my anger. I cursed him again and again. I wished that he and his wife could feel the pain that I was feeling. I wished that I could make him sorry for what he had done to me and to the other devotees in that hell. That was the first time ever that I wished that something very regretful would happen to another person. Slowly I forgot what had happened. The spine pain remained. Even now my right eye can only see light and dark and nothing more.

After this incident I didn't see that guard for a long time, which was very good not only for me but for all of us. One day, just before they took us to the Russian jail from Armenia, we heard from one of the guards an amazing story about him and his family. First he said that he had heard that I had cursed him for his abusiveness, and it must be that my curse had really worked out. Another thing he said was that there must really be God, who can see all that we are doing here and punishing accordingly. I told him that I did not know what he was talking about and asked him why he was telling me all this. By this time, everyone in the room wanted to know what was going on. The guard was acting very strangely, and he seemed scared as well. Placing his hands on the little food door and placing his sharp chin on his hands, he told us what had happened to the guard who had beaten me severely. He related how one Saturday he, his wife, and two children went to Leninakan (now Gyumri) city for a wedding party. On the way back, he was driving the car while he was drunk and had a very serious accident. The car plummeted over a cliff, and everyone was killed. The car was smashed so badly that people had to cut the car into many pieces to get the bodies out of there.

"Yeahhhhhhh!" everyone in the room cheered. The other inmates started to laugh and curse him even more. They were telling me that this must have happened because he had beaten so many innocent people, and God had punished him right away. "This is good!" they told me. "No more batons, no more pain!"

After he finished telling the story, the guard asked me if he had done anything offensive to me and if I had happened to curse him, as well, for it. "I have three small children to support, so please do not curse me," the guard said.

Everyone could see that he was very affected by the incident. I told him, "Sir, we as devotees do not usually curse anyone, but the Lord can actually see what you people are doing. And if you are too cruel, then the Lord will certainly punish you in many different ways both in this life and the next. Krishna's devotees never like to curse anyone. Rather, they will ask the Lord to help you guards to understand that what you doing is wrong and unnecessary. But if you do not understand, then sometimes Krishna Himself makes His own arrangements to take care of His devotees as well as the demons. When there is a very dire situation, the Lord will personally come to protect His devotees and punish the demons."

I asked him if he would like to listen to one wonderful story about such a situation, very similar to what we found ourselves in at that time, and he told me that he was really ready to listen to anything I had to say after such an incident. I went closer to the door and started to tell him the story of Prahlada Maharaja, who was protected by our Lord.

"This story took place many thousands of years ago. Prahlad's father was the most atheistic ruler history had ever known. His name was Hiranyakasipu. Hiranya means gold, and kasipu literally means soft bed, indicating illicit sexual connections. These were Hiranyakasipu's constant meditations. He had performed great austerities in order to get a boon from the chief of the demigods, Brahma. He asked for immortality, because he wanted to enjoy forever. Brahma said, 'My life span is greater than the entire creation, but even I must die. Ask for something else.'

"So Hiranyakasipu asked that he would never be killed by man or beast, not in the day and not in the nighttime, not by any weapons, not on the land, not in the water, and not in the sky, or inside or outside. All these benedictions were granted to him. He became the king of the heavenly part of the universe and was thinking he was God, the controller of everything in this material world. He thought that because of his benedictions, he would not die. While Hiranyakasipu was away doing his austerities, his young son, Prahlad, had learned all about Krishna consciousness. Prahlad would always chant the holy names of Krishna with great faith and bliss.

"Naturally, as the king of material heaven, Hiranyakasipu sent his son Prahlad to a school where the teachers were very materialistic. They used to teach Prahlad and his friends topics connected to this material life and body. Since Prahlad was a devotee, he knew what was right and wrong in this material world and knew the Supreme Personality of Godhead, Sri Krishna. Prahlad's chanting and later preaching of love of Krishna enraged his father so much that he ordered his soldiers to kill the five-year-old boy. Krishna protected His pure devotee, and therefore no one could harm him at all.

"The soldiers put Prahlad in a pit of poisonous snakes, but the snakes would not bite him. They directed an elephant to crush him, but Krishna, who is in the heart of the elephant, directed the animal to pick up Prahlad and place him on his back. Time and again, Hiranyakasipu tried to kill Prahlad. He threw Prahlad off a cliff, but Krishna caught him. He tried to poison Prahlad, but the poison could not affect him. Finally, Hiranyakasipu challenged, 'Where is your God, Prahlad?'

"Prahlad said, 'Krishna is everywhere, Father.'

"'Everywhere? Then, let Krishna come out and fight me.' Pointing to a nearby pillar, Hiranyakasipu asked, 'Is He there? Is He here?'

"'Yes, father, He is here and He is everywhere, even in your heart.'

"Hiranyakasipu struck the pillar with his sword. First there was a great noise, and then the pillar split apart, revealing Krishna in a fearful form to protect His devotee. The Lord had a frightening form as a half-man, half-lion. This is one form that Krishna has, called Lord Nrsimhadeva. It is Krishna's anger personified. After fighting with Hiranyakasipu, Lord Nrsimhadeva took Hiranyakasipu upon his lap and killed him by ripping open his belly with His sharp nails.

"All the benedictions of Brahma were kept intact by the Lord. Hiranyakasipu was not killed by man or beast, but by the Lord in His most unique form. He was not killed in the day or in the night, but at sunset. He was not killed on the land, on the water, or in the sky, but upon the lap of the Lord. He was not killed by any weapons, but by the long, sharp nails of the Lord. And he was not killed inside or outside, but just on the threshold or entrance to his palace. Prahlad was such a wonderful devotee that he stepped before the angry Lord and requested the Lord to forgive his father's many offenses and grant his father spiritual perfection. The Lord did this, and thus Hiranyakasipu became the most fortunate person."

As I told this story, the guard standing on the other side of the door listened very carefully, without commenting. When he left, he told me that he would keep the food door open all day so we could have some fresh air blowing through the cell, for which everyone was very grateful. Usually the prisoners had to pay to have that door open for a while, which also allowed them to talk to the other cells.

We used to receive at least two letters from the other devotees every day. Some letters were passed in the shower room, some through our "post office" system, and some by paying the guards to deliver them. Soon the administration, guards, and inmates were all talking about nothing but the guard's punishment and Krishna's real protection of His devotees. This was a very nice preaching opportunity for all of us, and we took it very seriously.

I personally felt bad about him and his children, but not for his wife, who used to tell her husband, "If you don't beat the Hare Krishna devotees today, then you can't sleep with me tonight." I could never understand that lady's mind and wondered what bad things she must have heard or seen about devotees that she wished our death, though the opposite happened. I believe even she had never met any devotee in her life but that the radio, television, and newspapers' false information was the main reason for her hatred towards the devotees of Lord Krishna.

I asked myself why they had died and what was Krishna's plan. None of the guards randomly beat us or used bad words while talking to us anymore, but at the same time they were trying to hide the reason they were not beating us. They did not appear afraid of us, but they behaved as if they no longer had such an angry mood or like they were busy with other duties. The entire jail was peaceful and quiet after that incident, and many of the inmates thanked the devotees for it. The only bad thing was that this was only six or seven months before we were sent to Russia.

Sachisuta felt bad about the guard's death, trying to guess which type of new body he got after leaving his demoniac body. He told me that he had kept count of the times that Manukyan had cursed him and Krishna, or used Krishna's name inappropriately, and it had been over one hundred and fifty times. Sachisuta told me that, according to the scriptures, if one chants the holy name of the Supreme Personality of Godhead even once, then he will not attain a body in the lower species after leaving this present one. Such a fortunate soul gets the opportunity to continue his chanting and service to Krishna in the next life. So Sachisuta wished him good luck and a better body in the next life.

I was personally worried very much about my own body with no time to speculate about where he was or which type of body he had. I didn't think about it then and have never considered it during all these long years since. I was just happy that after this incident the other guards were not as inclined to beat us like they had been before. The only lasting misfortune was my eye problem. The lack of vision was a huge change in my life, and I had to get used to my new situation. I would have to go through life half-blind and almost disabled.

After some weeks, my prosecutor, Armen, came to see me. He asked me many new questions. There was a room set aside for prosecutors to meet the prisoners and fill out papers. The room had only one small table and two chairs, all of which were bolted to the ground. Armen noticed that I was walking slowly and asked me what was wrong with me. I told the whole story to him, and he said he was sorry to hear of it. But he also told me that my suffering was my own fault because I did not give up chanting and preaching even in jail. He then asked if he could do anything for me.

"Yes," I replied. "Please bring one Pancha Tattva picture from the police station where a lot of our stuff is kept."

He told me that doing that is very dangerous. He could do that only if I promised that if anyone asked me where it came from, I would never tell them that it was he who gave it to me. After a week he brought a Pancha Tattva picture for me. I was incredibly happy to have this! I appreciated his help very much and promised to never tell anyone who gave it to me.

One day the guard knocked on our door and called my name. I thought this could be bad news, but fortunately he was calling my name to receive a parcel. I could not believe my ears! I was so curious to know whom it was from and what was inside. He handed me a paper to sign and gave me a huge bag. He told me, "Your friends are very stubborn and finally succeeded in sending you this food. They tried for many days but the administration did not allow it."

I wrote, "Hare Krishna and thank you," on the paper and gave it back. My hands were shaking from happiness, not so much from thinking about eating it but because all these prisoners would be able to enjoy the prasadam, which I had told them about so many times. I also felt good that someone outside was thinking about me.

One guard said, "The prison manager did not allow any parcel for you men. Your friends used to come every single day trying to send you a parcel. Finally today they could do so. I guess they have a lot of money to pay the guards down there."

Later I found out that the devotees had paid three times the usual bribe at that time to send us a parcel full of wonderful prasadam. On a paper were two names—Tigran (Prana das) and Armine (Damayanti devi dasi).

All the prisoners were happy too, because after hearing so much glorification of the prasadam, now finally they would be able to taste some from the temple! I quickly opened the bag and started to place the preparations on the table. All of a sudden our little cell was filled with unbelievable fragrances!

Khatsik, my friend, was breaking up the bread when he found two letters secretly hidden in it. One was from our Guru Maharaja, and there was a long letter from other devotees.

I was more interested in the letters than the prasadam. I started to quickly read the one from the devotees in the corner of the room so if a guard looked from the door hole he wouldn't see me. It was all about how the devotees outside were thinking, caring, and praying for us in jail and how they were trying to help us to get out of there. They encouraged us to be strong, never forget Krishna, and continue to chant and follow the rules as much as possible in our difficult situation. Tears were running down my cheeks while reading their sincere sentiments and my hands were shaking.

Next, I read the letter from Gurudeva, which was even more encouraging. He particularly appreciated all his disciples who were struggling in the different jails in the Soviet Union, thanking them for taking such a difficult mission on themselves. He encouraged all of us to be strong and never lose faith in Srila Prabhupada and Lord Krishna. At the end, he told us that these sufferings are very temporary and that soon we will see each other and chant and dance together.

This statement seemed so amazing and unbelievable at the time that I did not even think about it for long. I thought that I would be in jail forever, we would never see the blue sky without bars again, and that everything was over. It was hard to believe or even dream that in three years we would all go to India and have a wonderful pilgrimage with fifty devotees. It was even hard to believe that one day we would sit down and eat as much as we wanted, like normal human beings, what to speak of anything else in ordinary life.

The package contained incredible sweets for people in prison, sweets such as halava and burfi. There were also breads cooked by Prana das and some vegetable pakoras made by Damayanti. There were lots of fruits as well. Oh, everything was so tasty! At least that was what everyone told me; I had only a very little from the bag.

I wanted to send some prasadam to my devotee friends in other cells as well. But before I did anything about it, someone knocked on the top floor and we received, together with other mails, some burfi from Sachisuta along with a letter to me full of great appreciation to all our friends outside.

After some time, Adwaita sent some sweets along with a letter written on a cigarette box. Everyone was very happy that, after hearing so many times about the taste and qualities of Krishna prasadam, they got a chance to taste it. By paying a lot of money, the devotees outside had sent more weight of food than was usually allowed and arranged for the guards not to break the bread into pieces, as they usually did, to see if there were any drugs or letters. The irony is that the guards themselves used to sell drugs to the prisoners every single day. Really, prisoners could buy anything they wanted, whatever was available outside, from the guards there. Not only that, if you paid enough they wouldn't even check what was sent in or out.

### Bhagavat Maha-Prasadam ki Jaya...

# CHAPTER THIRTEEN

# The Court Decision

*Out of many thousands among men,*
*one may endeavor for perfection,*
*and of those who have achieved perfection,*
*hardly one knows Me in truth.*

*–Bhagavad-gita, 7.3*

After a while, Armen came to give us his last papers to sign and informed us that this was his last visit to us. He said his job was over, and he wished us all the best, as he would be handing over the papers to the court. I asked him if he could guess how many years we could expect. He said he had no idea, but it surely could not be more than three years because the sentence clearly said we were to be imprisoned from two to three years. I was preparing myself for the worst, but hoping for the best.

After about a week, we were asked to sign some new papers, which already had the court date printed on them. So we were ready the morning they came and took all of us to the truck, where we were together again for a while. They put us in an ugly truck, and after a half an hour or so we were parked in front of the courthouse. We all had some items with us from the cells. As soon as they opened the truck door we saw Prana and some others waiting for us. We were instructed to throw our belongings to our friends. They caught them and ran away with our letters and things.

Then the court case started. It was very sad to see my mother and brother there. They were looking at the floor, and my mom was crying, her handkerchief constantly in her hand. Adwaita's mother and sister were there too, but the members of Sachisuta's family had refused to come to court.

Damayanti's mother was the main one who brought complaints before the judge. She told the judge that her daughter became mad because of the preaching and books of Srila Prabhupada. We came to know that Damayanti had been arrested a month before and was being held in a psychiatric hospital. An interesting part of that procedure was a forty-year-old man who complained that Adwaita forced him to take a book, and after reading it and chanting, he became crazy.

During a break time, we were loudly singing Hare Krishna, which everyone could hear from outside. My brother then came close to the window and told me that he had a conversation with a judge who told him that if we pleaded guilty, they could let us go home after two months' time, one third of what they were planning for us. I told him that it is impossible for me to plead guilty, and he left unhappy. My mom kept crying, asking me how I was doing in the jail. She wanted to come and embrace me, but the police did not allow her. She looked helpless, confused by false information from the KGB and police.

It took three days to finish all the court procedures. For the other group of devotees, the proceedings took over forty days, but they could not find any fault. Therefore, after keeping them in the psychiatric hospital for all that time, they let them go free. But for some reason they did not let our group out. On the third day, they announced two years of colonial sentence for Sachisuta and me and three years of work colony for Adwaita. Because he had been in jail twice before for some other crimes, automatically they gave him one extra year.

From then on we started to count our time by making a pin hole in our small calendar each day. Every one hole would bring us one day close to our freedom. About seven months had passed since we were arrested in Yerevan, and that meant we had only seventeen months of our sentence more to go. After a formal judgment, prisoners were usually taken to a different cell. I said goodbye to my old friends, took my mattress and belongings, and followed the police to a room where people who had already been judged were waiting to go to the prison colony to spend the rest of the time. Some of the men were from my cell, but others were new and started to ask me questions about Krishna consciousness.

Two days later, one of the guards came and asked me to follow him. While we were walking in the corridor, he asked me if I knew where he was taking me. I told him that I had no idea whatsoever, but I was not expecting anything good. He told me that the head of the KGB was there to see me, which was very rare. He said that he had never seen him come to the jail personally before, and if he was here to see me, there must be very special circumstances. We came to a room, and after offering me a chair, the guard took permission from the KGB man to leave. After looking at and observing me for some time, he finally said, "How are you doing, Gagik?"

"Very well, sir."

"Do you know me?"

"No, sir, and I do not want to know you either."

"Why do you say that?"

"I know many like you, and there is absolutely no use to know one more, sir."

"No, I am not one of them that you have seen before."

"Then who are you, and what do you want from me? What can I do for you?"

"I am the chief of the Armenian KGB," he said, telling me his name, "and I came specifically to see you and talk to you personally. My people talked to your parents, and they agreed with our decision. I would like to share it with you and see what you think."

He then handed me a paper. "This is important. Please read and see what you think. If you like, sign it, in which case I personally promise you that after just one month you will say goodbye to this dark place and go home! But if you refuse to sign...then, my dear, we are going to send you to Siberia, the land of the white bears, where you will die from hunger. I promise you that 100%!"

I took the paper and started to read it. It was full of lies against ISKCON, Srila Prabhupada, and Harikesa Swami. It stated that I was very unfortunate to have met devotees and that the movement brought me so much trouble. It said that Harikesa Swami forced us to distribute books and that my mind was not functioning properly. I did not even finish reading it. I gave it back and told him, "I would rather go to the white bears any day than sign this garbage!"

He then asked about my cell and my life. Then he asked me if I had any complaint or question or if there was anything he could do for me.

I said, "Those are just useless words. You are not going to do anything. When I had really needed help, no one was there to help me out. As far as complaints, which kind of complaints are you interested in if you are planning to kill me from hunger? What is the use of asking something from someone if you are sure that he is not going to do it for you anyway?"

"No," he replied, "Please ask me anything you want, and then you can judge if I can and will do it for you."

I thought a little bit, trying to think of something nice to ask and test this guy, and then I said, "I have one question and one request."

"Go ahead," he replied.

"Is it true that you will take me out of Armenia?"

"Yes sir, if you don't sign this paper, then we have no choice but to send you out of Armenia."

"Okay, then my request is that you arrange for my friend, Sargis (Sachisuta), to be with me in my cell for the rest of the time we will be staying here."

"Okay, I will do that for you. After fifteen minutes, he will be in your room. Anything more?"

"Please tell the guards to give us some raw grains to eat."

"Okay, I will order them to do so, although we want you to have a hard time. But just to prove to you that I can do what you ask, I am going to do it for you."

"Okay, sir. I will soon see how much power your words have."

"Good luck, Gagik. You are a nice person, and I do not see why you have to be here. My people have reported that you are from a decent family and never had anyone in your family who had committed any crime; so I do not understand why you should stay here for nothing. Take care of yourself and be prepared for worse to come."

"Thank you, Hare Krishna."

"Hare Krishna," he replied and pushed the button under his desk. A guard came in immediately and took me back to my cell.

In less than fifteen minutes, the guard opened my cell door and brought my best friend to me. We embraced each other, crying, and then we had a long talk about everything that had gone on during those long seven months in that hell. It was a momentous occasion for both of us. We both were so happy to be together in one cell after being separated such a long time. The other prisoners were doing nothing but hearing our conversation, happy to see how much we respected each other.

For the next three weeks, we chanted together, ate together, and preached together. We remembered all our good and bad days outside and planned what we were going to do after coming out. We had many kirtanas and shared everything we had. Soon, we acquired some rice and yellow split peas, which we would put in a pot mixed with sugar and water and keep three or four days. After that, we would eat it. Once, we tried to cook a little bit in an aluminum pot over a fire, but it took a long time and filled the room with smoke. Sachisuta told me that it was not a wise idea to make the rest of the inmates breathe toxic smoke just for the sake of our bellies, although others were making tea in a similar way daily. He was a very kind and humble person who would never allow himself to do something that would give others even the slightest inconvenience.

Sachisuta wanted to keep himself very clean because, as he said, "Krishna is in everyone's heart; therefore the body is a temple of Krishna." In order to bathe daily, he would save the plastic bags that the inmates' mail came in, using the plastic bags to stand in. He would fill another bag with water from the little sink. He would then dip a little plastic cup into the water from the bag and pour the water on his body so it would go into the bag at his feet. It was a big austerity to take a shower in such a small bathroom, which was hardly one meter square and above the ground level about half a meter.

Once, during our daily kirtana, three guards took both of us out and kicked us for making noise in the "institution," as they used to call it. One of them was drunk, smelling very dreadful. He started to slap Sachisuta. I tried to protect my friend and told the guard that this was not a fair thing to do. He turned to me and started to slap me heavily too, cursing.

I tried to explain that he was drunk and should not do that to me, which made him even angrier. As he beat me, he was shouting, "Stop talking, dog! You gave up Christianity, our religion, and accepted the Muslim religion. You should do what I say, and I won't allow you to sing crazy songs here!" As soon as I would say something, he would beat me even more. Then he would go to Sachisuta and beat him up. Sachisuta would not say anything to the guard, but his silence and humility would make this man even angrier than my words. The guard screamed at him, "Why you are not saying a word, man?" And he would beat and beat even more.

After seeing this, I thought, "Oh it is much better to curse this man and get beat up than say nothing but still get beat up like Sachisuta is doing!"

Soon the day came that we were supposed to start our trip to the white bears in Russia. On August 26th, my birthday, we started our trip to Russia by train. Sachisuta made a beautiful gift for me, which he had been working on for about three days without showing me what he was doing. It was a pen on which he wrote, "A present to Gago prison 1986," which I still have. We keep it in our family as one of our most important treasures.

Guards came and opened the heavy door for us. After saying good-bye to all the people in our cell, we left that hell not knowing that we were going to an even more horrible place. We took our mattresses to where we had received them the very first day about eight month before and signed the paper stating that we had given them back. I was wondering about the need to sign a paper for such a junky pillow and mattress. Within these mattresses prisoners often hid their small but important belongings, such as money and letters.

Downstairs we met Adwaita. In a big room we then waited for all the prisoners who were supposed to go on the same trip. The room had dark walls, one of which had names and numbers written on it. It seemed that people, having to wait there bored for hours, had written on the wall whatever came to their mind. There were beautiful poems with colored frames, a love story by one prisoner, as well as curses of the police or others. Most of the writing was numbers and dates detailing a prisoner's arrest, the date of release, and the reason for being sentenced.

We spent several hours in the room during a time of hot weather, breathing the smoke of the hundreds of cigarettes. Finally, guards started to read our names one by one, directing us to go to an open door which led to a truck's side door that was touching the outer wall. We waited in that truck about an hour or so for all to be seated. There were a lot of trucks. The first people who sat in the trucks had to wait with the sun heating up the metal walls until the last truck was filled.

The trucks took us to a train, a horribly unforgettable experience. It was one coach connected to the middle of a long passenger train going from Yerevan to Baku in Azerbaijan. It resembled any other train except that, instead of doors, all the way through was a strong iron net so the guards could see everyone inside. And where the space was designed for six people, they put twelve. There was no air. Oh, if you wanted to go to the toilet, you had to wait many hours! Instead of our regular guards, there were Russian army special soldiers taking us from jail to jail. They had automatic guns and batons in case of emergency.

The truck had parked about a hundred meters away from the train. All the way to the train, solders were standing, counting us. First they let one prisoner out of the truck while loudly calling, "One." The next soldier the prisoner encountered on the way to the train screamed again, "One" as soon as the prisoner passed him. When a prisoner reached the train, the last soldier also screamed, "One." After that they let the next person come, calling, "Two," and so on.

They fed us bread and fish, which smelled so putrid that it was impossible to breathe, what to speak of eating. Chanting was very difficult, and sleeping was impossible. We slept by placing our heads on each other's shoulders and resting a little bit. All the time there was ear-splitting noise, and the non-stop smoke stayed in the train car like a thick cloud. Our eyes were burning. Everyone was speaking loudly, so it was hard to understand what was going on or who was talking to whom. We were trying very hard to practice tolerance. Soldiers came and hit the bars with their batons, which produced quiet for a while, but in a few moments the pandemonium started again. Someone was singing, someone was crying, and others were laughing loudly. Some were cursing Soviet rules or fighting. There was a women's section in between the men's. Some men and women were telling each other how much they love and will miss one another.

I was terrified, thinking this was not a happy birthday for me. I told my friends that I must be a very unfortunate and sinful soul to be in this hellish condition on my birthday. Sachisuta tried to convince me that actually I was very fortunate to be suffering for Krishna. Adwaita told me that the situation had nothing to do with me being pure or impure, but simply we had to do this as a service for our spiritual master and Krishna.

According to what I have seen in prison, the women prisoners were more aggressive and criminal than the men. They were acting like mad people in the train, and it was unbelievable what they were capable of doing in those critical conditions. I am embarrassed to tell everything they were doing there, but I will give one example of some of the milder things. When it was the ladies' turn to go to the bathroom, they would walk through the corridor. As soon as they reached the men's cage, they would open their clothes and stand there naked, holding onto the bars so tightly that the soldiers could not pull them off. When the guards tried to pull them away, they screamed hideously. After one or two baton hits from the guards, they would start to walk towards the bathroom. Men would scream and make a big happy noise after seeing women naked.

After eighteen hours or so our train stopped in Baku, and again black trucks took us to the jail, putting us in a transit cell. We were the first ones to come out from the train. This was the worse situation, since the first ones out had to wait in windowless trucks in the hot sun for a long time. The truck was filled up with criminals, some of whom were smoking. The metal roof was so hot that if you touched it, you could burn yourself. It was dark. The truck stank, since everyone was sweating with perspiration practically pouring out all over our body. We could hear sweat dripping from our fingers onto the metal floor of the truck. Before we reached the jail, everybody was as wet as if they came out from a swimming pool. At the jail they separated Adwaita from the rest of us, but Sachisuta and I were happy to still be together in one cell. They gave us better bread than in the Armenian jail, and altogether we ate much better in the transit cell.

The main problem with the transit cell was that it was totally dirty and smelly. Since no one was living there permanently, no one cleaned the toilets, which made everything intolerable. There were also no mattresses or pillows at all. Everyone slept on wooden or metal beds, which were extremely uncomfortable. We all had red sores on our bodies as well as bites from all kinds of bugs.

When one of the guards brought lunch for us, Sachisuta humbly asked if he could have one more piece of bread. The guard looked into Sachisuta's eyes and asked him why he was in jail. Sachisuta explained not only our situation, but also began a long conversation about Krishna and devotional life. The guard told him that the people who placed him in jail were the real demons and will never ever have peace in their lives. "You have not committed anything wrong, and they are all crazy people!" he said in Armenian.

He promised Sachisuta that he would take care of him nicely, bringing him as many pieces of bread as he wished. Indeed, every day he used to bring us lots of bread and ask many questions about our philosophy and religion. Soon we had lots of bread, which we distributed to others, too. This guard was a devout Muslim. He became so attached to Sachisuta that he started to come often to talk to him through the little food door. For Sachisuta's sake, he allowed the tiny window on the door to be kept open for more ventilation in the hellish cell, for which everyone was grateful. As in the Armenian jail, usually we had to bribe guards for such a privilege.

This guard would beg us to give up chanting. He would say, "Don't think of me as a policeman; I am just an ordinary man. I am just like your father, begging you to please stop practicing your religion in order to go on living. These police will kill you here!" But Sachisuta would just smile and tell that he is happy to do this for God.

Once Sachisuta asked the guard to look at our documents in the office to see if all of us devotees would go to the same camp or not. He came back with bad news, "You guys are going to be in different camps but will not be far from each other."

We inquired whether there was anything we or he could do to change that plan so we could be together. "No," he told us. "That it is impossible. Now, only Allah can change that, no one else. If the KGB decrees something, then the police cannot do anything else. The KGB are always superior, and if they have instructed so, then it is going to be like that only. You will be separate."

We also learned from him that after some days they would take me out, and two days after me they were going to take Sachisuta to the other camp by a different train. So we knew that we were spending our last days together. Soon those days became only hours and then minutes. We were supposed to say goodbye to each other soon, and neither of us knew that it would actually be our last goodbye in this lifetime.

The day before I left, some of the prisoners had spent the night gambling. One of them had lost everything he had, including his socks and jacket. He was gambling with a guy known in the Armenian jail as one of the best card players, but he was hoping to win at least once. He was borrowing money to keep playing. After he lost everything, he could not return the money he borrowed. In the middle of the night, we heard this guy screaming as five guys beat him mercilessly. Sachisuta and I woke up very afraid as we saw this horrible scene in the middle of our cell. Sachisuta wanted to try to pacify them, but one of the prisoners told him that he had better be quiet or else he would have his hand placed in the fire! So we were forced to watch five prisoners almost kill another, who was screaming so loud that the entire jail was vibrating.

The victim was also a decent fighter. With some expert boxing he left the face of one of the five opponents twisted and bleeding. But that aggressor would not be beaten. Rather, he came to his bed and took his sharpened aluminum plate off the wall. He ran towards the gambler and stabbed him with the sharp part of it. The poor gambler fell down on the concrete floor without any more sound or movement. Blood was all over the cell. Soon guards came and took the gambler, handling him like a piece of trash. We never knew what had happened to him after that. Sachisuta was shaking and chanting Hare Krishna. His eyes were closed and his face was white. We did not talk to each other for a while.

The next day, I was supposed to go. We exchanged some of the little possessions we had and tried to remember to tell each other the most important details before they separated us. I knew Sachisuta liked the red sweater that my mom gave me on my birthday. So I gave it to him, and he gave me his old sweater. Since he had only Harikesa Swami's picture, I gave my Pancha Tattva picture to him, and he gave me his new socks. I wanted to give him my thick jacket, but he refused. We found some nylon thread and tied pieces of it on each other's wrist as if they were talismans, burning the knots so they would never come off. We knew that we had less than a half hour to spend together, and we were both deeply disturbed. I told him, "The sixteen months will fly like anything, and we will be again together!"

He did not say anything to me for a minute. Then after a long silence, he looked at my eyes and started to speak slowly. "You know what I am most afraid of Gago?"

"What?" I asked him.

"I am afraid that I will never see the Armenian Bhagavad-gitas and distribute them."

I told him that the other devotees told us that Harivilas Prabhu, an Armenian devotee from France, had just finished the translation and printing ofBhagavad-gita in Armenian. It will take some time for him to smuggle them to Armenia. By then we would be released.

As he looked at me, tears started to run down his cheeks. I took his tears with my finger and touched them to my forehead, and then embraced him very tightly with love and compassion. Everyone was looking at us, but no one spoke a word. Some of the prisoners also started to cry. After a while, he told me that his second worry was that he would never see his guru.

"No." I replied, "After only sixteen months we will be out of this hell, and will be able to see him as well. Who knows, the state of this world may one day change as our guru told us in his letter, and we will be able to chant and dance together sooner!"

I requested one more time that he keep the jacket, which would be a nice pillow and mattress on the way to camp, but he refused again. He said, "Please take care of yourself well and have faith in the future. As soon as you reach the camp, write a letter to Prana das and give him your address. I'll do the same so he can give your address to me and mine to you. We can communicate with each other there." And he added, "I hope the demons will allow that."

Soon we heard the sound of the guard's shoes as he came through the long corridor towards our cell. I looked through the little window and saw he was slowly coming for me.

I looked at Sachisuta's face, and both of us started to cry. The hellish sound of the keys made us cry even more because we knew that now he would take me out. The guard opened the door and stood there like a statue. He took hold of my hand but could not pull me. Then he held Sachisuta's hand and started to speak: "Please don't put me in a bad situation, guys. I don't want to separate you by force, but I have my duty. You must come out of the cell without any force. Let's go; the truck is waiting for you."

It was such an unusual and emotional situation that everyone was touched. Somehow, the guard pulled me out gently towards the door. Sachisuta gave my little bag to the guard and handed me my jacket. With his other hand he was holding my hand, walking with me towards the door. As soon as we came to the doorstep, the guard asked me to go out and Sachisuta to stay in. He pushed me out the same time as he closed the door.

Sachisuta put his head out of the window and tearfully called out, "Hare Krishna, brother. Hare Krishna, my best friend. Thank you for giving me this Krishna consciousness, and thank you for everything you have done for me. I hope one day I'll be able to do something for you as well, and if not in this then in the next lifetime. Please forgive me for all the offences that I committed to you. Be strong and always remember Krishna and never forget Him!"

I walked backwards through the long corridor, waved my hand, and just told him, "Hare Krishna! Hare Krishna, brother. I will see you soon; please keep in touch!" All the hairs in my body were standing up. I somehow kept myself from loudly crying and screaming.

Then the time came that I was supposed to make a turn at the end of the corridor, and that was it—I would not be able to see Sachisuta, my best friend, any more. That was the most painful moment in my life. I do not know why, but I was trying to think of some way to make that moment last a little bit longer, somehow. Right at that moment, Krishna gave me an idea. I told the guard that I had accidentally taken Sachisuta's jacket and wanted to return it to him. He did not want to let me go back, but at the same time, he did not want to refuse me at the last minute and be seen as a bad guy.

"Okay, quickly give it back to him and come back. I'll be waiting for you here."

I started to run through the long corridor with my hands wide open, calling out, "Hare Krishnaaaaaaaaa!" Sachisuta somehow pushed out his long hands through the narrow window, scratching his shoulders, and with a smiling face called out, "Hariiiiibolll Hariiibolll!" Once more, for the last time, we embraced each other. Then many prisoners called loudly, "Hare Krishna! Hare Krishna, brothers, you were good friends and go on all the rest of your lives like that!"

I did not want to misuse the guard's kindness, but I did not want to be separated from my best friend either. Finally I told him, "Okay, now is the time for our temporary separation. Good luck to you." I handed over to him my jacket and turned to run back. He took it and threw it on me and told me to take it immediately. We both knew what it meant to have an extra pillow or blanket on such a long trip. So I wanted him to keep it, and he wanted me to keep it. Finally, I threw it to him and went back so far that he could not throw it to me anymore.

He took it, pressed it to his face, and started to cry very loudly, "Okay, brother, then I will return it to you after a year and a half, okay?"

"Yes, that's what I want you to do. Please use it for yourself during that time; you know, you are expert at using everything for Krishna and His service."

At the end of the corridor I stopped once more. I could clearly see my friend's face wet with tears. He had one hand out of the window, gently waving my jacket. For the last time, we told each other "Hare Krishna." After that, I never saw my friend, my brother, and this wonderful devotee.

After I turned to walk straight instead of backwards, I looked at the guard, who was crying and walking in front of me, instead of behind as they usually do. He looked at me and said, "Hey guy, you melted my heart and made me cry! No one yet made me cry in this hell but you. I wish these sixteen-months will fly as if sixteen days so you will be together again outside. In this hell, no one has ever made any guard cry; you were the first one! I can never possibly forget the friendship between you two. Please always stay like that. I wish that you will never come back to this hell again! Good luck to you!"

As I remember that day, I must end this chapter here, dear reader. My son has turned off the tape recorder and stopped typing, and I can only cry.

**SACHISUTA PRABHU KI JAYA!**

## CHAPTER FOURTEEN

# Entering the Labor Camp

*From the mode of goodness, real knowledge develops;*
*from the mode of passion, greed develops;*
*and from the mode of ignorance develops*
*foolishness, madness, and illusion.*

*–Bhagavad-gita, 14.17*

I t took me twenty-eight days to reach my destination, starting from my birthday, and it was the most disgusting experience I have ever had. Sometimes we stopped at a jail for twenty hours and then continued again with another train. But sometimes we stopped in the transit jails for three or four days. It was terrible to spend any time at all in the old Russian jails, which were built by Empress Ekaterina the Second (1762-1796). She was very famous in Russian history for her cruelty when torturing prisoners. Her prisons had almost no natural light in the cells, and the ceilings were made in a half-round shape, which created the illusion that they were pressing you down. When we walked there we always crouched down so our head would not touch the ceiling, even though the ceilings were quite high. It was a horrible feeling. We knew very well that we could never touch the ceiling with the tip of our fingers even if we jumped, yet we were always bending down, as if against our will.

The bunk beds were right in the middle of the room, not next to the wall as in other jails, and had three layers. The distance between the first and second bed was so tiny, that once you laid down there you did not have enough room to turn yourself on your side. The toilet was in the corner. It was completely open, three feet above ground; so it resembled a stage. In other jails there would be a wall, or at least a cloth, in front of the toilet. Since at least thirty-five people were living in one room, almost every ten minutes someone was using the toilet. It was such a disgusting place. The floor was made out of concrete and thick iron bars to prevent any holes or digging.

We stayed in one jail like that for three and a half days, and to my good fortune, I met a Christian, Warren, who was also there for illegal religious book production. He belonged to the Jehovah's Witnesses group and was a wonderful person. He was a little older than I was. We exchanged our knowledge and experience. In the course of our sweet, long conversation we never got tired at all. He was just starting his journey to Siberia, where he was supposed to stay for two years. We were both very different from the rest of the criminals; having committed no crime, we had almost nothing in common with them at all. We became very close friends in three days, making it very hard to be separated from each other.

In that jail was the first time I saw policewomen. They were very bad-tempered. They were actually more cruel than men. If for some reason they did not like you, they had a weapon called the crapaudine they could throw on you. It had three mouth-like pieces connected with a string. After it caught on you, they would pull it very hard, leaving a person with great pain and suffering.

On the positive side, since I left Armenia it became easier every day to preach to people without getting in trouble with the guards. One reason was that because the guards changed very often, hardly anybody knew who I was or what I was doing.

Finally, I arrived at the work camp where I was supposed to spend the rest of my sentence. We were fifteen prisoners all together in a long, narrow room where everyone waited for his appointment with the chief of the camp who would sort us into the existing work groups. There were ten different groups, each performing a different type of work. We were supposed to work eight hours every day. The prisoner who was serving the food told us that best place to work was the tenth group, because they do not do any heavy and dirty jobs. Those prisoners sewed with sewing machines. They are working inside, the best place to be in the cold winter.

I had been in the cell for a while before I had my appointment to get my work assignment. The chief was sitting at his desk and reading my thick file of records. He asked me to sit down, while he kept reading what I was charged with. Then he looked at me with a question mark on his face, took off his glasses, and said, "I've never seen such a file as this. Armenians are crazy, or what?"

"I think so, sir."

"What were you doing there?"

"Printing and distributing some books."

"What books?"

"Indian philosophy and religion. Very nice books, sir. They did not like that; they considered everything we were doing to be anti-Soviet propaganda and gave me two years."

"Why did they send you here to me, then? Why couldn't they keep you there in your country? There was no room for you guys?"

"I do not know, sir. The KGB gave me some papers to sign. I refused to do so, and that is why they sent me here."

"Why didn't you sign them?"

"It was all against our leaders and philosophy, and everything was a lie. So I did not like it."

"So, now you like it here? You could sign it and get out of this hell and do whatever you wish to do outside. Are you a fool?"

"No, sir. The TV, radio, and newspapers were going to use the papers for many bad reasons; so I did not want to do that."

"Krishna would not forgive you for that?"

"Krishna may have forgiven me, but I couldn't forgive myself."

"Nobody signed the paper?"

"No, sir, nobody. I do not even think they asked others, since they knew no one would sign."

"How old are you?"

"Twenty-three only sir."

"Where are the other two guys with you?"

"I have no idea. They didn't want us to be together. That's all I know."

After looking at the papers, he said, "That means just recently it was your birthday, right?"

"Yes, sir, I was in a hellish train at that time."

"Well, you chose that. What can I say? You are certainly a good boy; I wouldn't sign the papers either! What were you doing outside? What is your profession?"

"I did not study, sir; there was no time for it. As soon as I came back from the Army, I joined the movement and could not study. I didn't even like to study."

"That's what Krishna wants you to do?"

"No, I just decided to do so. We have a lot of learned people in our movement, such as scientists, artists, and many musicians. My mother and brother are both tailors and have their own businesses in my country. I used to help them sometimes to make some money."

This was already spoken as if Krishna Himself had inspired it. I could not believe that I was saying all this, and wasn't prepared! Indeed, my mother knew how to sew, and my brother was actually a tailor. But I learned very little from them. They didn't have any business, either. He looked at me and started to write something on my papers and put them back in my envelope.

"So you know how to sew?"

"Yes sir, of course."

"Okay then, you may go to the tenth group and work there. You are too skinny to work outside with the welding group anyways, I think."

"Thank you very much, sir. I appreciate that."

I couldn't believe my ears. I had prayed to Krishna that He would make some arrangement that they would take me to the tenth group, and here

He very kindly did that for me. I was so happy that my Lord was making all the necessary arrangements for such a fallen soul like me. I was very thankful to the chief, and I told him that I owed him something for giving me such an opportunity. I promised that as soon as I got out I would send him a Bhagavad-gita, and he was very happy. He told me also about a guard who is an Armenian, and said that I might want to meet with him so that I could talk in my own language. That was the first and last time I saw the chief of the camp. Usually, he was in his office, and everyone else was doing their job to keep the place operating.

Next, the guards sent me to the bathroom. They shaved my head completely and gave me new, black clothes. My other clothes were put in a bag with my name on it. I was very unhappy. Now I really felt like a fish out of water. I wanted to see how I looked in the new uniform with shaved head, but there were no mirrors in that place; so I waited until they took me to the camp.

Another guard took me to my new cell, and finally I saw the sky again after a long time. I could walk freely anywhere in the camp area, and although it was not a big territory, I felt very happy because it was many times bigger than a prison cell. It was like a huge village of 1,800 prisoners with 1,800 different reasons for being there. There was a long, three story building punctuated by all kinds of aluminum doors with electronic locks on them. After each section, the guard asked another officer who was sitting on top of the tower to push the button to open the doors. In this way, he took me to the third floor and told the prisoner in charge to take me to work next morning. They showed me my bed. I started to put my belongings in a drawer and put the bed sheets on my bed. There were about seventy-five people crammed into one long room. The stench was very severe. Huge, green mosquitoes used to come from a nearby river at night. They were so aggressive that even if you pushed them away, they would come back again and again. From the very first day, I wanted to be prepared to tolerate the difficulties there. I still had the gray notebook that Khatsik had given me, and I started to regularly record my thoughts in it. The diary was some comfort to me.

After I had settled in, some of the inmates started asking me questions about my case and crime, as usual. Soon almost everyone was next to my bed hearing my history. I answered them humbly. Everyone was satisfied that they knew who I was, why I was there, and where I should sleep.

I walked to the bathroom to see myself in the mirror with my new black uniform with my name and number displayed on my chest. I felt like a different person with my new hairstyle! I washed my face and then came back to my bed.

After a while, a bell started to loudly ring, and everyone started to rush downstairs. I asked one guy what this was all about, and he explained, "Three times a day, we all have to do this procedure. We have to go to the main square and make a perfect line of men in order to be counted, no matter if it is terribly hot or unbearably cold. The guards come and count all of us, and then we walk in a line to the eating hall. Three times a day we get pretty much the same old stew to eat."

I started to follow the crowd, but because there were so many people, I was unable to walk fast. Suddenly, one fat man pushed me and caused me to fall. Another one told me that this was my "exam." Everyone was laughing at me, and I was praying in my mind, "O Krishna, please help me here! I do not want to hurt anyone, but now I have to fight with this stupid man. Please, Krishna, help me. Help your helpless servant, please!"

I knew some rules already by listening to stories about camp life from criminals during the past eight months; so I knew what I had to do in such a situation. I did not want to fight or hurt anyone, but if you didn't stand up to some of the tough men, then they would abuse you and make you their servant. You would have to make them tea every day and clean their desk, and so on. So I turned back, ran towards the fat guy, and pushed him very hard. He fell back against the bathroom door, which was right behind him, knocking it open and falling down on his back on the floor. I could understand clearly that he was not expecting that from me. I ran towards him and did not let him stand up. I started to kick him as hard as I could several times. Immediately many prisoners came to the door and started to watch the scene. I knew it was very painful for him, but at the same time I felt I had no other choice but to do this at least one time. He started to curse and scream at me, but I didn't care and kept kicking him and hitting him as hard as I could. Finally, another man, Vanya, came and held back my hands. He told me that this was enough and asked me to stop fighting and just walk downstairs.

On the way downstairs Vanya told me, "You did a fine job, and that guy will never bother you again. Not only him, but no one will ever do anything to you because they have seen that you know how to protect yourself. This is very important for any one who comes to this world for the first time; this was your exam."

A police officer came, showed me a spot on the ground, and told me to remember that this was going to be my standing place until the end of my last day in there. Then, after being counted, I was pushed and shoved into the eating hall. I could not call it a dining hall or a cafeteria, or any civilized term, because this was not a place where anyone enjoyed visiting or eating. The food, mainly made out of meat and fish, stank to high heaven. The aluminum plates and cups were so dirty that I couldn't imagine how it was possible to eat or drink from them. There was also a tumultuous noise in the eating hall. Try to imagine the sound of 1,800 sets of aluminum spoons, cups, and plates all scraping and clanking at once. Overall, it was disgusting.

As soon as we entered, everyone took his seat. I was just carefully watching what was going on there. It happened that I was asked by one criminal to sit at the end of the table, where right in front of me was placed the big pot of nasty food that was prepared for everyone. Steam rose from the pot, almost choking me.

I had no choice but to sit and tolerate the situation, thinking, "In some ways a jail was better, since at most twelve to fifty people were eating." As I looked around, I noticed that on the front wall there was a large painting of a blue sky, a forest, and a small pond. The wall was so dirty and oily that some parts of the picture were shining and some weren't. Then a person next to me started to push me with his arm, bringing my attention back to the table. When I asked him what he wanted, he indicated with his eyes that he wanted the pot and the plates. I made a gesture to show that I didn't understand. My lack of understanding seemed to make him and the rest of the ten people at our table angry.

I looked for Vanya to see what he would suggest I do. After finding him two tables over and catching his attention, he moved his head to indicate that I should not distribute the food.

Someone from the end of the table called loudly, "Hey, Armenian, distribute the food to all the plates now. We have a limited time here. Hurry up."

I replied that I am a strict vegetarian and cannot even touch this pot, so you should take care of it yourself. I added that I was not going to do this even if we had to fight over it. He took his spoon and showed me that he was going to throw it at my face if I didn't cooperate. I took my spoon and showed him that I was going to do the same to him if he tried anything.

It took only a minute before someone in front of me was told to do the job. Vanya was looking at me, smiling and nodding. On the way out, he came to me and told me that he purposefully didn't tell me anything about it to see how I'd overcome the situation. He said I did a good job. If I would have served the food one time, they would have forced me to do it all the time.

The first day, I refused to eat anything in the eating room, preferring to take my piece of bread to my room. But on the way out, the police officer noticed, took my bread, and threw it in the trash. He told me that I was not allowed to take food to my cell, and if I wanted to eat I had to do it here only. I stayed hungry for the day.

After I returned to the room, Vanya came, sat with me, and asked me to tell him a little bit about my case. He was a gentleman, and he taught me a lot about the unwritten law of the camp. He said, "Feel free to ask me anything you'd like to know, and I'll help you out." I was very thankful. He told me that the only way to take bread out of the eating hall is to hide it under my hat. He asked me why I couldn't eat there, and I explained, "Because I can only eat dry bread; after a few bites it becomes very difficult to swallow. I need to eat it with salt to produce some saliva in my mouth. I need some water too. There was no water on the table, and the cups were so dirty!"

When I mentioned water, he told me I should never drink any water without boiling it because it came directly from the nearby river, which was full of industrial waste dangerous to one's health. As I later learned, the water there was so foul that if you kept it for three or four hours you could see thick dirt settling on the bottom of the pot.

I had nothing to boil water in, so he gave me an empty one-liter glass pot and taught me how to make a heater from two razor blades. He took two small pieces of pencil wood and put them between the two razor blades and tied the whole thing with a simple thread so the blades could not move and contact each other. After that, he connected two wires, one to each blade. We filled the pot with water and placed the heater in it. We connected one wire to the negative and one to the positive side of the current at the electrical outlet, which was melted almost open. The water started to bubble. In about five minutes, it was at a rolling boil. I smiled at him with thankful eyes. It was a very nice method to kill all the bacteria. Then he told me only to drink water after the first batch. The first time one boiled water with a new heater, he explained, harmful chemicals came from the razor blades.

Every day I went to work, returning to sleep in the same place. The work zone was just a five-minute walk from the living zone, but the zones were separated from each other by a tall fence. Each time we went to work, they took us through a tunnel where many guards checked our pockets and our body so that we would not take anything from one place to the other. Soon I learned everything and everyone I needed to know to live there.

Vanya and I were in the same shift. I could ask him about anything I wanted to know about that camp. He had been there for the last five years and knew everyone. He introduced me to his "family man," who was called "Small" because he was so short. Small had come from another camp two years before, where he spent one and half years before he was sixteen.

Vanya told me that usually in a camp you live as a family, and eat with someone, sharing whatever you have together. That is the way prisoners help each other, and also protect each other from unwanted situations. When I asked if I could be in their family, they told me that they had no objections. So we started to become closer and closer to each other and started eating together. I secretly brought my bread from the kitchen and ate it with boiled water. They were drinking tea while I was eating my bread and talking about Krishna or life in general.

Sometimes when we were eating together, Small looked at me over his cup of tea as if he wanted to have some of my bread. When I would offer him some, he would try to refuse by saying that I had nothing else to eat. But when he finally took some at my insistence, my portion became even tastier. Spending my days like this, I counted the time to my 730th day.

One of my biggest concerns was about my beads. So that no guards would confiscate them, I chanted my rounds every day in the morning while everyone was sleeping. But once a week soldiers would come and inspect. They would search everywhere for narcotics, money, and any other restricted items. They would open all pillows, mattresses, drawers, and even floors. One day they found my beads in my pillow and took them away from me. Then, like I had done countless times since being in prison—God knows how many times, I started to make my beads from my bread. But Vanya told me that he knew of a better way to do it, which he would help me out with the next day when we would go to work camp.

That day he started to teach me some tricks, such as how a sewing machine can be transformed into a drilling and polishing machine. He took a plastic clothes hanger and started to cut it into small pieces just the same size as I liked to have my beads. He then took a tool that had been hidden under the floor and connected it on the side of the sewing machine, turning the machine into a drill. Then he made a tiny hole in each plastic "bead." I was astonished to see how smart people could be in difficult situations such as this. I got some plastic thread and started to make the most sophisticated and best beads I had ever had in jail. The brown plastic reminded me of Tulasi beads, and it was super fun to chant my rounds on them. I was so thankful to my friend for that great help.

The foreman in the work camp taught me a few simple sewing techniques. In the summer it was fine, and all the windows were open. Winter, however, was a completely different situation. Because sewing is so sedentary, we suffered greatly from the cold weather. Our fingers became frozen while sewing. But we had our daily quota of garments to finish. If we did not meet our quota, the guards got very angry and hit us with their batons or sticks. So we all wanted to learn to do everything quickly with all results of an acceptable quality. We used to sew some stylish jackets, to which the supervisors would attach a false label that said that it was made in such and such factory.

We used to work three different shifts. The worst was working the night shift, since it's very hard not to sleep while working, no matter how hard you tried. After working for a while one night, I heard loud screaming. It was terrible! One prisoner who had fallen asleep and could not feel his fingers any more from the cold had sewn three of his fingers together, breaking the needle inside one of his fingers. After that, I tried to be even more careful not to push the sewing machine pedal too hard. I was very fortunate that in sixteen months I sewed through only one finger. That also happened during the night shift in the bitter cold. I wore gloves with the fingers cut off so I could feel and hold the cloth, but one day I fell asleep and woke up with a needle stuck in my index finger. I ran to the drawer where our tools were, pulled the needle out with pliers, and then went back to work after putting some iodine and a bandage on it.

Sometimes it was so cold that it was impossible to be outside for even a minute. From time to time, the temperature was -42 to -52 Celsius (-43 to -61 Fahrenheit), which was very frightening. All the windows would get covered with ice about five inches thick on the inside and more than ten inches on the outside. It was always dark, even in the daytime, and it generally snowed in an unbelievable manner. The toilets were outside and were so cold that we often preferred to tolerate some discomfort than go outside to use them. We did not work when it was so cold, but stayed in our main place, doing nothing. Whenever we did go outside in the cold weather, we used to play like schoolboys in order to waste time. We would be amazed at how thrown water became ice before it touched the ground, and then made a sound like breaking glass.

My teeth started to get weaker and weaker every day because I did not have any nutritious food at all and ate too much salt, which damaged my gums, making my teeth very loose. I could easily wiggle them all with my tongue. Sometimes, even while I was eating my soft bread, they would move.

Vanya told me that I must eat some garlic with my bread if I didn't want to loose all my teeth. At first I was completely against that idea because it is against Prabhupada's orders of, "No onion, no garlic." Also, since childhood I hated garlic and never ate it. But once while I was eating my bread I accidentally swallowed one of my teeth, and a few weeks later I swallowed another. Then I started to use some garlic. I used to just place it on my bread and eat or rub it on my teeth and gums.

I wrote some letters to my parents and Prana das just to get a reply, so I could see whether the camp mail system worked. I soon got replies from both. Prana also sent me Sachisuta's address, and I was very happy to learn that he was not very far from me. I wrote to him, receiving his reply after a long time and obviously opened by the police. They checked everything we wrote to each other. We were thus able to write to each other only six to eight times within sixteen months. In his letters, he always spoke about his health and the very difficult outside work he was doing there. They were forcing him to work very hard. Soon I got a letter from him saying that he was very sick and had completely refused to work. That was not such a good strategy; the police would heartlessly beat criminals who did not want to work. He was fasting to protest the heavy nature of the work. He would always write that he was doing well spiritually, chanting his sixteen rounds every day, and following all the rules. His diet was the same as mine, three pieces of bread a day with salt and boiled water.

In one of his letters, he mentioned that they took him to a prison hospital where analyses showed that he had tuberculosis. In another letter, he told me that the best plan would be if we could meet each other on the 24th of January somewhere in the city so we could return to Armenia together. But in his last letter he wrote that he was very sick, in the hospital in very critical condition. He said he didn't know if he was going to be able to walk out alone, so he might need some devotees to come to pick him up from there. He told me that he already wrote about his health situation to Prana das in the hopes that Prana would make some arrangements to get him. He said that our plan was still the same, with the same post-prison meeting place.

I prayed to Krishna to please help my friend recover from his disease. There was nothing else that I could do. After all, my situation wasn't any better than his. I got very sick also and suffered from malaria, jaundice, and typhoid several times. All I ate daily was my three pieces of bread and salt. My health got worse, day by day. At one point I was so skinny and weak that I was unable to walk straight and often had difficulty climbing up the staircase to my room. Once, I asked the guards to escort me to the camp doctor. I collapsed in the middle of the walkway and opened my eyes in the doctor's room. He smiled at me like a beast looking at his prey.

"So how are you, Armenian Krishna?" he asked me.

"I am very critical, doctor. Please help me to recover! Please!" I replied.

There were about ten other criminals waiting for the doctor's help. He took out an old box of medicine and started to distribute two vials of the same medicine to everyone who was there. He said, "This is the best medicine for all of you guys, and it will help you out if you drink it."

He seemed to be making fun of us. One boy told me that once one criminal beat up the doctor out of frustration, for which he got another three years in an even worse camp. The doctor appeared to be a heartless creature. He told me, "Since they sent you to this place to die, there isn't any medicine for you this time. Sorry." Feeling very disappointed, I did not know what to do. I stayed there for a while. Then I stood up somehow and walked out by holding the wall.

At one point during this time, it was so hard for me to walk that someone helped me to work and back. My back started hurting, too, and I thought, "Now, I am totally finished." For a few weeks, I somehow chanted my rounds while lying down, praying and begging for Krishna's help. My friends were boiling water for me and helping as much as they could. By Krishna's mercy, I gradually got better and started to stand without assistance. It was amazing how I survived. Even today I can't figure out how I came out alive from that hell.

One day I wrote in my diary, "I do not know if I will be able to survive these terrible conditions, and I am praying to Krishna to take me back to His eternal abode." I had mentioned in my diary three times, "It would be better for me to die than to live like this. What is the point of this kind of life?" So, honestly speaking, for a time I was unable to mentally maintain my sense of spiritual determination. There was not much support from inside the camp, and I did not know what was going on outside. The only information I got from the police was that all my friends were in jail.

I remember this as a most critical time. I felt really helpless. Maya, or illusion, was whispering in my ear, "Hey you! What are you doing here? Do you think it is wonderful to die from hunger and suffer so much for Krishna? No, give it up and stop chanting this mantra. You are young and full of energy! Get out from this hell before it's too late, before you die. Get out and enjoy life like everyone else in this world. Do not be stupid—give it up now!" It was so real that I could feel her breath on my face.

I met the Armenian guard several times, but he was not a nice man. Once he found out that I was a Hare Krishna devotee, he did not want to have anything to do with me. I guess he was afraid of what his bosses would think. Once, I happened to find out that he was going to Armenia for a vacation; so I humbly asked him to get some money from my friends and relatives there and secretly give some of it to me so that I could purchase medicines and extra food for myself to perhaps survive my sentence. He did not seem happy with the idea, but he took my paper of addresses without question or comment.

I had some hope then for my material well-being, but when he came back he did not even come to see me. He worked in a different part of the camp, and it took many weeks before I could get close enough to him to ask secretly whether or not he could contact my friends. He said, "Oh, I was very busy with my family in Armenia, and I did not have time to meet anyone. But, don't worry—I will be going back there in a year, and maybe then I can arrange something." He knew well that after a year I would be either outside or dead and never need his help again.

Later, Vanya told me that there was one soldier there from Armenia who might help me out. The soldiers stood on very high watchtowers to guard us day and night. Once, during our night shift, Vanya and I went to find the Armenian soldier and started to talk to him from the ground. He was from a town near to mine and was friendly. So we made an agreement with him, throwing him some interesting products that he could use or sell outside, with the understanding that the next time he came he would throw us some money and some tea for my friend.

These types of arrangements were typical for the criminals there. Everyone used his intelligence to create incredible things for sale. Some made beautiful automatic knives, panes of plastic mosaic figures, and hundreds of different things. They had two different buyers. First, there were the permanent buyers, who were the police officers. They bought things at very cheap prices or exchanged with tea or narcotics. Then they sold the crafts for high prices outside the prison. Second, the soldiers bought things from time to time, or just while they were stationed there. They might also exchange the goods for tea or pay a somewhat higher price than the police officers. Unfortunately, after a couple of transactions, they moved this Armenian boy to some other place, and I never saw him again.

So, then I could understand that Krishna just wanted me to depend on Him rather then some spoiled police officer or a soldier, who was in many ways also like a prisoner, spending eight hours every day with us there. I thought then of the story of Draupadi, a devotee of Krishna in ancient India. Her husband, Emperor Yudhisthira, was a very humble, truthful man whose only fault was that he could not refuse an opportunity to gamble. His cousins challenged him to a game of dice wherein they cheated him of everything—his inheritance, his freedom, and even his chaste wife. His cousins then wanted to drag Draupadi into the assembly and shame her by pulling off her clothes. Srila Prabhupada said that such an abominable act had never even been thought of before. She looked around at those who had assembled to watch the match, asking for help and mercy, but no one came forward to help her. At first, she clutched her garments, trying to defend herself. But then she realized, "These are great, powerful warriors trying to disrobe me. What can I do?" So she raised her arms up high and prayed sincerely, "Krishna, I am your surrendered devotee. If You desire, then You can protect my honor."

Krishna immediately came there, unseen to all, and supplied an unlimited length of sari cloth to cover Draupadi's body. Those warriors pulled and pulled with disbelief until the room was piled high with cloth and they were exhausted. Only then did they understand that she was protected by God, Krishna, and they would never be able to disgrace her. Thinking in this way, with revived and greater faith in Krishna, I surrendered my fate into His lotus-like hands.

I somehow found the energy to chant the holy names and go on with my practice. One day, Krishna came in my dream and played His transcendental flute. He held my hand and spoke very gently and sweetly. Krishna said to me, "Please do not worry; you are my devotee. Just continue what you are already doing, and I will personally take care of you."

The very next day, an inmate brought me a magazine called Science and Religion in the Russian language. It contained a very prejudicial article about devotees. The good part was that it included a nice picture of Srila Prabhupada and some devotees. I immediately cut the photo out; it made a nice altar for me in my drawer. Although the article was against the Hare Krishna movement, when I read it, sentence by sentence, I mentally reversed whatever they wrote to make it a very nice article.

The most intolerable situation during my illness was having to walk all the way from the third floor to the ground floor and back again to use the toilet while I was having constant diarrhea, thus needing the toilet frequently. I had to go there many times a day because of my weak stomach. Sometimes in the middle of my return journey up the stairs, I had to go back and use the toilet again. Sometimes I would feel as if I was going to fall unconscious, so I would sit down on the stairs while my whole body was shaking. But sitting on the cold concrete wasn't a good idea either, so somehow I would bring myself to the third floor, and as soon as I lay down on my bed, I felt like going to the bathroom again.

Anyway after some time I started to slowly recover and walk properly by Krishna's mercy. I put all the suffering behind me, but I had gotten so skinny that I was afraid to look at myself in the mirror while shaving in the morning. It was a big task for us to shave, since they didn't give us any razorblades yet asked us to shave our faces at least every two days and shave our heads every week when we took a bath.

The prisoners often got into heartless fights, and sometimes people got killed. One particular incident really affected me. There was a boy who came from the town very close to the camp. He had been in camps for four years, out of which the past year had been in our camp. Since he had just become a teenager, they had transferred him from the children's camp to the adult's.

Vanya told me that from the very first day this boy argued and fought with another criminal who was from his village. Some other criminals told me that the man, who had been in this camp for a long time, was the one who was trying to make the boy's life miserable. One day, while this man was sleeping, the boy took a thick iron bar from the fire stove and hit him on his head. The man died on the spot. The boy then went to the guard and told him what he had done. The guards took care of the body and then put the boy in the underground cells for about one month. After that, right in the camp they had a court and gave him another twelve years. For many months I used to see the killing in my dream, and I felt like the dead man's spirit was always in our room.

## CHAPTER FIFTEEN

# The Special Mercy of Krishna

*Pride, arrogance, conceit, anger, harshness, and ignorance—these qualities belong to those of demoniac nature, O son of Prtha.*

*-Bhagavad-gita, 16.4*

T he day I felt the most helpless was the day I especially felt the Lord's help and mercy. I was still in my bed at noontime and, for the first time ever, I had not finished my rounds. I thought, "Maybe I can finish my rounds tomorrow, just this one time only." I was resting with closed eyes after doing my night shift, but I could not sleep. Then I heard my name called over the speakers!

At first I thought that I was going crazy, and that my ears were just making up all kinds of sounds. But after a while they called my name again, "Gagik Buniatyan, come to the office for an appointment." I could not believe it! I jumped up and started to run out into the cold and unpleasant weather.

I ran to the automatic door and screamed to the guard that I had an appointment. He pushed the buttons one by one. I passed through one door after another until I came to the office building. My heart was beating very fast, and I didn't know what to think or what to expect. "Who might be there waiting for me on the other side of these ugly walls? Whom might Lord Krishna send to me, and why just now when I was so depressed and in a helpless condition?"

One of the police officers asked me to wait in the corridor. After about ten minutes, he opened a door and asked me to enter. My heart started to beat even faster as I entered the meeting room—behind the thick glass I saw (Ivan) Haridas Thakur and (Vardan) Nityananda Ram standing and waiting for me! I couldn't control my tears as I came closer to them. We touched the glass with our heads and told each other "Hare Krishna." We were all crying for a while, in silence. There were absolutely no holes in the glass. Even if a person would scream, they wouldn't hear anything on the other side of the glass. Nityananda picked up the phone and asked me and Haridas to do the same. I took two phones and they took one each, and we started to speak to each other. Haridas started to ask me questions first.

"How are you, Gago?"

"I am okay, tolerating. How are you doing?"

"We are doing all right and waiting for you prabhus to come out."

"How is Sannyasa, Kamalamala, and the others?"

"I hope you know that they are going to record this conversation, so please—no specific questions," said Haridas Thakur.

"Okay."

"You look too thin. You are not eating?"

"Yes, what to do? These guys are not giving me even my monthly parcel from my parents. It is not so easy here."

"What are you eating, then?"

"Just bread and salt."

"That's it?"

"That's it for a long period of time."

"Can't you ask for anything vegetarian from them?"

"No, they won't give me anything, even if I will die tomorrow without it."

"Are you working?"

"Yes, of course."

"What work are you doing here? Is it too heavy?"

"No, I am just sewing and sewing, eight hours a day."

"What would you like us to do for you?" Nityananda asked.

"Pray for me, please," I said.

"No, no we are serious!" he insisted. "What would you like us to do for you, materially, so you can feel better here?"

"Give me some money if you can so I can buy some bread, sugar, and a shaving blade. I do not remember when the last time was that I ate sugar, or shaved with a new blade. In the jail it was better because they would give me a spoonful of sugar, but here they mix everything in the tea, so it's impossible for me to eat sugar. I do not know what else to ask from you. If you have money, you can buy a lot of things here. So money is the most essential thing here, just like everywhere else, I guess. Here if you have money you can buy practically everything you desire."

"Okay, we will try to arrange something for you. We have been here in this hellish place for more than a week, and every day we have been trying to come to see you. But these people had no heart and did not let us come in. We offered them a lot of money too, but they all refused to help us."

"Why did they not let you come to see me? What did they tell you?"

"They said that only relatives are allowed to come and see the inmates."

"That's stupid! The rule is that anyone can come once in six months to see anyone if both sides agree to it."

"Anyway, today's guard was a bit better. He told us that he can see how hard we are trying to come and see you, and had some compassion towards us. Somehow his heart was melted, and he agreed to give us two hours with you."

"Did he charge you, too?"

"Oh yes! Without money, it is impossible to do anything from this side."

"From this side, too," I replied.

"Do you have any news from Sako?" I asked.

"Yes, before coming to you, we visited him too."

"How is my brother Sako doing? Please tell me everything you know about him. I got my last letter from him about a month ago, and it wasn't so good."

"He is doing okay, but ..."

"But what?"

"Well, he was very ill, and skinnier than you are. He was having some health problems, but spiritually he was doing great, just like you."

"Oh, you do not know how I am struggling here! This is too much for us, I think."

"Is there any news from Gurudev?"

"Yes, we have great news for you today!"

"What's that? Tell me quickly."

"You are already initiated! The guru gave you a spiritual name. Your name is Sachisuta dasa!"

"Really! How did that happen?"

"Tulasi dasa took our names to the Moscow devotees, and they sent all of our names to Sri Visnupad. He held a very special ceremony in Mayapur on March 25th, 1986. As you know, it was Lord Chaitanya's 500th anniversary too; so on that special day he initiated us!"

"Who else was initiated?"

"Sako, Tigran, Vardan, Agvan, and me from Armenia, but all together we were twenty-six devotees, said Haridas."

"What is your name?" I asked Ivan.

"Haridasa Thakur dasa, and Vardan is Nityananda dasa, Tigran is Prana dasa, Agvan is Adwaita dasa."

"What is Sako's name?"

"Sarvabhavana dasa."

"Wow! That is very interesting! What is my name again?"

"Sachisuta dasa."

"What does it mean?"

"It means son of Mother Sachi. And you know who Sachi Mata is, no?"

"O, yes, of course."

"How is Armine doing?" I asked.

"She is in a psychiatric hospital, doing okay, and soon they will let her out."

"That's good they did not take anyone else to jail," I thought. "So where are Sannyasa and the others in that group now?"

"They are also going to be out soon. We are waiting for some papers from Moscow, and then they will let them out. Devotees are doing very active demonstrations all over the world for you guys, and that's helping a lot. Sri Visnupad is worried about you guys very much and doing everything necessary to get you guys out of here."

"How are the devotees doing in Russia? How many devotees are behind bars?"

"Nearly about fifty all together."

"Oh, that's too much, Prabhu..."

"Yes, what to do ..."

"Are there any ladies in jail, as well?

"Yes, about six or seven ladies are there. Premavati is there, and her baby daughter died in the jail. I guess you knew that already?"

"Yes, demons, demons."

"Did they arrest Mamu Thakur?"

"No, I do not think so; he is traveling and preaching all over."

"Were you able to give some money or prasadam to Sarvabhavana (Sako)?"

"Yes, there it was much easier to do these things than here."

"That's good. At least my brother got something. He is very sick. I really worry about him, but I don't know what to do from here. I do not feel as if Sachisuta is my name, but what can I do? Let me write it down," I said.

I started to write all the names they told me on a piece of paper. It was interesting to know that one and a half years ago I was initiated, but I didn't know anything about it for all this time. Not only that, but taking initiation in a jail must have been somewhat of a new occurrence in ISKCON.

So anyhow, we talked for more than two hours, and at the end they told me, "We brought a lot of nice prasadam for you but could not pass it to you. Tomorrow morning we will try again, and if we are not successful, then at least we are going to try to send some money in."

"Oh, thank you very much. I really appreciate that very much."

I told them what they could do to pass some money to me, and then said, "Thank you very much for coming such far distances to see me, Prabhus! You gave me some hope and life today; actually you saved my life!" I think I desperately needed such a meeting.

A police officer came in and said that our time was over, and we must leave the room immediately.

We offered obeisances, and my friends left. That was one of the most wonderful days.

I was nervous about getting the money for a few days, but then I gave up hope. I learned months later that my friends tried to pass money to me the next day, but the guard who usually brokered money for the inmates did not show up. Another guard took all the money for himself.

Still, the visit from the devotees gave me new hope and a will to live. I found some energy to tolerate my last five months in the labor camp. In fact, I was so hopeful that I started to write several pages a day in my diary. The most interesting entry was that when they told me that my name was Sachisuta das, I did not feel as if it was my name. After being released, I came to know that the devotees in Moscow had accidentally changed the order of the names during the translation from English to Russian and Sachisuta's name and my name got mixed up. They wrote my name as Sachisuta dasa and Sako's name as Sarvabhavana dasa. Sachisuta left his body believing his initiated name was Sarvabhavana dasa. He never found out that Sachisuta dasa was his real initiated name.

# CHAPTER SIXTEEN

# Behind Birth and Death

*And whoever, at the end of his life, quits his body,*
*remembering Me alone, at once attains My nature.*
*Of this there is no doubt.*

*–Bhagavad-gita, 8.5*

Slowly, my days were coming closer and closer to the end. The only problem was that the closer the end got, the slower the days passed. The last days were the most difficult. One month before my release, they allowed me to grow my hair. Anyhow, I passed all the days of my sentence, one by one, and made a hole on each of the 730 days on my calendar. Finally, it got to a point where there were only two days left before I could come out and look at this hell from the other side. I wondered how I would feel at that time. I was very fortunate to be released two days early. Since anything could happen in that place in one day, I was very happy to miss any day at all. I came out on the 22nd of January, which translated to two days, or forty-eight hours, or 2,880 minutes earlier from the camp. They couldn't let me out on the 24th because that was a Sunday and the office was closed on weekends.

On the morning of my release day, January 22, 1988, I was ready. I was sitting on my bed, looking at the speaker on the top of the long posts, which might call my name at any minute. Everybody was coming to say goodbye and Hare Krishna to me. Some were joking, some were serious, but it didn't matter because everyone was at least chanting Krishna's holy name. It was hard to believe that after just an hour or so I wouldn't see all those ugly fences around me.

Finally they called my name, and I was ready to leave that horrible place forever. I started to walk towards the gate with some of my friends.

From time to time I turned back to see the inmates who were looking from the windows and waving their hands. Then, from the first gate Vanya and Small embraced me saying, "Hare Krishna" and "Goodbye." They returned because the police would not allow them to walk more towards the next gate. They extended me wishes for a list of great things in my future life, the best of which was, "Never come back again." At the end of the walkway, before entering the office gate, I screamed loudly, "Hare Krishna!" Everyone who was watching screamed back loudly, "Never come back again!"

I next went to the office, ready to sign my liberty papers and retrieve the clothes that I gave them the day I entered. Inmates are paid a little for the work they do so that they will have some money to pay for their tickets to their home and to make a new start in life. I was also given this. The guards were all smiling now, instead of their usual angry mood, and they also told me, "Never come back again."

It is practically impossible to describe my feelings at that moment, so I am not going to even try. I was like a seven-year-old boy, running this way and that, kicking snow around, laughing loudly, and calling, "Krishna Krishna."

I prayed to Krishna, "O Krishna, I am out now and I will serve you eternally because you are my only Lord, no matter how hard you deal with me, your servant. Thank you, Krishna, for protecting and taking care of me, Hare Krishna. But please, Krishna, never again bring me back to this hell, please."

I went to the nearest hotel and booked a room for two days. It was very close to the camp. In the daytime I could see the black walls and long buildings of the work camp, and the black aura on top of it. It was terrible and scary to see the vastness of that place. I could hardly believe that I was looking at it from the other side of the fence.

Sometimes I felt that the KGB might change its mind and take me in again. The mind itself is so terrible. As a free man, I wanted to scream to everyone to appreciate their freedom, no matter how hard life is. I had paid my dues to society for my so-called crime. I was thinking, "Krishna must have a plan to still use me in his service in the future, too." I was a survivor; I had not seen the white bears as the head of the KGB had warned me. Two years before, this powerful, heartless man had said, "My dear sir, we are going to send you to Siberia, the land of the white bears, where you will die from hunger. I promise you both 100%!" But fortunately it did not happen.

I made a phone call to my friends and asked for some money for my expenses to reach Armenia. I soon received it. I took a train to Moscow where Sachisuta and I were supposed to meet. I did not find him there, and after waiting for some days, I took a flight to Baku, Azerbaijan, where I had promised to meet a cellmate's brother and give him an important, secret letter. Then, since I was very close to my hometown of Meghri, I took a train there. The next evening I was with my family, feeling that Sachisuta would have some good surprise there for me just like he did years ago.

My parents were very happy to see me. Everyone was asking me how I felt and other small talk. Having a general idea of when to expect me, they were pretty much prepared to receive me. Soon, all our neighbors and relatives were in our house sharing my parents' happiness as they had shared their grief two years back when I was arrested.

My first question for them was if they knew anything about Sachisuta and if there was any news about when he was going to be back. My mom told me that there was not only no news, but he hadn't even called his parents. That seemed very strange to me. I started to think of everything that could explain where he could possibly be. One certain thing was that we were supposed to come to the police station in our home town within about fifteen days of release to turn in our papers and receive our passports back. If we were late then there would be a penalty and various legal problems.

My mom started to feed me daily with lots of vegetables and vitamins so I could recover quickly. Every day she would force me to eat one or two 500gram cans of condensed milk, as well as honey with butter, nuts, and bread. It was a relief to eat such things after so many hungry days, but it had its side effects too because my stomach had become smaller. It felt like I was overeating every day.

One day I went to the police station to get my passport. I met the same police officers who had arrested me several times. They were more pleasant than before, shaking my hand and mildly asking how I was doing. There was a big reason behind that "kindness." I had been told in camp that the police are usually afraid that a released prisoner may sometimes take revenge on the officers who made the arrest. Former prisoners often become even more dangerous than before their arrest, attacking the arresting officers at night if they see them alone. There were many cases where they would try to hit the arresting officers by slamming them with a car, or throwing acid in their face to make them blind for the rest of their life. After I signed many different papers they gave me my passport, and I returned home.

The next day, I phoned Sachisuta's home to see if he was back and ask his parents about his return if he was not. I felt very uneasy that I had not heard anything for so long. As soon as I picked up the phone, my mom quickly came over to me and asked where I was calling. When I told her that I was trying to call Sachisuta's parents, she told me not to do that because it was too late at night. She then took me to her room, asked me to sit down next to her, and then started to cry and curse the KGB. My dad asked her to stop crying and tell me why she was cursing. She kept saying that she did not know how to tell me. I started to get very nervous. Then my brother came in with his wife and somehow, with their support, my mom told me that one month ago Sachisuta passed away in the jail. He had been very sick. I do not remember exactly what happened to me, but I fell unconscious on the sofa and started to cry very loudly after some water was thrown on me.

Everybody was in a panic trying to do something to help me, but I was in a different world—a world of very deep pain and suffering, suffering and separation. After a while, they brought me back to external consciousness and I started to cry as if I was a ten-year-old child. I could not believe that I had lost my friend Sachisuta forever! I did not want to even consider it. That was the most painful kick the KGB gave to me. To this day, I have been angry and full of poison in my heart against them. I felt as if the KGB had shot me full of bullets.

A movie started playing in my mind of our last days and the sad separation in the Baku jail. I was doing everything possible to remember all the details, since all I had of him was my memories and heart connection. I could not yet accept a life-long separation from my very good friend. I kept saying, "That means they killed my brother! They killed my brother, and they killed my best friend! That means they killed my brother, and I'll never see him again! They killed my brother, and they killed my best friend! That means they killed my brother who was such a nice person! They killed my brother, and they killed my best friend. Ohhh, terrible!"

After a while, I went out and started to walk towards his parents' house to see them and share their grief. My mom was following me, crying. Soon I was standing in front of their door, where I was horrified to see a black cloth hanging. A black cloth indicates that because a family is in grief people have to be respectful and keep a low noise level around their house.

My mom knocked on the door, and Sachisuta's sister Anush opened it. As soon as she saw me, she called her mom and told everyone that I was there. Sachisuta's mother ran to meet me with open arms, crying loudly and calling, "Welcome home, my son, welcome home Sako-jan!" She meant that she accepted me as her son that day, and she embraced me tightly. I could not tolerate seeing her in such a sad condition and everyone dressed in black, so I fell unconscious again, right in front of their doorstep.

His father came and started to shake me, calling my name and sobbing. "Please," he told me, "do not do this! Do not make it worse for us, Gagik! Come inside; we are your family. It would be better to let us sit and talk about your brother and friend." Sachisuta's father and my mother somehow helped me to come in and lay on the sofa. The ladies put some ice on my forehead. After some time, I was able to sit with them in their living room, where they had Sachisuta's picture draped with a black cloth and some candles burning next to it. As we exchanged questions and answers, his father started to tell the story of Sachisuta's experiences in the Russian labor camp according to what the camp authorities had told him and what he witnessed there himself.

He said that Sachisuta wrote him a letter saying that he was in a hospital jail and needed his family's help and support. So his father traveled to the camp hospital to do whatever he could. They stayed in a visitor's room together for three days and nights in November 1987. He told me that his son was very ill at that time, almost eating nothing. He was chanting the Hare Krishna maha-mantra and speaking very little about his health or anything else.

He said that he knew his son's condition was very serious and had a feeling that he was not going to live much longer if he continued like that. He had tried hard to convince Sachisuta to eat, but Sachisuta told him that he was having a chronic problem with his stomach and he refused. He was also suffering from tuberculosis, coughing all night long. After three days, his father had returned back to Armenia with no hope that his son would survive.

On December 24th, he got a telegram from the jail hospital again urging him and his wife to come immediately to see their son since his condition was very critical. He tried to rush there, but he was one day late. They told him that Sachisuta had died on December 26th. They also told him that according to some law he was not allowed to take his son's body at that time. After several months, they would be able to get his body in a stainless steel coffin with a seal that if you opened you could be jailed. They gave him Sachisuta's clothes, which included the jacket I had given to him in jail. He was only twenty-three years old, and he was scheduled to be released on January 22nd, 1988. He died just twenty-seven days before his release date.

When the father returned back with only some of his son's clothes, the whole family was in mourning. I spent a long time in their home talking until late at night. After a while, there was nothing more to say.

I was in shock, and did not know what to do or where to go. After two days I received a phone call from Atmananda das from Yerevan. He was happy to know that I was back and invited me to Yerevan for a large gathering in Damayanti's (Armine's) house. She had just recently been freed from a psychiatric hospital and was using her house as a center. I told him that I had been waiting for Sachisuta only and since there was nothing that held me in my home town any more, I could leave the next day to meet the devotees.

Damayanti came to meet me at the bus stop to take me to her new apartment. We were so happy to see each other that we both had tears in our eyes. She was like an elder sister to me and to many Armenian devotees. People at the bus stop sadly watched us cry, and when we discussed the passing of Sachisuta, some ladies started to cry too. We started to walk towards her building, unable to speak.

I was amazed to find almost twenty new and old devotees gathered at her apartment. I was especially happy to see Sannyasa das, Kamalamala das, and Atmananda das. Haridasa and Nityananda were there as well. They apologized for giving me the wrong information about my spiritual name and told me the correction. They also told me that Harikesa Swami had sent our new japa beads to Moscow along with our names, but the KGB had confiscated them and so none of the devotees had their initiated beads.

Then Sannyasa had everyone sit down. First, we remembered Sachisuta's wonderful heart and dedicated service to guru and Krishna. Everyone who had ever met him had something wonderful to tell about him. Unfortunately, no one had been able to find out any details about how he had passed away, although no one had a doubt that he left his body in a very auspicious way.

After that, Kamalamala set up the video camera and started to ask me questions about everything I had gone through. At that time, I was still so angry and upset with the KGB that I could not even look at their faces on the street. It was difficult for me to relate my history in such a way that was not disturbing to the ladies and younger devotees.

I was very anxious to hear about everything that had happened at the temple and ISKCON while I was away. As soon as Kamalamala had finished recording me I started to shower my questions. I was especially excited to see the Armenian translations of the Bhagavad-gita and Sri Isopanisad, which we were able to have due to the help and encouragement of Harivilas Prabhu. He had done so much for the Armenian devotees. He found an Armenian professor in France, Dr. Gegam Sahinian, who successfully translated Bhagavad-gita As It Is, Sri Isopanisad, Coming Back, etc. in 1982. It was only by his endeavor and investment that all those books were printed in Germany and later on sent to Armenia for distribution. Sannyasa was already having some printed for mass distribution. I was so happy to see his devotion and determination. He had just come out of jail for printing and distributing books, yet again he had started to print new books. They also introduced me to a new devotee Brahmananda Puri das who was actively helping Sannyasa das with printing Srila Prabhupada's books.

Then, we had a great kirtana and sat down to honor the wonderful prasadam they had been cooking from early morning. I could feel the enthusiasm of all the devotees. It was especially wonderful to see all the new people who had become devotees in the two years I was imprisoned. Damayanti's apartment was decorated with Krishna's pictures. I noticed Sachisuta Prabhu's picture in a frame on her small and attractive altar.

The devotees served me first, bringing me a little from each preparation. It was a grand feast with at least thirty different kinds of prasadam. As I sat on the floor, looking at all the plates, I did not know where to start. My emaciated stomach had to stop after I had hardly tried three or four preparations. But because I had not had a meal like this for two long years, I wanted to eat all of it. There was no place for even one more cherry! Oh, it was such a satisfying feast anyways.

One day Kirtana Rasa das (Arsen) and his wife Rukmini devi dasi (Marianna) invited me to their house to watch videos about Mayapur, India, and ISKCON in general. Up to then, I had seen only some black and white clips about Harikesa Swami and a little bit of Srila Prabhupada. The simple pleasure of spending the day with these devotees and sharing prasadam with them filled me with gratitude after my imprisonment.

In these ways, I stayed there for a while with devotees, and slowly came back to a normal life. I thought of my friend, Sachisuta dasa all day, every day, even during my chanting of japa. I even grew a little beard out of respect for him, according to Armenian tradition. Then Sannyasa told me that as devotees we do not follow such traditions, and he asked me to shave. I obeyed whatever my elder brother would tell me. Devotees were constantly doing demonstrations all over the world with Sachisuta's picture, and finally in May 1988, the government officially registered ISKCON as a sanctioned religion in the Soviet Union. My understanding is that someone was supposed to sacrifice his life in order to register our movement, and Sachisuta das was the one who had been ready to do so for Krishna. Krishna surely took him back home, back to Godhead.

I was always trying to find some way to honor my friend. I also wanted to make sure that the devotees knew about him and appreciated his great sacrifice. I had an idea to marry, have a son, and name him Sachisuta, as a way to honor my best friend and say his name daily in my home. I wanted to have him always next to me in my own way and remember him all my life.

Soon after that, by Lord Krishna's special arrangement, I met my wife, Dayanvisha devi dasi, who had become a devotee when I was in jail. We had the same feelings and understanding about spiritual life and marriage, and she agreed with my original plan. We married on the 18th of May, 1988. On September 21, 1990 we had our dear son, whom we named Sachisuta. We were very happy that Lord Krishna sent him to us to take care of him as well as we can and try to do everything to make him a nice person and a devotee of Lord Krishna.

One day, Brahmananda Puri, who just returned from Georgia, came to my house and told me that he had something extraordinary for me, but that he would not give it to me unless I gave him something in exchange. I offered him some maha-prasada from our Gaura Nitai Deities. He handed me a cassette tape and asked me to play it right away.

He told me that the quality wouldn't be clear because it was recorded on the street, but I would understand it well anyway. The devotees had been doing harinam sankirtana in Georgia, chanting and dancing in the street, when one man came and told them that he had been with one of our devotees who had died in jail. He told the devotees everything in detail about him, and one of the devotees happened to have a tape recorder. It turned out that he had been in the same cell with Sachisuta das the last three months of his life while he was in the prison hospital. He told the devotees how humble Sachisuta dasa was and about the unique qualities he had. Brahmananda Puri brought the tape to Yerevan for me. Even today, I remember every word on that tape.

The former cellmate said, "Sachisuta was very sick and hardly walking to the bathroom when they brought him to the hospital, but he was chanting his sixteen rounds every day and only talking about Krishna. A unique quality of Sachisuta was that he could transform any conversation into a talk about Krishna. We were the only two in the cell, so we became very close friends. I do not believe in God, but after having so much association with him, I started to believe in Krishna and was asking him more and more about Him and devotional life.

"It was simply wonderful to have him in my cell! He was a great person and a real Krishna devotee and believer. But his health was getting worse and worse, day by day, and he was hardly eating anything. He kept asking the guards only for a glass of milk and a couple of boiled potatoes a day. They refused to give even that to him, although it was actually part of our prescribed diet in the hospital. Even the bread the guards brought had sometimes been touching fish; so Sachisuta would refuse to eat it and would give it to me. I felt ashamed to eat his bread, but I knew that he would never eat it, so I would accept it.

"He was somehow always very happy, and didn't feel his pain and suffering at all. At least he would never show me that he was suffering. Any time I asked about his health he started to preach to me about the differences between the spirit soul and the material body. Sometimes we would sing the maha-mantra together in the cell, and I remember his sweet singing and happy mood at that time. He would become extremely happy during our singing, and his eyes were so different.

"One morning, he was feeling better and asked me for a favor. He asked me if I could shave his head and leave a little bit of hair on the top at the back. I asked him why he wanted that, but he did not explain anything. 'Just do what I say, please,' he replied."

The man then described how he had shaved Sachisuta's head, and then Sachisuta had managed to take a shower somehow in the narrow toilet, and then cover himself with a clean bed sheet tied as a dhoti. He made a nice garland by stringing some colored papers torn from magazines and used toothpaste to make tilak marks on his body. After that, he sat in a lotus yoga position and chanted Hare Krishna as usual on his bread beads, while looking at the Pancha Tattva and Harikesa Swami's very small picture in his left hand.

"He was happier than usual, and I was very happy to see him in that mood, thinking that he was recovering and feeling better. I was very sick as well at that time," the man continued, "so a guard took me out of the cell to give me my daily injections. It took hardly twenty minutes. When I came back, I saw that Sachisuta was still sitting in the same place in the same way, and it looked as if he was chanting. I lay down on my bed and read a newspaper. After a while, I noticed that Sachisuta was not chanting, but simply sitting and smiling. I asked him why he was not chanting but smiling, but he did not reply. I asked him that again and again, and I asked him different questions. But he was silent. I stood up and came close to him then. I pushed him gently and asked, "Why are you smiling, my friend, and not talking?"

"Then, I understood that he was not there, or that the soul was no longer there, as he would have said. I screamed and banged on the door. With tears in my eyes, I told the guards that they had killed this innocent boy! They came and took his body after some time, and I never saw him again. I do not know who Sachisuta was and who you people are! I do not believe in God, but I would like to die just like your friend died right in front of my eyes! He is a hero to me, and all my life I will remember him, all my life! He was an extraordinary and pure person."

After hearing this tape it was clear to all of us, with no doubt, that Sachisuta das was a pure devotee of Lord Krishna. He knew that he was going to leave his body that day and was really preparing himself—his body, mind, and soul—for it. He was detached from the demands of his body and mind and, as the soul, he was preparing to meet his dear Lord, Krishna. Everyone who heard this truly amazing story was touched and excited about it. Everyone was impressed with Sachisuta's great faith and devotion to Lord Krishna, Srila Prabhupada, and his guru and all the parampara (disciple succession). He certainly was a pure devotee of Lord Krishna, and Krishna personally took care of him as He promised in Bhagavad-gita.

## Sachisuta Prabhu ki jaya!

The same person also sent a letter to Sachisuta's parents in Russian offering condolences. A copy of that letter is in the picture section of this book.

My wife and I started to cry and then noticed that Brahmananda's tears were running, too. We thanked him, gave him gifts, and paid our obeisances to him. All night I could not sleep as I tried to imagine and understand my dear brother's feelings on his last day. My wife cried all night, and using the little bit of light that came from the streetlamps, meditated on the picture of Sachisuta that hung on our wall next to our altar.

From that day on our life has been changed. We wanted to do something and were feeling very much unsatisfied. For a long time I tried to figure out what was disturbing my mind, and one day I came up with an idea. My wife and I decided to have Sachisuta's statue in our home and set out to find out how we could do it. At first we were thinking of making a small statue of about ten inches high, but we ended up deciding to make a life-size statue with a beautiful seat for him. Vajra das (Volodya) then carved a wonderful vyasasana seat for Sachisuta Prabhu. We also found a good artist who quoted a price and said he was ready to start the work, though it was not done until a while later.

Although times had changed in the Soviet Union, there were still many troubles. It continued to be very difficult to distribute books and preach. It was hard to do any kirtana or gathering. Now, instead of calling themselves the KGB, government antagonists were using the word "nationalists," but the actual situation was not much different. Often the officials would come and create some disturbance for the devotees. Since our house was used as a center in Yerevan, there were problems from time to time and unnecessary fights. Our neighbors were working in some kind of criminal activity, and especially didn't like it when we were having kirtana. They used to come to our place drunk, start arguments, and curse the devotees. We were all trying our best to satisfy them and explain our program to them, but hardly anything was working out. Sometimes we got phone calls from strangers telling us to stop our gatherings and singing. The callers would tell my wife that they would kill me and burn our house if we did not stop the singing. In this critical situation we were trying to be extremely careful, going out only if it was necessary.

Books were stored in our home, and it was quite dangerous to distribute them, or to have a Sunday feast and invite many new people. There were hundreds of incidents on the streets of Armenia where our books were burned and devotees beaten. We kept informing the police about these things, but there wasn't even the slightest action taken to protect our rights. Rather, the police were working with our enemies.

One Sunday before the feast and kirtana started, my wife took some sweets and went to a neighbor's home. We were all waiting for a long time but she did not come back. After some time I went to see what was going on. I knocked on the door and, without waiting for an invitation, opened it and looked inside to see Dayanvisha sitting with about ten people surrounding her, listening to her preaching. They did not even notice me, since they were listening to her with full attention. I knocked on the door once more, and the father of the house invited me in while praising my wife and explaining that they liked her explanations. They all took prasadam and promised that not only would they not bother us, but they wouldn't even let anyone else disturb any devotee in that area. After that, sometimes they would come for our Sunday feast, participate in the kirtana, and take prasadam with us. Sometimes they even came to protect us from troublemakers.

People in our neighborhood started to respect us. Different groups would come to listen to Dayanvisha's preaching and singing. She was capable of dealing with extreme situations and would not even let anyone enter the temple room with their shoes or socks on. Sometimes when people came in an ill temper, with the seeming specific goal of creating arguments and problems, she would take care of them graciously, give them some prasadam, and speak to them in such a way that they would forget what trouble they had come for.

In our house we worshipped Nitai-Gauranga Deities. They were the first Deities in the USSR, which I heard Harikesa Swami had smuggled in when he came to the USSR the first time. These Deities had traveled all over the USSR, somehow protected from the black hand of the KGB. At one point, for a long time They were hidden underground in order to protect them.

During those difficult times, some of the fingers were accidentally broken. Once They were stolen from the temple for about two years, and no one knew where they were. Then one man brought Them to Adwaita Prabhu and requested him to not reveal who had stolen Them. Those Deities are still in Armenia today.

In 1988 or 1989 Prabhavisnu Swami came to Armenia. He was the first sannyasi, first guru, and first English speaking preacher to come to Yerevan. On the day he came, it was snowing for the first time that winter. We had organized a program for him in our home, to which all the neighbors came, in addition to the devotees.

We had planned a large public program for which we rented a big hall for Prabhavishnu Maharaj to preach and sing. Unfortunately, we received some phone calls from anonymous people warning that if we used this hall they would kill Maharaj. We informed Maharaj and he told us that there is no better opportunity to die than while preaching Krishna consciousness. We stationed some devotees by the gate so they could stop suspicious people trying to enter. At one point there was a big fight, and some devotees were seriously injured. At a later time, Gopal Krishna Goswami and Rohini Suta Prabhu came to visit us. I remember some bad incidents took place in Tridandi Prabhu's (Tadevos) house as well. Once, a fight broke out, and the whole street came out to look at what was going on. From time to time incidents such as these took place in Damayanti's apartment too.

In 1990, due to the help of Harivilas Prabhu, Harikesa Swami, Prabhavisnu Swami, Rohini Suta, Bhakta Aso, and others for the first time in Armenia we were able to purchase a house and made it into a temple. It was in a prestigious place and started a new life for Krishna consciousness. It was a big change for all Armenian devotees to be able to gather not in someone's home but in Krishna's home.

But unfortunately, it didn't take long for the Armenian Apostolic Church to find out about our new place. They attacked the temple several times, injuring many devotees and stealing everything from the temple, even the utensils. Once, they stole two temple cars full of our stuff.

Some of our lady preachers faced big troubles while distributing books, even in new regions. Once, Armenian priests arrested two Matajis and forcefully cut off their neck beads and religious paraphernalia as well as their clothes. They took these and their books and made a fire right in the city of Goris. Those so-called Christians didn't even care that they were dealing with women and harassed them like they would harass men. This is how they would follow the commandment: "Love your neighbor just like you love your self."

Another time, they had told us what time they were going to attack us; so we were all prepared for them. Devotees had sticks and iron rods. Bhakta Karen even prepared a small handmade bomb in case of a severe emergency. Then the temple president, Haridas Thakur das, informed the police that we were warned about a forthcoming attack at the temple and that if the police did not take any action then we would protect ourselves with sticks and iron rods. The police purposefully did not send any officers to the temple. When the people from the Apostolic Church came, exactly when they said they would, it seemed that they were not expecting any serious opposition from devotees, since they knew that we do not hurt any living entities. Perhaps they did not know that violence is religious when used to defend the innocent.

To their surprise, as soon as they entered the temple the devotees started to beat them, although outnumbered by about three to one. The devotees closed the temple door from inside so any others who were outside could not come in to help their friends. Those outside then threw gasoline on the temple door and started a fire. Some started to climb up the outside wall. Karen and Haridas, who were on the second floor, were trying to stop them. After some time, Karen took the bottle full of gasoline and was about to throw it on their car, which was parked right next to the temple. Haridas started to scream, "No, Karen, no, please do not throw it!" But it was too late, and as soon as it hit the car it started to burn. Everybody from the surrounding buildings was watching this terrible scene. After some time police officers arrived and arrested all the devotees and took them to the police station. After some hours, all the devotees were released except Kalidosha Pranashana dasa (Kamo) who spent a month in jail. They attempted to charge him with the offense of breaking a stick over the head of one man during the fight.

Despite this type of trouble, somehow or other, book production, translation, and distribution were going on constantly, non-stop. Mainly it was Sannyasa das and Brahmananda Puri das who were taking care of the book production. Damayanti devi dasi, Bhakta Gevorg, Amsu das, Gaganeshi devi dasi, and Atika Sataka dasi were actively translating Srila Prabhupada's books. Later on Harikesa Swami invited them all to Sweden where he provided them with modern technology to work more effectively. The rest of the devotees were actively participating in book distribution.

As a result of the sacrifices that all these great devotees have performed, nowadays there are over one hundred big and small temples established in the former USSR. By the sacrifices of the new generation many more will be opened, and this wonderful Krishna consciousness will be spread all over the world.

# Conclusion

*Wherever there is Krishna, the master of all mystics,*
*and wherever there is Arjuna, the supreme archer,*
*there will also certainly be opulence, victory,*
*extraordinary power, and morality. That is my opinion.*

*–Bhagavad-gita, 18.78*

After the registration of ISKCON, many conditions changed in the USSR. The previous mistreatment and death of Sachisuta Prabhu played a crucial role in all these positive changes. But that registration was not so easy to get. It was the result of countless demonstrations in front of many buildings and in various streets of Moscow. Generally, during these demonstrations there was some conflict with police and many devotees got arrested.

I remember one incident during the winter of 1988 in Moscow. It was too cold to demonstrate outside, so the devotees decided to do kirtana in one of the big metro subways. I was leading kirtana while playing mrdanga drum with my frozen hands, somehow tolerating the pain. The humidity had caused the mrdanga membrane to become loose; so in order to make a good sound I needed to bang very heavily. But how long can one play drums like that? Soon the mrdanga membrane was covered with blood from my fingers, but kirtana was going on in such a way that I felt it would have been a sin to stop it. Hundreds of people were surrounding us, clapping and dancing. After some time a group of police officers came and ordered us to stop the kirtana immediately. The devotees made a sign to me that I must go on. The police started to push and pull the devotees here and there, creating a disturbance. Two of them screamed in my ear to stop leading. I didn't stop. So one huge man with a big mustache grabbed me from my underarm and started to pull me out of the circle. The devotees came and caught my legs and started to pull me back into the circle again. So one big policeman was pulling me one way, and four devotees were pulling me the other way. I was totally in the air, still playing the drum, leading kirtana, and trying to also tolerate the pain of my body, which felt as if it was about to split in half. I was waiting to see what would happen next. My wife came to the policeman and asked him to leave me alone, but he started to curse her loudly. At that time Dayanvisha grabbed his big mustache, twisting and pulling it so strongly that the man dropped me and the devotees were able to pull me by my legs into the circle again. Everybody was laughing at the policeman and clapping their hands.

At that time Atmananda came to my wife and asked her to please try to do it once more so that he could take a photograph of it. We were all laughing. Similar incidents happened many times and in many different places, and the early Soviet devotees can tell many funny stories like this one.

I remember one humorous incident that happened in Moscow while Yagya devi dasi and I were distributing books. Two boys and two girls came across the street to where we were, and we decided to offer them a book. They looked at it, liked it, and wanted to take it, but they had no money to pay for it. I noticed one of them had a bottle of Cognac alcohol under his jacket. I asked him how they had money for such expensive poison but didn't have money for such an important medicine. They told me that they had put together all their money in order to buy that bottle and were going to drink it as soon as they went home. They said that there was no money left.

After speaking with them for a while, I saw that they were receptive to Krishna consciousness, and I wanted to give them the book. But then I would have been obligated to spend my own money for it, which I didn't want to do. So I came up with the idea of exchanging the book for the alcohol. They gave me the alcohol, took the book, thanked me, and left.

Yagya, who was standing next to me and watching the whole thing, started to scream, "Are you crazy, Sarvabhavana? What are you going to do with that now?" I said I didn't know, but I hadn't expected them to accept my offer. She decided that now we had to sell the alcohol in order to get the money for the book back. After some time she calmed down and took the bottle from my hand and said in my ear, "I know a guy, my next door neighbor, who is always drinking. Anyway, I'll sell it to him and save your situation." Thankfully it worked.

Moscow was and is the heart of USSR, and we knew well that it was the place to do all the demonstrations and harinama sankirtana processions. Many devotees would actively participate, which was always a kind of a challenge for all of us. Miraculously, whenever we were going out for harinama, the Russian Orthodox Church members would also be there standing in Arbat Street with anti-Hare Krishna posters, etc., as if they well knew that we are going there too.

Sometimes young Russian boys with shaved heads would come and stand in front of us and wouldn't let us to move forward on the narrow street. They wore special gloves on their hands with sharp irons on them. They were harassing the devotees, often getting into fights and dragging some ladies out of the kirtana and teasing them. All the other devotees were trying to protect them, and it was becoming a big mess.

Once they had a big surprise there, which I can never forget.During a harinama party we had Ambarish das with us, who had a black belt and had been practicing martial arts for a long time. So the same thing happened; they attacked us on Arbat Street. Ambarish came forward and asked them to stop this nonsense and let them go or else he would knock them all down. The boys were skeptical and could not believe that this skinny young man could actually take care of them all in a few seconds. So they started the fight with him. To our and their surprise, it took only a very short time for Ambarish to open the road for all the sankirtana devotees.

The next several times after that we didn't see them there again, but after a while they came again with an even bigger group to "protect Russia from getting spoiled by the Hare Krishnas."

In 1989, for the first time in history, a group of fifty devotees were allowed by the Russian government to go to India for a pilgrimage. Most of them had been tortured by the KGB some months before. A two-month tour was organized. I was fortunate to be part of that historic pilgrimage! Just a year before, I was suffering in a jail, but now we were chanting and dancing with hundreds of devotees from all over the world, just as our Gurudev had mentioned in his letter to all of us who were in a camp! Special credit for this tour is, of course, going especially to Harikesa Swami, Kirtiraj Prabhu and his wife Haripuja, Gopal Krishna Goswami, and Prabhavisnu Swami, who gave the pilgrimage tour a very intimate mood.

But the KGB gave us much trouble before they allowed us to go on that pilgrimage. Devotees from all over the Soviet Union had come together in Moscow about three or four days before our trip to India. It was very enlivening to see so many devotees from all different parts of the country. We were all very happy in each other's association. Although our tickets were ready, the Moscow officials still did not issue our visas and necessary papers. At first, they had promised to issue visas to us, but then for unknown reasons they refused to do so. Krishna Kaumar and other devotees were very busy trying to deal with the government.

The original plan of Kirtiraj Prabhu was for us to first participate in the Kumbha Mela festival. But since the papers were not ready and we missed our flight, we started a demonstration in front of the building of the Ministry of Foreign Affairs. We had prepared lots of banners and posters, as well as some big pictures of Krishna and Srila Prabhupada. We were singing and dancing in front of the big building across the street from the ministry. Soon some reporters surrounded us, taking photos and asking what this was all about. It was very cold, plus raining or maybe even snowing there that day, but all the devotees were very enthusiastically demanding that they issue our visas.

Soon Krishna Kaumar came out from the ministry with a large smile on his face and said that we should go to the airport and wait there with all our luggage so, in case they issued the visas, we wouldn't be late for the next flight. There were only a few flights a week from Moscow to India. So we went to airport Sheremetevo-2, where at least one hundred and twenty devotees started a huge kirtana. We had loudspeakers and microphones, and the kirtana was so loud that no one could hear any airport announcements in the entire hall. Soon airport officials came and requested us to stop the kirtana. None of us even thought to pay attention to them. They then called the police to stop us, but that didn't work either. After some time the airport manager came, personally requested us to stop singing, and promised he would help us to obtain our visas. So we stopped. The manager explained the whole situation to the visa department and asked them to help, since we were about to lose our tickets a second time. By the mercy of Lord Krishna, soon Krishna Kaumar Prabhu came to the airport with all fifty passports with visas.

The devotees started to bang mrdangas and karatalas, calling loudly, "Hariiiiboll, Haree Krishnaaaa." The lady devotees were crying and embracing each other as we finally were allowed to enter the airplane and take off to India. Those who had to stay in Moscow said goodbye to the ones who were fortunate to go to India for the first time, opening the road for the rest of them. Soon we were in the air in extreme jubilation for what we had achieved. I could hardly believe that after a matter of just some hours we were going to land in Kolkata airport.

We met many important people in India and told them about the Soviet regime's view of religiosity. Many press conferences took place in Kolkata, Mayapur, Delhi, etc. Among them was one with the prime minister of India (1984-1989), Rajiv Gandhi. A photograph was taken of all fifty Soviet Hare Krishna devotees with him in his residential courtyard. All the Indian newspapers were writing favorably about the Soviet Hare Krishna's, and this news was spread all over the world in many different languages in both print and video.

There was an incredible reception arranged by the devotees from all over the world, and it was a mind-blowing atmosphere in Kolkata airport that day. (This video is also on hkussr.com.) The first interesting thing we saw in the airport was Jagannath Deities. For us, from a repressive regime, we could not believe our eyes to see Deities in the airport.

Hundreds of reporters and photographers from newspapers, magazines, television, and radio were there to let the world know about this historic occasion. Many of them wrote big headlines, one of them saying, "BHAKTIVINODE THAKURA'S PREDICTION HAS COME TRUE." Bhaktivinode Thakura predicted that one day devotees from all over the world will come together and chant loudly the holy names of Lord Krishna in Mayapur Dham, the birthplace of Sri Krishna Caitanya. Devotees had come from all over the world but not from Russia, so the day we came to Mayapur his dream came true.

We all started quickly to fill out all the necessary papers, very eager to come out of the door where hundreds of devotees were waiting for us so we could all celebrate the historic event of the first Russian devotees' arrival in India. Somehow, Kirtiraj Prabhu, Jayapataka Swami, Krishnadas Kaviraj, and others managed to come into the hall where we were filling out our declaration papers and helped us to do it faster.

We could hear the ecstatic huge kirtana from outside, which made us even more eager to finish everything, come out, and touch the holy ground of Kolkata Dham, both the birthplace of Srila Prabhupada and where Caitanya Mahaprabhu walked on his way to Puri, Orissa.

When everyone was ready to come out, Kirtiraj Prabhu wanted us to go out the door one by one. As soon as the airport officials opened the door, a very loud sound of kirtana made our hair stand up. It was the first time we ever witnessed, what to speak of participated in, such a huge kirtana. In addition, for many of us, it was the first time we ever wore a dhoti or sari as well as a sikha and even tilak.

I was one of the first ones who came out of the door, and I could not stop my tears. Devotees started to throw flowers and offer us many flower garlands. We all paid our obeisances to each other, and they pulled us to the middle of the big circle, where we started to dance in ecstasy.

All our luggage was carried to the top of the buses for us, so our hands would be free to take part in the kirtana. Devotees were jumping up and down, some were crying loudly, and more and more flowers were pouring on our head like from heaven. They had given each of us kartals on which was engraved "ISKCON USSR," and we started to play and sing together in a sweet kirtana.

I do not know how long it continued, but at one point there was no choice but to stop the kirtana and sit in the buses with our luggage on top. All of us had never seen such buses or experienced the extremely hot weather. We were all wet as if we had come out of a swimming pool.

Soon our bus took off towards the Radha Govinda Temple in Kolkata, which was the first real temple we had ever seen. At the temple, there was another super ecstatic kirtana and reception waiting for us, and thousands of flowers fell from the balcony on all the devotees. We slowly came up the stairs and entered the temple. The entire scene made a great impression on all of us. This was the first time we ever had an opportunity to see such beautiful Deities and altar. The moon-like faces of Radha and Govinda were smiling at all of us as if to say, "Finally you are home. There is no KGB here, so please chant and dance as much as you like."

I can never forget the taste of my first charanamrita and maha-prasadam from Radha-Govinda. Lord Jagannath's big beautiful smiling eyes were looking at us, as if He were about to jump from the altar to take part in the heavenly kirtana. After a while one devotee pulled my hand and dragged me to the Lord Jagannath Deities to show me the tears that were dripping from the Lord's eyes. I couldn't believe what I saw! Indeed I saw tears in the Lord's eyes, shining like diamonds and slowly coming down His cheek.

**Handkerchief drawn using color pens by Sarvabhavana in Sovietashen's jail, 1986**

**Page from Sarvabhavana's prison diary**

**Sarvabhavana das by Sachisuta's grave in Meghri, Armenia, 1989**

**Sachisuta prabhu with his school friends**

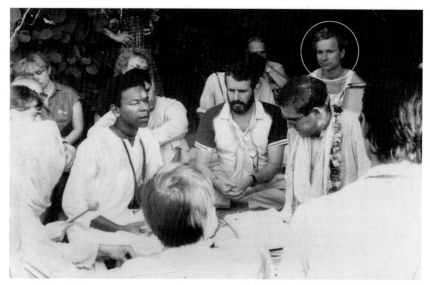

Prabhavishnu Swami during one of his first visits to Moscow. He is leading a kirtan in the forest. On the far right Ananta Shanti das is accompanying him.

The Soviet devotees during their historical visit to India in Kolkata next to the statue of Vladimir Lenin

One of the first public harinamas in Armenia. Sarvabhavana das plays on the Mridanga drum in a cultural center in Yerevan, 1988

The early Harinama in Russia , Acyuta Priya das in the left and Premavati devi dasi on the right

# Armenian Devotee Dies in Soviet Labour Camp

These photographs of Sacisuta dasa were taken by the KGB when they arrested him..

ORENBURG TERRITORY, Soviet Union — Armenian devotee Sacisuta dasa (Sirvis R. Ogadzhanyan) died in Soviet labour camp YU-K 25/7 "B" December 26, 1987. His death came just 11 days before his scheduled release. Sacisuta was 23 years old.

When the KGB arrested Sacisuta on January 5th 1986, they took pictures of him in his apartment for evidence, including one of him holding devotional pictures and one in which he posed before his altar.

Tried for his religious activities on July 4th, 1986, in the capital city of Yerevan, Sacisuta received a two-year sentence to a standard-regimen labour camp. He was due for release on January 5th or 6th, 1988.

Sacisuta suffered from diabetes and an insufficient diet and sometimes wrote to friends and relatives requesting food. Officials of the labour camp never delivered the parcels sent to him. During the winter of 1987, Sacisuta was admitted to a camp tuberculosis clinic.

According to Helsinki Watch, an international human rights organization, Sacisuta was the only Soviet prisoner of conscience known to have died in a labour camp in 1987. His body was not released to his relatives, nor was a death certificate or document stating the cause of death issued. A funeral was held in his home town of Megri, Armenian Soviet Socialist Republic, without the body.

In December 1987, Sacisuta's parents visited him at the labour camp. Although severely ill at that time, he told them he looked forward to going home.

Sacisuta's death was reported in the *New York Times* January 19th, 1988, but there was no mention of it in any Soviet newspaper.

**A page from the World news magazine dedicated to Sachisuta das**

**Historical pilgrimage of the 50 soviet devotees to India in 1989. The devotees had the great honour and pleasure of meeting the Prime Minister of India, Rajiv Gandhi.**

# A Life Offe

The only "prisoner of conscience" to die in a Soviet labor camp last year, Śacīsūta dāsa had led a life of heroic service to Kṛṣṇa.

by SANNYĀSA DĀSA

**At the time of Śacīsūta's arrest,** the KGB took the photos at right after having him pose with the incriminating evidence: his *Bhagavad-gītā* and his altar. Above, the author, Sannyāsa dāsa.

*Sannyāsa dāsa (Suren Karapetyan), a Soviet devotee of Kṛṣṇa, wrote the following short biography in memory of his heroic Godbrother who died last December in a Soviet labor camp in Siberia. Sannyāsa dāsa was himself recently released from a psychiatric hospital in Soviet Armenia, where he had been suffering severe persecution because of his participation in the Hare Kṛṣṇa movement. He is one of the main devotees responsible for the printing of many thousands of Śrīla Prabhupāda's books in Russian and Armenian within the USSR. The Hare Kṛṣṇa devotees in the USSR have earned distinction because of their courageous preaching. This is an account of one very special devotee by another.*

I first met Śacīs (Sarkis Ogac zhanyan) i... monia then, 1985. I had pneu- living at Ka... at reason I was and Sārvab... home. Śacīsūta came for the heard about ...ik Buniatyan) some imp... ...ching to ...ical matters—... They ha... we would usually spe... about. The two young men ...

Kamalamālā with great attention, with...ut saying anything. I thought that they ...uld not understand him, but I was ...ng. Although they appeared very seri... ...and did not express their joy, they ...onstrated it in another way: they gave ...smoking hashish that same day. ...acīsūta and Sārvabhāvana had been ...assmates in high school and were inti...mate friends. Before meeting the devotees, they had learned a little Indian philosophy. They were aware of the principle of

**Article fron the Back To Godhead Magazine about Sachisuta Prabhu**

# red to Kṛṣṇa

*ahiṁsa* (nonviolence) and were vegetarians. After graduating from high school, they were sent to the army. In the army it was very difficult not to eat meat, but they were determined. They even suffered persecution for being vegetarians. Śacīsūta was regularly beaten by soldiers and officers.

Śacīsūta would speak very little. One might get the impression that he had no emotion. But he was relishing deeper, spiritual emotions. He was so attached to

Kṛṣṇa that he would constantly chant the holy name of the Lord. I had never seen such a person before; I had only read about such devotees in *Caitanya-caritāmṛta*. I never saw Śacīsūta idle. He was always serving his spiritual master and Kṛṣṇa. If he was not engaged in producing and distributing books, he would wash the floor or the pots and dishes.

Whatever Śacīsūta did, he did very conscientiously. He would always chant while doing his service. After the devotees

took *prasādam*, it was usual for everyone to sit down and relax. Śacīsūta, however, would immediately get up and wash all the plates. He would never allow anyone to wash his plate. He took great pleasure in serving the devotees.

Once I was going to wash my pants and had put them into a bucket of water. I went to another room for five minutes, and when I returned I found that my pants had been washed and hung up to dry. When I asked Śacīsūta why he had washed my

**The historical visit of His Divine Grace A.C. Bhaktivedanta Swami Srila Prabhupada, Red Square, Moscow 1971**

The Soviet devotees' ecstatic arrival to the Kolkata International
Airport in 1989. Sarvabhavana das is third from the left.

# কৃষ্ণনাম নেওয়ায় কমিউনিস্ট সরকারের জেলে
# ভয়ংকর অত্যাচারের দিনগুলি ভুলতে চান জ্যাজিক

**সুপ্রকাশ মণ্ডল (বি এন এ), মায়াপুর (নদীয়া):** মাঝবয়সে পৌঁছে অতীতের ভয়ংকর
দিনগুলি আর মনে রাখতে চান না জ্যাজিক বুনিয়াটিয়ান। এখন তিনি সর্বভাবনা দাস। আদি
নিবাস সাবেক রাশিয়া। বর্তমানে আমেরিকার বাসিন্দা। যারা তার
জীবনের অনেকখানি সুখের সময় কেড়ে নিয়েছে, কৃষ্ণ নিবেদিতপ্রাণ
এই ব্যক্তি নির্দ্বিধায় ক্ষমা করে দিয়েছেন তাদের। সর্বভাবনা ইসকনের
একজন দীক্ষিত ভক্ত। কিন্তু যখন তিনি প্রথম কৃষ্ণনাম নেন, তখন সময় এমন সুখের ছিল
না। সোভিয়েত রাশিয়ার কমিউনিস্ট সরকার সে সময় কৃষ্ণ আন্দোলনে যোগ দেওয়ার
অপরাধে প্রাণে মেরে ফেলতেও চেয়েছিল তাদের। কিন্তু সমস্ত বাধাবিপত্তি সরিয়ে আজ তিনি
সত্যিই খুশি। কারণ, তিনি আজ চৈতন্য মহাপ্রভুর জন্মভূমিতে পা রেখেছেন।

১৯৭৪ সালের ঘটনা। স্কুলের পাঠ সবে শেষ করেছেন জ্যাজিক। সঙ্গে সঙ্গে তার ডাক
পড়ে রাশিয়ার সেনাবাহিনীতে। জ্যাজিকের জানালেন, স্কুলের পাঠ সাঙ্গ করে সেনাবাহিনীতে
যোগ দেওয়া রাশিয়াতে তখন বাধ্যতামূলক ছিল। দু'বছর পর সেনাবাহিনী থেকে ফিরে
আসেন তিনি। তারপর তাঁর বন্ধু ওহানজাওয়ানের মুখে প্রথম কৃষ্ণর নাম শোনেন।
ওহানজায়ান ছিলেন তাঁর সবচেয়ে কাছের বন্ধু। একই স্কুলে পড়তেন, একই
সঙ্গে সেনাবাহিনীতে যোগ দিয়েছিলেন, আবার একই সঙ্গে ফিরেছেন।

সে-ই তাঁকে জানায় যে, ভারত থেকে কিছু সাধু ব্যক্তি এসেছেন। তাঁরা মানুষকে ভগবান
কৃষ্ণের কথা শোনান। মানুষকে সৎ পরামর্শ দেন। বন্ধুর কথাতেই একাদন ওহ সাধুদের কাছে
যান জ্যাজিক। প্রথমদিকে সৎ পরামর্শ শুনে ভালোই লেগে যায় তাঁর। কিন্তু মুশকিল বাধে
একটি ক্ষেত্রে। জ্যাজিক তখন মারাত্মকভাবে ড্রাগ আসক্ত ছিলেন। তিনি ভেবেছিলেন, সব
কিছু ছাড়লেও মারিজুয়ানার নেশা ছাড়তে পারবেন না। কিন্তু মাত্র দু'দিন ওই সন্ন্যাসীদের
সংস্পর্শে এসেই তিনি ভুলে গেলেন সব নেশা।

এতক্ষণ পর্যন্ত সব ঠিকঠাক চললেও আসল গণ্ডগোল লাগে দীক্ষিত হওয়ার পরে। ধর্ম
প্রচারের খবর সরকারি গোয়েন্দাদের কাছে যাওয়ার পরেই রাজরোষে পড়েন তিনি।
রাশিয়ায় তখন গর্বাচভের জমানা। কমিউনিস্ট সরকারের নির্দেশে পুলিশ ধর্মানুষ্ঠানে যোগ না
দেওয়ার জন্য তাদের বাড়ি এসে হুমকি দিয়ে যায়। এতে কাজ না হওয়ায় থানায় নিয়ে
বেধড়ক মারধর করা হয় তাদের। তারপর কাগজে লিখে দিতে বলা হয় যে, তারা যা

করেছেন ভুল করেছেন। সে জন্য তারা দুঃখিত ও ক্ষমাপ্রার্থী। দুই বন্ধু সই করতে অস্বীকার
করায় তাঁদের পাকাপাকিভাবে জেলে পোরা হয়।

জেলে ঢোকার পর তাঁরা দেখেন তাদেরই মতো আরও অনেককে
একই অপরাধে জেলে বন্দি করা হয়েছে। তারপর থেকে তাঁরা জেলেই
শুরু করেন কৃষ্ণনাম। অত্যাচারী কমিউনিস্ট সরকার তাদের আট মাস
সময় দিয়েছিল হিন্দুধর্মের পথ ত্যাগ করার জন্য। এর মধ্যে রোজ নিয়ম করে শারীরিক
অত্যাচার চলত তাদের ওপর। রাবারের চাবুক দিয়ে তাঁদের মারা হত যতক্ষণ না তারা
মাটিতে লুটিয়ে পড়ে জ্ঞান হারাতেন। পুলিশের অত্যাচারের পরেও কোনও কৃষ্ণভক্তকেই
ধর্মের পথ থেকে সরাতে পারেনি রাশিয়ার পুলিশ।

এরই মধ্যে পুলিশ চাবুক দিয়ে বার বার আঘাত করে জ্যাজিকের ডান চোখটি নষ্ট করে
দেয়। ভেঙে দেয় পিঠের হাড়। আট মাস আমেরিয়ার জেলে কাটানোর পর সরকার তাদের
সাইবেরিয়ায় পাঠিয়ে দেয়।

মাইনাস ৫০ ডিগ্রি তাপমাত্রায় বন্ধু যক্ষ্মা রোগে আক্রান্ত হয়। জেল কর্তৃপক্ষের কাছে তিনি
এক গ্লাস দুধ চেয়েছিলেন। কিন্তু তাও দেওয়া হয়নি তাঁকে। সেখানেই মারা যান
ওহানজায়ান।

এই খবর জানাজানি হওয়ার পর সারা পৃথিবী থেকে রাশিয়ার ওপর চাপ আসতে শুরু
করে। অবশেষে দু' বছর জেলে কাটানোর পর আন্তর্জাতিক চাপে মুক্ত ঘটে ওহ বান্দদের।
সর্বভাবনা জানালেন, জেলে থাকার সময় রোজ তাদের একটি করে ইঞ্জেকশন দেওয়া হত।
তার প্রভাবে কয়েকজন বন্দি পাগল হয়ে যান। জেল থেকে মুক্তির পর প্রত্যেক বন্দিকেই ছ'
মাস আমেরিয়ার মানসিক হাসপাতালে কাটাতে হয়েছিল।

জেল থেকে মুক্তি পাওয়ার পর ভারতে আসার অনুমতি দেয়নি রাশিয়ার তৎকালীন
সরকার। অবশেষে ১৯৮৯ সালে রাশিয়া টুকরো হওয়ার পর সেখানকার প্রথম কৃষ্ণভক্ত
দীক্ষিতরা ভারতে এসে পৌঁছান। সর্বভাবনার কাছে সে দিন কখনও ভোলার নয়। তারপর
বহুবার তিনি ভারতে এসেছেন। কৃষ্ণ পায়ে প্রাণ মন সঁপে দেওয়া এই ভক্ত এখন
অত্যাচারীদের সব অপরাধ ক্ষমা করে দিয়েছেন। নিজের চোখ নষ্ট হয়ে যাওয়ার জন্য আর
কোনও আফসোস নেই তার।

**Bengali newspaper writes about Sarvabhavana das**

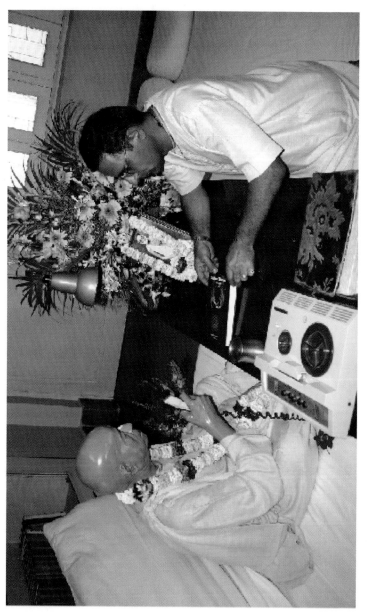

**Sarvabhavana offering the first advanced copy of his book to Srila Prabhupada in his room in Sridham Mayapur, Gaura Purnima 2007**

Здравствуйте семья

Осужденных. Просим Ваше принять наше первое соболезнование, по поводу Вашего сына и брата.

Он до последней минуты был себя ... верил своим ..., который он придерживался строго. Перед кончиной он был вздоровом уже, он ... и чувствовал приближении смерти и ... говорил ... великие слова. Это глядя у него были удлинённые зрачки, ... он ... в чистое белое, белого цвета. Папа ... подрядился с ним в ... части, он слабыми живо ни пону не передовал. После кончины у нас со ... ... фотографию и в ... на коечный более ... ... оставшего ... ... ... ... оставляем.

Ещё раз примите наше больше соболезнование от знакомых и близких ... него сына и брата.

г. Оренбург.
19__ 25/4
Заочные знакомые Варвара.

Dear family of Ohanjanyan's

Let us express our sincere condolences on the occasion of the demise of your son and brother. Till the very last moment of his life he maintained dignity, maintaining faith in his ideals pursued by him very strictly. Just
before his passing away he had a very clear mind. He knew that his death was coming, and he anticipated it. He passed away while murmuring the words of his prayer. He had flower garlands on his chest, and he was dressed in clean white clothes. Our fellow countrymen [in the labor camp] bade farewell to him, but he has not asked anyone to convey a message to you or somebody else. After his death we found with him a personal photo and the certificate which allowed him to have hair once again. We are asking the administration to send you all his remaining belongings. Again, please accept our deep condolences from the near and dear ones of your son and brother.

Orenburg,

Avetisyan Karapet

**Translation of the letter**

"Can we really be more tolorant than this tree?"
This photograph was taken by Sarvabhavana das in India. He
sees a lot of similarity between this tree and the early Soviet
devotees, because no matter how hard Mother Nature beats this
tree, it still stands there green till today and even grows through
the roots. The roots are more than three meters high because the
Ganges washes away all the dirt year after year.

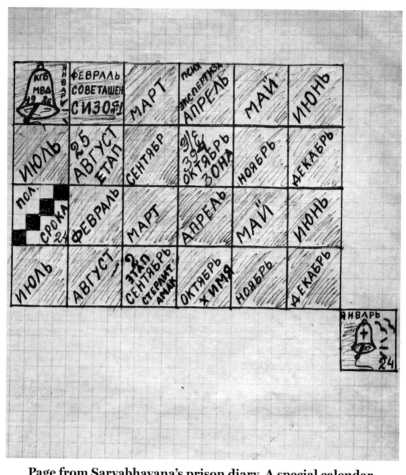

Page from Sarvabhavana's prison diary. A special calendar.

# UNITED NATIONS

**HIGH COMMISSIONER
FOR REFUGEES**

PHONE : 4699302
FAX : 91-11-4620137

14, JOR BAGH
NEW DELHI-110003
(INDIA)

# संयुक्त राष्ट्र
## शरणार्थी उच्चायुक्त

TELEX : 031-62885 HCR IN
CABLES : UNDEVPRO - NEW DELHI

Reference: HCR/AM000001

Original date of Issue : 04 May 1993
Renewed on : 01 May 1998
Valid Until : 30 April 1999

## CERTIFICATE

This is to certify that **GAGIK BOUNIATIAN**\*\*\*\*\*\*\*\*\*\*\*\*\*\*\*\*\*\*\*\*\*\*\*\*\*\*\*\*\*\*\*\*\*\*\*\*\*\*\*\*\*\*\*\*\*\*\*\*\*\*\*\*\*\*\*\*\*\*\*\*

a national of ARMENIA is on the basis of available information considered to be a refugee within

the Mandate of the Office of the United Nations High Commissioner for Refugees.

Any assistance provided to **GAGIK BOUNIATIAN**\*\*\*\*\*\*\*\*\*\*\*\*\*\*\*\*\*\*\*\*\*\*\*\*\*\*\*\*\*\*\*\*\*\*\*\*\*\*\*\*\*\*\*\*\*\*\*\*\*\*\*\*\*\*

**and his family,**

DOUSTRIK (WIFE) \*\*\*\*\*\*\*\*\*\*\*\*\*\*\*\*\*\*\*\*\*\*\*\*\*\*\*\*\*\*\*\*\*\*\*\*\*\*\*\*\*\*\*\*\*\*\*\*\*\*\*\*\*\*\*\*\*\*\*\*\*\*\*\*\*\*\*\*\*\*\*\*\*\*\*\*\*\*\*

SACHISUTA (SON) \*\*\*\*\*\*\*\*\*\*\*\*\*\*\*\*\*\*\*\*\*\*\*\*\*\*\*\*\*\*\*\*\*\*\*\*\*\*\*\*\*\*\*\*\*\*\*\*\*\*\*\*\*\*\*\*\*\*\*\*\*\*\*\*\*\*\*\*\*\*\*\*\*\*\*\*\*

RASALILA (DAUGHTER) \*\*\*\*\*\*\*\*\*\*\*\*\*\*\*\*\*\*\*\*\*\*\*\*\*\*\*\*\*\*\*\*\*\*\*\*\*\*\*\*\*\*\*\*\*\*\*\*\*\*\*\*\*\*\*\*\*\*\*\*\*\*\*\*\*\*\*\*\*

BALARAM BOUNIATIAN (SON) \*\*\*\*\*\*\*\*\*\*\*\*\*\*\*\*\*\*\*\*\*\*\*\*\*\*\*\*\*\*\*\*\*\*\*\*\*\*\*\*\*\*\*\*\*\*\*\*\*\*\*\*\*\*\*\*\*\*\*

during their stay in India would be greatly appreciated.

This certificate is valid for a period of one year.

\*Added on 05 May 1998.

N L NARASIMHA RAO
Associate Legal Officer
**For UNHCR Chief of Mission**

Signature verified

S. Sehgal/S. Jose

# UN certificate of Sarvabhavana and his family

THE WHITE HOUSE

WASHINGTON

January 15, 1992

Dear Mr. Boutelle:

On behalf of President Bush, thank you for writing to let him know
about the outstanding work being done by the Hare Krishna Food for
Life Program.

Letters such as yours are a reminder of what can be achieved
when ordinary Americans claim our nation's domestic problems as
their own. Although it is not possible for the President personally
to recognize each of the many worthy individuals and organizations
as "Daily Points of Light," I was delighted to forward your letter
to the committee here which reviews examples of outstanding community
service initiatives. They will contact you should they require
further information about the Food for Life Program.

From homelessness to teenage pregnancy and from illiteracy to
drug abuse, we can solve our nation's most pressing social problems
only with the kind of direct and consequential action which you
describe. As the President said during his address to the Congress
on January 29, 1991, "The problems before us may be different, but
the key to solving them remains the same: it is the individual, the
individual who steps forward."

The President appreciates your taking the time to write him. You
have his best wishes.

Sincerely,

C. Gregg Petersmeyer
Assistant to the President &
Director, Office of National Service
(The White House Points of Light Office)

Mr. Ronald E. Boutelle
National Coordinator
Food for Life, Denver
1400 Cherry Street
Denver, CO  80220

# Appreciation from the White House, USA

Finally, Kirtiraj Prabhu came into the temple room, and with a microphone, asked all the devotees to stop the kirtana and come to the balcony for lunch prasadam. Krishna Kaumar Prabhu, who was Kirtiraj Prabhu's right-hand man, was translating everything into Russian for all of us. But the kirtana was going on in such a powerful way, like it would never end, that no one could stop it. It took them many announcements to stop the kirtana and start to serve prasadam.

They made a beautiful arrangement for all of us. We had never eaten from banana plates and drunk from clay cups. After eating, many devotees did not throw the cup away, thinking that they were meant to be used multiple times. We were very surprised to see how the Bengali devotees threw them in the trash can carelessly and then washed their hands.

The prasadam was of extraordinary variety, and the flavors of the many different preparations delighted us. Devotees kept coming and coming with new preparations, forcing us to take at least some of each new item. After eating a little from each we could hardly stand up from where we sat on the floor. Some devotees lay down on the floor, unable to stand up at all.

After prasadam, we were told to go to our buses and be ready to start our trip to Sri Mayapur Dham, the transcendental holy birthplace of Sri Caitanya Mahaprabhu and world headquarters of ISKCON. This was one of the most important events for all of us. We had all been waiting for this glorious day when we would get the causeless mercy to visit the holy dhama, the real dreamland. On our way to the buses, next to the temple entrance, two or three rickshaws were parked, and the drivers were cutting the tops off of green coconuts for us to drink the sweet juice. For most of us this was a new experience, since there are no coconut trees in the USSR. Soon we had started our journey, with kirtana, to Mayapur, which took a little more than four hours. Two or three buses full of devotees started from the Kolkata temple and took off in the direction of Mayapur. The roads were bad, and the drivers drove very fast, so we were bounced up and down in our seats. We had never had a ride like this.

After three and half hours, at the juncture of the main road and the left turn to the Mayapur road, a group of devotees was waiting for us. As soon as the bus stopped next to them, they came up to the windows to offer us garlands and flowers, their surprised eyes full of happiness. After they talked to Kirtiraj and others, we again went towards Mayapur with increased anticipation. We were all waiting to see the dhama with our own eyes. We had seen Mayapur only in pictures, 8mm short films, and in our dreams.

We reached Mayapur at dusk. We were amazed to see a huge crowd of devotees who had waited a long time for us Soviet devotees. They were having a lively and sweet kirtana.

At that moment something happened which makes me laugh each time I remember it. In Moscow we were asked to buy different important things for our trip to India. All of us were well prepared for physical problems such as malaria, dysentery, and cholera. Everyone had a first aid kit, as well as some very ugly and stinky anti-mosquito creams and liquids.

Some devotee—I do not remember exactly who it was—came up with the idea to be extra careful about Mayapur mosquitoes. He told us that we must take honeybee protection hats with us in order to avoid mosquito bites. Someone brought them for all of us, so that everyone got one of them for their protection. So upon our arrival at the main entrance at the Mayapur ISKCON temple, we were asked to put the hats on before coming out of the bus.

So now, please imagine hundreds of devotees waiting with flowers, flower garlands, and kirtana for the first Soviet devotees, who now came out of the buses one by one, some of them wearing those hats. All the devotees who greeted us were calling loudly, "Haribol!" and "Hare Krishna!" with surprised wide open eyes, as we looked like some kind of aliens stepping for the first time on the earth. Kirtiraj was also looking at us with wide open eyes and asking, "Sto eto tokoe?" (What is this?) while doing a brief movement of his hand indicating that we should take the hats off. Some devotees were throwing endless flowers from the top of the main gate on everyone, which also included two decorated elephants.

During the huge kirtana and reception for the Soviet devotees, the sound of the drums and cymbals sounded like it was coming from heaven. Gurukula students were blowing conches and chanting auspicious mantras. Some were holding flags and fire lamps. Soon they opened the narrow entrance, asking us to enter the ISKCON land and stop in front of the bhajan kutir of Srila Prabhupada. This was the first residence that the devotees built for Srila Prabhupada. This thatched hut is still kept as it was in Prabhupada's time, with a twenty-four-hour non-stop kirtana there every day.

We all paid our obeisances and continued moving towards the main temple. We started to move slowly along with the kirtana party, following the festive elephants on the main road. As soon as we entered the temple, we stopped the kirtana for a moment in astonishment at Sri Sri Radha Madhava's moonlike faces. We then heard the famous recording of "Govindam Adi Purusam" from the Brahma Samhita, and all the devotees were dancing and swaying like ocean waves in the temple room, which was so packed that there was no room even to stick one needle.

Soon after that, another kirtana started. This was something that I am unable to describe completely and so will not make much of an attempt. There was a big circle where all the devotees were participating with great enthusiasm and ecstasy. The many mrdangas and kartals made us feel like we were in Goloka Vrindavan. Kirtana was going on in such a way that it would never have stopped, so Krishna Kaumar came and told us, one by one, that we must come out, get the keys for our rooms, and take our luggage there. It was hard to stop such a kirtana voluntarily and go to our rooms, but we had no other choice. We all got rooms in the Long Building, which is close to the temple. After refreshing ourselves, we went for the glorious prasadam especially made for us.

The next morning was again amazing for us. We attended the mangala arati, somehow trying to stand in the completely packed temple room. For the first time we saw the big and beautiful sun of this low latitude rising early in the morning on the flat horizon right behind the temple, accompanied by hundreds of different birds.

Everything from that day on was programmed specially for us. Daily there were many interesting pilgrimages, as well as press conferences with reporters from many newspapers, magazines, and television stations from all over India and abroad. Kirtiraja Prabhu had organized a very tight program of non-stop spiritual enthusiasm.

After seeing the holy places close to the Mayapur temple, we traveled by trains, buses, and boats to reach more distant sacred sites. During these well planned tours in Bengal and Orissa, we met a number of prominent people. One was the king of Orissa. In his house, we took prasadam that was brought from the main temple at Puri. Upon arrival in Kolkata on the way to Puri, we had a kirtana near a park with Lenin's statue. We had a long and thick garland especially made for Lenin. Two devotees somehow garlanded him, and then we went round him several times with kirtana.

This was mostly a joke for all of us, but the story was published in the newspapers. After Orissa, we returned to Mayapur where we participated in an installation ceremony for the main gopis and took part in the annual Gaura Purnima festival. Then we started our journey towards Vrindavan, the holy place of Lord Sri Krishna's birth and pastimes.

This was another well organized trip full of the amazing experience of witnessing India's holy places and culture first-hand. In Vrindavan, as in West Bengal and Orissa, we had many press conferences, association with great devotees, and meetings with well-known people. One of the most unforgettable meetings was, as I mentioned before, with the then prime minister of India, Rajiv Gandhi. We made a special trip to Delhi from Vrindavan to meet him. He was very happy to see fifty Russian devotees, most of whom had been released from prisons recently. A photograph of our group with him became one of the top pictures and stories of the week, not only in the Indian press, but in many other countries as well. It was, no doubt, something none of us would have imagined or believed—that persecuted Russian devotees would be having a meeting face to face with the Indian prime minister. He gently smiled at all of us, and in his short speech, expressed gratitude to Russian devotees, who had risked their lives for spreading Hindu dharma in a communist country.

We returned back to Vrindavan where we spent another week or so, and then prepared for our return to Moscow. Although we were saddened to be leaving, at the same time we had so much to share with our brothers and sisters who had not been able to come with us. We had beautiful gifts and maha-prasada for each and every one there. We had collected maha-prasada, holy dust, rocks, and holy water from everywhere we had visited. Kirtiraj Prabhu and his wife Haripuja also prepared many gifts, Deities, and everything possible for us to take with us.

Some of the rich devotees in India, like His Grace Radhapad Prabhu, Mr. Tulsian, distributed to all of us all kinds of gifts like dhotis, saris, shawls, etc. He had also donated Radha-Krishna and Gaura-Nitai Deities and money for the big Deities, Radha-Moscowishvara, that were to be made in India for the future Moscow temple.

In the last days in Vrindavan, Kirtiraj Prabhu wanted to have an idea of approximately how much overweight we were going to be at the airport in New Delhi. So he went from room to room, talking personally to all the devotees and asking them kindly not to carry unnecessarily heavy things, since overweight would be very costly. In the process, he also visited our room where we were packing our last purchased items from Loi Bazar. He knocked on the door, and without waiting for an invitation, entered our room with a wide smile, asking if we were ready and had removed unnecessary things from our luggage.

We all nodded our heads and continued our packing. Then he took our luggage one by one and weighed them. He took many things out of Haridasa's, Nityananda's, and Prana's bags and told them to leave them. Tridandi Prabhu told us that Kirtiraja was very strictly checking everyone's bags and had taken lots of things out already, so we should not be upset if he did the same to us.

At last he pointed to my red bag in the corner of the room and asked whose it was. I told him that it was mine and walked together with him towards the bag. He tried to pick it up with his right hand but could not. He tried it again and looked at me with surprise and asked, "Sarva, sto eto takoe?" (What is this?) I told him that it was maha-prasada that I had collected from all over the holy places we had visited during our pilgrimage. He asked me to open it, which I humbly did. He took out, one by one, plastic bags with items that had full descriptions about each particular place. He sat down on the corner of the bed, looking at each item, putting to one side each package while smiling and shaking his head.

He was very happy to see how everything was nicely organized and looked around and said to all the assembled devotees, "This is the heaviest bag so far, but I have no words to say to Sarvabhavana Prabhu and cannot take anything out from his bag, since everything is maha-prasada and connected to Krishna." He did make one change. He found a white piece of marble from Srila Prabhupada's samadhi in Vrindavan that I was planning to keep on our altar in Armenia. He hit the corner on the edge of the window, broke a small piece from it, handed that piece to me, and remarked that if every devotee were to take one big piece of marble like I did, there wouldn't be any marble left to finish the samadhi. Then he told me to take the big piece back to where I got it from, which I did immediately. We had one more day in Vrindavana, filled with shopping and seeing the Deities.

Then, with tears in our eyes, we returned back to Moscow and from there to Yerevan, filled with great enthusiasm and energy to again work on book production and distribution. We had a gathering in our home with all the Armenian devotees, where I gave to them the maha-prasada and gifts one by one. We spoke for a long time, and some devotees decided to stay not only that night but also for several days to hear about our trip to India. I tried to tell them each and every detail so they would visit there mentally. Everyone was especially happy to see the more than 2,000 black and white photographs that I had taken during our pilgrimages.

After returning from India, I decided to follow through on my previous desire and research to have a statue of Sachisuta Prabhu in my home as a special honor. I gave the artist several photographs of him. The artist did an excellent job, such that everyone who had known Sachisuta Prabhu told me that the statue looked just like him. In this way, I hoped to fulfill Sachisuta Prabhu's last desires. He had wanted to see and distribute Armenian Bhagavad-gitas, so I put one in the statue's hand. And because he had wanted to see his guru, I brought the statue to Harikesa Swami and also pinned a badge with Harikesa Swami's photo on Sachisuta's heart. So they met through loving remembrance.

All the expenses for the statue were collected from the people who knew Sachisuta Prabhu. The success of the collection was especially due to the effort of my wife, Dayanvisha Devi dasi, who had enough courage to get donations from all the police and guards who had made contact with Sachisuta dasa or our case in Armenia. She also collected donations from the prison guards, prosecutor, judge, and the doctors in the mental hospital. She told them that because they had some connection to Sachisuta's death, they would surely suffer, but if they wanted to lessen the suffering they should take the opportunity to give some donation.

After completing Sachisuta's statue we had a big opening ceremony and feast. The sculptor came and received a framed picture of Krishna.

After I married, we developed a much closer relationship with my prosecutor, Armen. We met from time to time to talk about Krishna. By this time, he was in an important position in Yerevan. But he had not forgotten his old Hare Krishna friends, and he was always happy to meet me. Once, I went to meet him in his office in Yerevan. We had a lot to remember from the past, and our relationship was no longer that of criminal and investigator. Rather, he was very friendly. He told me that everything in those days had been totally controlled by the KGB, and there had been nothing he could do, although he knew well that we were innocent. He had all our books on his shelf, and in his drawer he had Sri Isopanisad, which he was studying at that time. He said that he liked the books and was learning a lot from them, although he didn't agree with many things.

I asked him how he was doing and about his family. He hung his head and told me that he had a family problem that disturbed his mind constantly, day and night. His daughter could not walk properly from birth. He said he tried everything he could possibly do and had taken her to many doctors in Armenia, Russia, and Canada. Two years previously he had been in America, where doctors gave her special treatments. He later called me on the phone to share his feelings and ask me if I could do anything for her. Once in our conversation he slightly admitted that his daughter's condition could be a karmic reaction to his treatment of Sachisuta. He asked me if I knew any doctor in India who could help his daughter. I told him that I didn't, but I'd surely pray for her. I explained that certainly there can be negative karmic reactions if one hurts Krishna's devotee, but if one prays and asks forgiveness then the devotee and Krishna may forgive him.

I also looked up my friend from the Armenian jail, Khatsik, who had given me the gray notebook in which I kept some important notes from those hellish days. He had been out of jail for a couple of years and was living comfortably in Armenia. He was very happy to see me; he invited me into his home. I told him everything that had happened to me, and I invited him to visit me in Yerevan. He came the next summer with his wife, and again we had a satisfying, long conversation about life and Krishna consciousness.

Now everything is so different. Of course, I really appreciate the political changes and the positive reaction of the Russian government. But one factor I miss really and deeply in my life is the challenge of the old days. Now it seems that I rarely have the "fired up" association and mood of urgency that was present in the preaching of the late 1980s. I have not had prasadam quite as tasty as we used to have or felt the same enthusiasm for preaching and spreading this wonderful Krishna consciousness. It may be that this early period was my time to "get the mercy," and now it is yours, my son, and also the readers of this story. I am living with the great memories and taste of those days and am happy to continue to be part of the important mission of Srila Prabhupada and Caitanya Mahaprabhu.

The only thing I am very sorry about is that I lost my best friend. This is pain that feels as if no time and no knowledge could possibly cure or even give some relief. A friend is a good thing, son. One must have at least one good and faithful friend in this lifetime. Sometimes I write poems whenever I remember my friend in various moods. I share these with my wife, some close friends, and Sachisuta's parents, who accept me as their own son. It has become our family custom that each time we go to our hometown we visit them.

Once when you were very small, hardly three years old, we paid them a visit when all their family members were there. After a while, Sachisuta's sister came in with her small children. Sachisuta's mother was playing with you, holding you, and singing for you. As soon as her grandchildren came into the room she told them, "Come, come, dear children; come and see. Your uncle is here," and started to cry. She is a wonderful lady, the mother of a pure devotee of Lord Krishna, and I respect her very much. I'll always be there for her whenever she needs my help and support. That is my heart's duty for the rest of my life. If she accepts me as her son, then I must accept her as my mother.

I am not sorry for whatever happened to me. Rather, I am grateful that this useless man, Sarvabhavana dasa, was used for spreading Lord Chaitanya's sankirtana mission in the former Soviet Union. Several times, devotees insinuated that it was actually the fault of Harikesa Swami and some other leaders that devotees suffered so much in the USSR, but I personally do not like to think in that way. I am one hundred percent sure that whatever happened at that time was Krishna's plan and arrangement.

Harikesa Swami once told me that he felt that it is his fault that I have a blind eye and bad spine. He even gave me money to have eye surgery, but I couldn't do it because there was a chance to lose even the sight I had. Anytime he asked me about my eye and back and tried to help me out, I told him that I don't want him to feel guilty or bad about it. I donated my eye to Krishna, and that's it. Without his dedication, this mission wouldn't have been successful. I am actually thankful to him that he could find the courage to preach in such an atheistic and demoniac country and use me for that great mission. Anyway, we well know that "without the will of Krishna, even a blade of a grass cannot be moved."

I seem to have this incurable spine and eye disease which will always remind me of my Lord Krishna. To this day and probably for the rest of my life I will always remember Lord Krishna each time I sit and stand due to hellish pain on my spine. Some devotees came to know about this and tried to help me take care of my health problems and supported me financially so I could go on with my devotional life.

I would like to especially thank, Harikesa Swami, Niranjana Swami, Bhaktivignan Goswami, His Grace Dayaram das and his good wife Prema Manjari devi dasi, Radhajivan Prabhu, Harivilas Prabhu, Kashiraj Prabhu and his wife Ambhoda, Kirtiraj Prabhu, etc. By the mercy of those wonderful devotees I was able to get treatment for my eyes and spine and cover some immediate expenses for my family. I am eternally grateful and indebted to all those devotees. May Lord Krishna's causeless mercy always be upon them.

I would like to also thank His Grace Shyamasundar Prabhu, for sharing in detail with me during his short visit to Armenia about his visit to Moscow with Srila Prabhupada. We had a wonderful time, enjoyed his association, and were pleased to hear from him some nectar, like stories about Srila Prabhupada, George Harrison, Guru das, Jamuna devi, Mukunda Maharaja, and many other early great devotees of the 20th century.

Thank you very much, Dad, for sharing all these wonderful and unique stories. Thank you for your time and help in publishing this book. I am sure Lord Krishna is very pleased with your service and devotion to Him, and your experience will certainly help many people to become strong and serious devotees of Lord Krishna. I know that by the mercy of Srila Prabhupada and Lord Caitanya, you will go back to the spiritual world at the end of this short life to be with Krishna and His devotees for eternity. That is the perfection of life, and I must learn it from you, as everyone who reads this story must learn it and practice it. Thank you very much, Dad.

After hearing all these stories I asked my father, "What would you wish the readers of this book to know?" And, this is what he told me.

"I would wish to thank all of you who have taken your most valuable time to read this book. Remember that one of the most important factors in spiritual life, and even life in general, is faith. Without faith and determination no one can achieve the highest goal of life.

"Krishna's external energy, maya, is always testing us in many different ways in our life. Be conscious of the fact that Krishna knows everything that has happened before, what is happening now, and what is going to happen in the future. Do not lose faith or be discouraged under any circumstances. And last, we need to remember that eventually we are all going to die. So it is best to take the time we have now to read the holy scriptures and learn the art of dying, just like my friend, Sachisuta dasa, and serve Krishna just like Harikesa Swami wrote to me in this letter:

September 3, 1988

Dear Sarvabhavana das.

"Please engage in the process of Krishna consciousness as if this day were your last day. In this way become more and more sincere. Always remember that Krishna is the Supreme controller and enjoyer and serve Him with love and devotion. Krishna will always help you if you depend on Him."

I hope this meets you in good health and a happy serving mood.

Your ever well-wisher,

**Harikesa Swami**

Srila Prabhupada ki jaya! Sachisuta Prabhu ki jaya!

Hare Krishna

# APPENDIX I
# Srila Prabhupada in Russia

*(from Prabhupada-Lilamrta by Satsvarupa dasa Goswami)*

Srila Prabhupada, on a world wide tour to spread Krishna consciousness, visited Moscow, the capital city of then United Soviet Socialist Republic for five days in June, 1971. He had been corresponding with a Russian Indology professor, Dr. Kotovsky at Moscow's USSR Academy of Sciences for over a year.

Krishna dasa in West Germany, with the help of Dr. Bernhardt of the University of Hamburg, had obtained the names of other Russian scholars. A letter to Krishna dasa in December of 1970 revealed Srila Prabhupada's plans for preaching in Russia:

"I am very encouraged to see your enthusiasm for preaching this message to the Russian people, and your idea to send letters with Dr. Bernhardt is also quite good. He is a big scholar, and he also appreciates our movement. So, if you arrange a tour of Russia for me, I am prepared to accept. Let us see what Krishna desires ...

"If we can go to Russia with our World Sankirtana Party, I am certain that it will be very much appreciated, and people will see the real peace movement is this chanting process—chanting the holy names, Hare Krishna, Hare Krishna, Krishna Krishna, Hare Hare, Hare Rama, Hare Rama, Rama Rama, Hare Hare. So try for it."

Srila Prabhupada had personally replied to Professor Kotovsky:

"...it was understood that you and your university are interested in hearing about Krishna culture and philosophy. This ancient Krishna culture and philosophy is the oldest in the world or in the universe. At least from a historical point of view it is not less than 5,000 years old.

"Perhaps you may know that I started this cultural movement in 1966, and it is already spreading all over the world... My life is dedicated to spreading this Krishna culture all over the world. I think if you give me a chance to speak about the great Krishna culture and philosophy in your country, you will very much appreciate this simple program with great profit. This culture is so well planned that it would be acceptable by any thoughtful man throughout the world."

For Srila Prabhupada and his traveling companions, Shyamasundara and Aravinda, getting tourist visas for Russia was simple. They would take a five-day, government-controlled tour with every activity planned by the Soviet Tourist Bureau and everything paid for in advance. The Hotel National, near Red Square, Lenin's Tomb and the Kremlin was expensive but plain. Srila Prabhupada found his room dingy and cramped, with barely space for a bed and two chairs. Aravinda told the hotel manager that they would not eat the hotel fare, but would have to cook their own meals. The manager refused at first, but finally allowed them use of the maid's kitchen.

That problem solved, the next was getting food. Srila Prabhupada sent Shyamasundara out. He found a milk and yogurt store, but he returned without any fruit, vegetables, or rice. Srila Prabhupada sent him out again, and this time he was gone practically all day, returning with only a couple of cabbages. Srila Prabhupada sent him out the next day for rice. When Shyamasundara returned with rice after several hours, Srila Prabhupada saw that it was a poor North Korean variety, very hard. Srila Prabhupada asked for fruit, but Shyamasundara had to hike for miles through the city to find anything fresh—a few red cherries. Wherever Shyamasundara went, he would have to stand in long queues to purchase anything. Usually, however, someone in the queue would notice that he was a tourist and bring him to the front of the line. Everything Shyamasundara purchased was with coupons.

Srila Prabhupada remained peaceful and regulated, keeping to his daily schedule. He would rise early and translate the Vedic scriptures into English and then go out for a walk through the all but deserted streets. Srila Prabhupada, wearing a saffron shawl, strode quickly, Shyamasundara sometimes running ahead to photograph him.

As they would pass Lenin's Tomb, a queue would already be forming. "Just see," Srila Prabhupada commented one morning, "that is their god. The people don't understand the difference between the body and the spirit. They accept the body as the real person."

Srila Prabhupada appreciated the sparseness of the traffic—some trolleys and bicycles, but mostly pedestrians. As he walked among the old, ornate buildings, he saw elderly women hosing the wide streets. "A good practice," he said. The Russian people appeared to live structured, regulated lives, much more so than the Americans. These simple, austere people, unspoiled by the rampant hedonism so common in America, were fertile for Krishna consciousness. But, devoid of spiritual sustenance, they appeared morose.

Srila Prabhupada met with Dr. Kotovsky for several hours, but Dr. Kotovsky could not arrange for Srila Prabhupada to speak publicly in Moscow or distribute his books. After only three days, Srila Prabhupada's mission in Moscow seemed finished.

Shyamasundara: Srila Prabhupada is eager to lecture here at the Academy of Oriental Sciences.

Professor: No, he cannot lecture here. It would never be allowed. (Shyamasundara turns on the tape recorder, Professor Kotovsky eyes it suspiciously but does not object.)

Prabhupada: The other day, I was reading in the paper, Moscow News. There was a Communist congress, and the president declared that, "We are ready to get others' experience to improve." So I think the Vedic concept of socialism or communism will much improve the idea of communism. There are many good ideas in the Vedic literatures about the socialist idea of communism. So I thought that these ideas might have been distributed to some of your thoughtful men. Therefore I was anxious to speak

Professor: You know, there is a great interest in modern society today in the history of old, old thought. We have published some of the Puranas and parts of the Ramayana, also the Mahabharata and Manu-smriti, and such was the great interest that all of these publications were sold out in a week!

Prabhupada: Modern society is missing the point of human life. They do not know what is the next life. There is no department of knowledge or scientific development to study what is there after finishing this body.

Professor: Swamiji, when the body dies, the owner also dies.

Prabhupada: No. This fact you must know. Why is there no department of knowledge in the university to study this fact scientifically? That is my proposition. That department is lacking. It may be as you say, it may be as I say, but there must be a department of knowledge. Now recently a cardiologist, a doctor in Montreal and Toronto has accepted that there is a soul. I had some correspondence with him. He strongly believes that there is a soul. We accept knowledge from authority.

Professor: In the Communist system, authority has to be backed by empirical knowledge.

Prabhupada: Krishna consciousness and communism are in agree-ment. Both stress surrender to an authority. The devotee surrenders to Krishna, the communist to Lenin. Our life is by surrender, is it not? Do you disagree with this point?

Professor: To some extent you surrender.

Prabhupada: Yes, to the full extent.

Professor: You have to surrender to the society, for instance—the whole people.

Prabhupada: Yes, to the whole people or to the state or king or government or whatever you say. The surrender must be there.

Professor: One either serves a king, who is a single person or the whole society.

Prabhupada: The principle of surrender is there. Without surrender there is no life. So we are educating persons to surrender to the Supreme, wherefrom you get all protection. Just as Krishna says, "sarva dharma parityajya." So surrender is there. No one can say, "No, I am not surrendered to anyone." The difference is where he surrenders. Therefore, in the Bhagavad-gita it is said, "After surrendering to so many things, birth after birth, when one is factually wise, he surrenders unto Me."

Professor: Yes, but surrender has to be accompanied by revolution. The French Revolution, for example, was a revolt against one kind of surrender and yet the revolution itself was another surrender, surrender to the people. So it is not enough to come full stop. Surrender is to be accompanied with revolt against surrender to other people.

Prabhupada: Yes, the surrender will be full stopped when it is surrender to Krishna. That is full stop: no more surrender. Just as, I'll give you one example. A child is crying, and people change laps: "Oh, he has not stopped." But as soon as the baby comes to the lap of its mother?

Professor: He stops crying!

Prabhupada: Yes, full satisfaction. The final surrender is to Krishna and then you will be happy.

After only three days, Srila Prabhupada's mission in Moscow seemed finished. The meeting with Professor Kotovsky over, what was left? The government would allow nothing else. It had not allowed him to bring in books, and now he had been refused the opportunity to speak publicly! Foreigners were not allowed to talk with the Russians. He could go nowhere, unless on an accompanied tour. So with no preaching and no prospects, he stayed in his cramped room, taking his massage, bathing, accepting whatever food Shyamasundara could gather and cook, dictating a few letters, chanting Hare Krishna, and translating Srimad-Bhagavatam.

Srila Prabhupada took a guided tour of Moscow, riding with other tourists on a crowded bus. He saw elderly Russians going to church, armed guards at the door; he surmised that the guards were to prevent the younger generation from entering to worship. He soon tired of the tour, however, and the tour guide got him a taxi and instructed the driver to return him to the Hotel National.

Shyamasundara continued to spend most of his day looking for fresh food. Hearing that oranges were available at a certain market across town, he set out across the city. With his shaved head and his white dhoti and kurta (shirt) he drew stares from everyone he passed, and as he was returning after dark, uniformed men accosted him, taking him to be a local deviant. Grabbing him, they pinned his arms behind his back and shouted at him in Russian. Shyamasundara caught the word dakument (document, passport).

He replied, "Dakument, hotel! Hotel!" Realizing Shyamasundara was a tourist, the officers released him, and he returned to the hotel and informed Srila Prabhupada of what had taken place. "There is no hope in Russia without Krishna consciousness," Srila Prabhupada said.

Once Shyamasundara was standing in line at the yogurt store when a man behind him asked about yoga. "I really want to talk with you," the man said, and he gave Shyamasundara his name and address and a time they could safely meet. When Shyamasundara told Srila Prabhupada, he said, "No, he is a policeman. Don't go."

Standing at his window, Srila Prabhupada glimpsed a parade in nearby Red Square—troops, tanks, artillery, and missiles parading through the streets. "By always preparing for war," Prabhupada said, "the Russian leaders keep the people motivated and thus avoid a revolt." He compared war-loving Russia to the asuras (atheists) in the ancient Vedic histories.

One day, two young men, one the son of an Indian diplomat stationed in Moscow, were loitering near Red Square when they saw an amazing sight. Out of the usual regimented routine of traffic, a tall young man with a shaved head, a long, reddish ponytail, and flowing white robes approached. It was Shyamasundara. Familiar with Shyamasundara's dress, the son of the Indian diplomat stopped him. Shyamasundara smiled, "Hare Krishna, brother," and he began talking with the Indian, whose name was Narayana. The Russian, Ivan, knew a little English and followed the conversation as closely as he could. The talk grew serious. "Why don't you come up and meet my spiritual master?" Shyamasundara asked. Honored, the boys immediately accompanied Shyamasundara to the Hotel National. When they arrived, they found Srila Prabhupada seated on his bed, glowing and smiling, Aravinda massaging his feet. Shyamasundara entered, offering obeisance's before Srila Prabhupada. Ivan was completely fascinated.

Ivan was interested even more than his Indian friend, and Srila Prabhupada began explaining to him the philosophy of Krishna consciousness, while Narayana helped by translating. Ivan inquired with respect and awe, and Srila Prabhupada answered his questions, teaching as much basic information as was possible in one sitting. Prabhupada explained the difference between the spirit soul and the body and described the soul's eternal relationship with Krishna, the Supreme Personality of Godhead. He spoke of the scripture Bhagavad-gita, of his network of temples around the world, and of his young men and women disciples all practicing bhakti-yoga.

Srila Prabhupada mentioned his desire to preach in Russia, which was a great field for Krishna consciousness because the people were open-minded and hadn't been polluted by sense gratification. "Krishna consciousness philosophy," he said, "should be taught to the most intelligent people, but because of government restrictions it would have to be done discreetly. Devotees will not be able to sing in the streets, but they could chant quietly together in someone's home."

Prabhupada then began singing very quietly, leading the boys in kirtana. Ivan's taking to Krishna was similar to a hungry man's eating a meal. After several hours, however, he and his friend had to go. They would return the next day.

Shyamasundara began spending time with Ivan and Narayana. Ivan, a student of Oriental philosophies, was very intelligent and eager to know what was going on in the outside world. He was fond of the Beatles, and Srila Prabhupada told him of his association with George Harrison and John Lennon. Ivan and Shyamasundara had long talks about the ambitions and hopes of young people outside Russia, and Shyamasundara explained to him how Krishna consciousness was the topmost of all spiritual paths. Shyamasundara also taught him the basic principles of bhakti-yoga, such as chanting the prescribed sixteen rounds of japa daily, and gave Ivan his own copy of Srila Prabhupada's translation of Bhagavad-gita As It Is.

Srila Prabhupada showed Ivan how to make rice and chapatis (flat bread) and asked him to give up eating meat. Joyfully, Ivan accepted the chanting, the new way of eating—everything. Ivan was being trained so that after Srila Prabhupada left, Ivan could continue on his own. Ivan would be able to see himself changing and advancing in spiritual life, and after practicing for some time he could be initiated. Ivan said that he would tell his friends about Krishna consciousness. In this young Russian's eagerness and intelligence, Srila Prabhupada found the real purpose of his visit to Russia.

Srila Prabhupada gave the analogy that when cooking rice, the cook need test only one grain to determine if the whole pot is done. Similarly, by talking with this one Russian youth, Prabhupada could tell that the Russian people were not satisfied in their so-called ideal land of Marxism. Just as Ivan was keenly receptive, millions of others would be receptive also.

Canakya Pandit says that one blooming flower can refresh a whole forest and that a fire in a single tree can burn the whole forest. From the Marxist point of view, Ivan was the fire that would spread Krishna consciousness to others, thus defeating the communist ideology. And from Srila Prabhupada's point of view, Ivan was the aromatic flower that would lend its fragrance to many others. Srila Prabhupada's visit to Russia was no obscure interlude but had become an occasion for planting the seed of Krishna consciousness in a destitute land.

Caitanya Mahaprabhu had predicted that the sankirtana movement would go to every town and village, yet for hundreds of years that prediction had remained unfulfilled. Srila Prabhupada, however, in the few years since his first trip to America in 1965, had again and again planted Lord Caitanya's message in one unlikely place after another. And of all places, this was perhaps the most unlikely; during a brief, government-supervised visit to Moscow, he had planted the seed of Krishna consciousness within the Soviet Union. He was the needle, and everyone and everything connected with him was like the thread that would follow.

Professor Kotovsky had remarked that Srila Prabhupada's stay in an old-fashioned hotel would not prove interesting. But Srila Prabhupada, unknown to Professor Kotovsky, was transcendental to Moscow or any other place in the material world. Srila Prabhupada had come to this place, and Krishna had sent a sincere soul to him to receive the gift of Krishna consciousness. This had happened not by some devious espionage against the Soviet government, but by the presence of Krishna's pure devotee and representative and his natural desire to satisfy Krishna by preaching. In response to Srila Prabhupada's pure desire, Krishna had sent one boy, and from that one boy the desire would spread to others. Nothing, not even an Iron Curtain, could stop Krishna consciousness. The soul's natural function is to serve Krishna, and Krishna's natural will is to satisfy the pure desires of His devotee.

In a letter to Tamala Krishna, on the 25th of June, 1971, Prabhupada summed up his Moscow visit:

"The city is well-planned. There are big, big houses and roads, and in the daytime the streets are busy with buses, cars, and underground trains that are far better than American or English. The underground streets are very neat and clean. The surface streets are also daily washed. But there is some difficulty in collecting vegetarian foodstuffs; still we are cooking meals by the cooker, which has saved our life. We talked with one professor, Dr. Kotovsky, and Shyamasundara talked with many great writers and musicians. Two boys are working with us; one Indian and one Russian. So there is good prospect for opening a center, although the atmosphere is not very good. The embassy was no help. So our visit to Moscow was not so successful, but for the future, it is hopeful."

# APPENDIX II

# The Story of Haridasa Thakura

*Summary and commentary by Radha Damodara dasa*

Haridasa Thakura was born in a Muslim family about 500 years ago in the village of Bhuvana in India, before the coming of Lord Caitanya (the Golden Avatara of Lord Krishna). He took the association of Lord Krishna's devotees and always chanted the holy names of Krishna with love.

At that time, the entire human society was totally devoid of any spiritual aspirations; they were immersed in base and perverted enjoyments of the body. Those who held discourses on the scriptures were scarcely better for they did not instruct people on the essence of those scriptures, the congregational chanting of the holy name of the Lord. Seeing the hopeless plight of the living entities, the devotees of the Lord often met together, away from the public view, to clap their hands and chant the holy name in ecstasy.

Haridasa had absolutely no attraction for material enjoyment. The holy name of Lord Krishna continuously vibrated on his tongue, creating an extraordinary beauty about his mouth. Never for a moment did he feel any apathy towards his chanting of the holy name of Krishna; he remained absorbed, tasting the nectar of devotional service. It was common to see Haridasa Thakur dancing while he sang the glories of Lord Krishna's name. People would gather around him just to see the unrestricted tears of love of Godhead that flowed profusely from his eyes, drenching his entire body. Even the strictest atheists marveled at his behavior. The local Muslim authority known as the Kazi became envious of Haridas Thakur's popularity and reported to the king, "This man is acting like a Hindu; arrest him and punish him appropriately." The envious words of the sinful Kazi sparked an immediate response from the equally sinful king, and Haridasa Thakur was arrested. Having received the mercy of Lord Krishna, Haridasa had no fear of the Muslim authorities nor even of death itself. With the name of the Lord on his lips, Haridasa appeared before the Nawab.

Previously many religious people had been terrorized and jailed by the Muslims, and those prisoners were happy to learn that Haridasa might be joining them. They thought that his presence in their miserable situation would certainly relieve their suffering!

When Haridasa was brought to the prison, he glanced compassionately upon them. His long, graceful arms, which extended to his knees, his lotus eyes, and his charming moon-like face enchanted everyone. They offered their most sincere respects to the saint, and love for Krishna stirred in their hearts. Srila Haridasa Thakura was pleased with the tremendous devotion that had grown in the hearts of the prisoners, and he blessed them, "Just remain as you are." But the miserable prisoners could not grasp the depth of that blessing, and they felt quite angry. Some of them thought that Haridasa was cursing them.

Haridasa could see the misunderstanding and compassionately explained himself, "My blessing to you is that you will remain as you are, but please do not feel disappointed. I could never wish you any misfortune. I simply desire that the love you now feel for Krishna should always remain the same. From now on, chant Lord Krishna's name and constantly remember His pastimes, inspiring one another."

"I certainly do not want you to remain prisoners forever, but I do pray that you develop distaste for material pleasures. Please chant the holy name of the Lord. My blessing was meant to free you from your present miserable condition and to insure that you remain happy in love of Krishna. I look upon everyone equally and wish the best for all living entities. I pray that you may develop unflinching devotion for Krishna. Do not be sad; you will one day be freed. Once you leave the prison you may live in the forest or you may live in your home, but always think of Krishna and try to cultivate spiritual life."

Then, Haridasa went before the king. Because of his purity, Srila Haridasa Thakura radiated a certain effulgence, which the king could not fail to notice. He rose respectfully when Haridasa entered and offered the saint a seat. He asked Haridasa, "What sort of madness has overcome you? By good fortune you were born a Muslim. Why do you behave like a Hindu? We do not even accept rice touched by a Hindu, yet you want to ignore your high birth and become a low-caste Hindu? To discard your own race, land, and religion for another is perverted! How do you expect to attain the liberated platform if you behave in this way?"

Haridasa Thakur answered, "My dear Sir, there is only one God for all living entities. The difference between the Muslim God and the Hindu God is in name only. According to knowledgeable Hindus and Muslims and according to every scripture, be it the Koran or Purana, God is one. He resides in everyone's heart. My dear respected Sir, please consider these points seriously, and if you still find me guilty then punish me."

The king said, "My friend, just speak from your own scripture and accept the path. Then you will have nothing to fear. Otherwise, the Kazis present will force me to punish you; they will revile and insult you. Why should you let that happen?"

Haridasa fearlessly replied, "Whatever the Supreme Lord desires is destined to happen; there is no one who can check it. Even if my body is cut into pieces and I loose my life, I will never give up chanting the Lord's holy name."

The king said, "I cannot allow this Hinduism to spread and degrade our community. I have decided to punish you according to the mandates of the Koran so that you will be freed from your sins."

He told his soldiers,"Lash him in twenty-two market places until he dies. If he lives despite the punishment, then I will conclude that he has spoken the truth."

From one market place to another, they beat him mercilessly, so that everyone would see the punishment and be afraid. But Haridasa was a pure soul, completely protected by the Supreme Lord. He was so absorbed in the chanting that he did not feel any of the blows of the whips!

Throughout his ordeal, Haridasa's one emotion was pity for the soldiers! He prayed, "O Lord Krishna, please be merciful upon these poor souls so they may not go to hell because of me."

At last the guards had to stop in amazement. "How can a human being survive such a brutal beating? Any ordinary man would have died after the beating we gave in the first two or three market places. We have lashed him continuously through twenty-two market places, and he still shows no sign of either pain or death. Occasionally he looks up to smile at us." They concluded that he must be a saintly person.

"Oh, Haridasa," they pleaded. "because of you we shall certainly be punished. When the Kazi sees that despite our beating you are still alive, he shall certainly kill us instead."

"If my survival brings such terrible misfortune to you," replied Haridasa, "then I shall definitely give up my body. Just see how I die."

Haridasa Thakur immediately fell into trance. A pure devotee of the Supreme Lord possesses all mystic power; so without any hesitation, Haridasa fell lifeless, without a trace of breath. The Muslim soldiers gladly threw the body of Haridasa into the Ganges. Haridasa was directly protected by the Supreme Lord Krishna Govinda, therefore who could harm him?

Haridasa floated downstream on the currents of the Ganga, and after some time he became conscious, by the Lord's desire. Fully awakened and overwhelmed with ecstasy, he climbed the bank of the Ganga and proceeded towards the king's palace, loudly chanting the name of Krishna as he walked. When the Muslims saw Haridasa they were convinced that he possessed extraordinary mystic powers. Pure, happy feelings replaced the envy and hate in their hearts. They offered him obeisances, worshipping him as a very saintly person. By this worship the Muslims became free from material entanglement.

In a humble and meek voice the king said, "I can now understand that you are truly a saintly person. You have realized the absolute truth, and you have seen the one Supreme Lord everywhere and in everyone. Kindly forgive me for the offenses I have committed against you." Haridasa Thakur forgave the king and went back to his chanting and dancing, and many people became influenced by his purity.

Haridasa Thakura arranged his apparent death to protect these soldiers from punishment.

This history is significant in that Haridasa Thakura's concern extended to the material well-being of the soldiers and was not conditioned upon their acceptance of any religious practice or philosophical perspective. Haridasa did not dismiss the potential suffering of his tormentors as material illusion, nor did he dismiss the potential consequences to the soldiers as their karmic reaction for the harm they had inflicted on him. His concern for his tormentors transcended considerations of his own well being. Knowing of the Supreme Personality of Godhead and His merciful love for us, we cannot be indifferent to the suffering of others, because Krishna is never indifferent toward us.

Our understanding of how to relate to others springs from our understanding of our own nature and of our relationship with our creator. Almost without exception, people in general gain their sense of how they ought to act in the world, of what is right and what is wrong, from their religious worldview. For the Vaishnava, identity is clear. We are spirit souls, parts of our Supreme Lord Krishna, and we are His eternal servants. Such an identity has immediate implications for our relationship to other living entities. If, as we are taught, all living entities are spirit souls, then we are all interconnected by virtue of our relationship to Krishna.

Moreover, there is an inherent equality of all living entities because we all share the same spiritual essence. Thus, our relations with others must be guided by principles of concern for others. Indeed, our Vaishnava tradition gives specific injunctions for behavior, the foremost of which is compassion. Indeed, it is the duty of the Vaishnava to become the humble servant of other living entities. This duty of service to others, while not the main tenet of bhakti-yoga, follows logically from our objective of serving the Supreme Lord. The Lord describes Himself in Bhagavad-gita as the well-wishing friend of every living entity. If we desire to please the Lord, then we must accept as our mission the roles of friend and helpers of others in their various material manifestations.

Haridasa Thakur, associate of Sri Caitanya Mahaprabhu and the teacher of the holy name, embodied concern for others in his response to the soldiers who were ordered to execute him. Because of his great spiritual potency, their severe beatings did not have the expected effect of ending his life. However, when they informed him that failure to carry out their instructions and execute him would cause them suffering, Haridasa Thakur arranged his apparent death to protect these soldiers from punishment.

Haridasa Thakur's example of extreme tolerance and compassion perfectly embodies the instructions of his spiritual master, Lord Caitanya, who instructed His followers on the behavior required to reach transcendence. He said, "One must think himself lower than the grass. One must be more tolerant than a tree and always prepared to give respect to others."

Our philosophy makes clear that we who practice bhakti-yoga are not superior to other living entities. In reality, all spirit souls are minute parts of the Supreme Lord. Devotional service is the eternal duty of every living entity. Some souls are more entangled in material illusion than others. However, our true identities are similar and equal. How can we be superior to others on the basis of an illusion?

Indeed, the less covered we are by material energy, the more we should fulfill our duty of serving other living entities. We are enjoined to work for the highest welfare of others. To bring others to Krishna's service, we must first attract them to hear our words and consider our example. Thus, we must be involved and caring members of society. Otherwise, we remain on the fringes of society, without the influence that will permit the Vaishnava message to be heard.

Vaishnava ethics do not differ greatly from the ethics of other major religions. Moreover, they are easily discernible by the exercise of basic common sense. When in doubt, we can always refer to the four moral precepts which uphold our regulative principles. Truthfulness is preferable to dishonesty. Kindness and compassion are preferable to cruelty. Generosity and renunciation are preferable to greediness. Order and cleanliness are preferable to the shabbiness and littering that sometimes result from our failure to maintain the facilities we have been given.

Srila Prabhupada wanted his followers to be recognized as perfect gentlemen. As we make our way in the larger human family, we should be welcomed on the basis of our kindness and consideration for those around us. If we remember to treat others with the kindness we have received from the devotees who inspire us, our temples will not be large enough to hold all those who wish to enter.

*It is said that great personalities almost always accept voluntary suffering of people in general. This is considered the highest method of worshiping The Supreme Personality of Godhead, who is in everyone's heart...*

# Names of Some Early Glorious Devotees in the Former Soviet Union...

Without whose endeavor the Krishna consciousness movement wouldn't have spread in the former USSR:

1. Ananta Shanti das
2. Amsu das
3. Advaita Acharya das
4. Amala Bhakta das
5. Alalanatha das
6. Ananda Chinmayi devi dasi
7. Armen Sarkisyan
8. AcyutaPriya das
9. Atmananda das
10. Ambarish das
11. Akinchanadhana das
12. Ayravata dasa
13. Ajanabahu das
14. Amritahartha das
15. Bhaktivignana Gosvami Maharaj (Vaidyanath das)
16. Brahmananda Puri das
17. Bharadvaj das
18. Damodara das
19. Damayanti devi dasi
20. Dayanvisha devi dasi
21. Ekadasi devi dasi
22. Gargarishi das
23. Gaganeshi Devi dasi

24. Haridas Thakur das
25. Ishani devi dasi
26. Japa das
27. Jagannatha devi dasi
28. Kamalamala das
29. Krishna Kaumar das
30. Kirtan Rasa das
31. Lilavatara devi dasi
32. Laxmi Priya devi dasi
33. Mayuradvaj das
34. Mamu Thakur das
35. Mukunda datta das
36. Maha Mantra devi dasi
37. Madhava ghosh das
38. Marika dasi (Premavati's daughter)
39. Martik Martirosyan
40. Nityananda Rama das
41. Premavati devi dasi
42. Parjanya Maharaj das
43. Purnamasi devi dasi
44. Prana das
45. Rupanuga das
46. Rama Bhakta das
47. Rukmini Devi dasi
48. Rantidev das
49. Ranga devi dasi
50. Sanatana-Kumara das
51. Sashakari das
52. Sannyasa das
53. Sashu das
54. Senik Adamyan
55. Sachisuta das
56. Shyamakunda das
57. Sarvabhavana das

58. Tridandi das
59. Urjaswati Devi dasi
60. Udarakirti devi dasi
61. Valmiki muni dasa
62. Vrindavan das
63. Visvamitra das
64. Vakta das
65. Vedavyasa das
66. Vakreshvar Pandit das
67. Yamaraj das
68. Yagya devi dasi
69. Yagyanga das (Yura)
70. Yamunangi devi dasi

**AND MANY OTHERS THAT I DO NOT KNOW PERSONALLY, BUT LORD KRISHNA KNOWS THEM ALL FOR SURE.**

My humble obeisances and apologies to all of them
whose names are missing from this small list.

## OM TAT SAT

# Sanskrit Words Used in Salted Bread

**Aratika** - a ceremony of singing and worshiping Lord Krishna's Deity form in the temple.

**Bhagavad-gita** - literally "The Song of God." This is the "Bible" of the Hare Krishna Movement. It was spoken by Krishna to guide us. Srila Prabhupada translated the Bhagavad-gita into English and purported the verses so that we could easily understand and follow Krishna's instructions.

**Burfi** - a sweet made from milk and sugar.

**Darshan** - the wonderful event of being able to look upon the Lord and have the Lord look upon you.

**Dasa** - a male devotee- means servant of God.

**Devi** - a female devotee - means servant of God.

**Dhoti** - the simple cotton cloth worn by male members of the Hare Krishna Movement. Single students, called brahmacaris, wear orange or saffron cloth. Married men wear white or yellow cloth. The senior men called Swamis, Goswamis, or sannyasis wear orange or saffron cloth. Women wear a cloth called a sari. Single and married women wear colorfully patterned saris and widows wear white saris.

**Gaura Purnima** - the anniversary of Krishna's appearance on Earth as Lord Chaitanya.

**Guru** - the spiritual master coming in direct disciplic succession from Krishna to you.

**Hare Krishna maha-mantra** - the holy names of Lord Krishna which are the key to spiritual realization in this the Iron Age (Kali-yuga):

**Hare Krishna Hare Krishna Krishna Krishna Hare Hare
Hare Rama Hare Rama Rama Rama Hare Hare**

**Haribol!** - means "chant the holy names!" or "go on chanting!"

**Harikesa Swami, Srila** - at the time of Sarvabhavana's imprisonment, this disciple of Srila Prabhupada was the leader of Eastern Europe.

**Japa** - repeating the Hare Krishna mantra softly as a meditation on your beads.

**Jaya** - "All glories." A cheer such as "Hip Hip Hooray!" or "Hallelujah!"

**Katha** - talks or lectures about Krishna philosophy.

**Ki Jaya** - invoking exuberant cheers.

**Kirtana** - singing the Hare Krishna mantra in the temple.

**Maha** - very large or special.

**Maha-mantra** - the great mantra; the Hare Krishna mantra.

**Mangala-aratika** - the Sanskrit word mangala means auspicious or advantageous for spiritual advancement. Aratika is a ceremony to worship Krishna in the temple. Devotees of Krishna rise early and chant, study, serve, etc. in the early morning hours because these hours are most conducive to increasing our spiritual life. Mangala-aratika takes place every morning around 4:30 am in every temple.

**Mantra** - a series of words or holy names of God; prayers that can be used to glorify God.

**Maya** - illusion, especially thinking that we are the body, not the soul.

**Mrdanga** - the traditional two-headed clay drum of West Bengal, India.

**Navadwipa** - technically meaning "nine islands," it is the area in West Bengal where Lord Chaitanya appeared five hundred years ago and displayed His pastimes for twenty-four years.

**Pakoras** - vegetables coated with a spiced batter and deep fried in ghee (clarified butter).

**Pancha Tattva** - Lord Krishna's incarnation of Lord Chaitanya and four of His principal associates. "Pancha" means five and "Tattva" means Truth. Lord Chaitanya appeared in Mayapura, India, just over five hundred years ago to spread the chanting of the Hare Krishna mantra. This chanting is the recommended means in this age to achieve love of Krishna, and thus perfect one's life and go back to home, back to Godhead (the spiritual world, where one serves Krishna eternally.)

**Parampara** - transcendental knowledge is carefully passed from guru to disciple in a chain of disciplic succession called the Param (supreme) para (order).

**Prabhu** - means "master," and devotees of Krishna commonly use it to address one another to show respect.

**Prabhupada, Srila** - the founding guru of the Hare Krishna Movement. Please see the mini-biography below, "Who Is Srila Prabhupada?"

**Prasadam** - the remnants of food offered to Krishna.

**Sankirtana** - congregational singing of the holy names of the Lord, often the Hare Krishna mantra. Hare Krishna devotees often perform sankirtana in public places to benefit all that hear.

**Sanskrit** - the oldest language in the world; the Vedic scriptures were written in this ancient, scholarly language.

**Srila** - a respectful title for one's guru or a saintly person.

**Swami or Goswami** - literally means "one who controls his senses." This title is given to one who takes a vow of celibacy and is committed to use all his facilities to make spiritual advancement and spread Krishna consciousness.

**Tilak** – clay from the banks of a sacred river, such as the Ganges or Yamuna, used to mark the body as a temple of God.

**Vrindavan** - the place of Krishna's appearance and pastimes 5,000 years ago located in the state of Uttar Pradesh, India.

# Who is Srila Prabhupada?

is Divine Grace A. C. Bhaktivedanta Swami Prabhupada (Pronunciation - the "bh" is pronounced like the "b" in English but with an extra puff of breath. Bhuck-tee -vay-DAHN-ta Pra-bhoo- PAHD) appeared in this world in 1896 in Calcutta (currently Kolkata), India. He first met his spiritual master, Srila Bhaktisiddhanta Saraswati Goswami, in Calcutta in 1922. Bhaktisiddhanta Saraswati, a prominent religious scholar and the founder of the sixty-four branches of the Gaudiya Matha (Vedic bhakti-yoga institute), liked this educated young man and convinced him to dedicate his life to teaching Krishna consciousness. Srila Prabhupada became his student, and eleven years later (1933) at Allahabad, he became his formally initiated disciple. At their first meeting in 1922 Srila Bhaktisiddhanta Saraswati Thakura requested Srila Prabhupada to broadcast the science of devotional service through the English language. In the years that followed, Srila Prabhupada wrote a commentary on the Bhagavad-gita, assisted the Gaudiya Matha in its work, and in 1944 started Back to Godhead, an English fortnightly magazine. Maintaining the publication was a struggle. Single-handedly, Srila Prabhupada edited it, typed the manuscripts, checked the galley proofs, and even distributed the individual copies. Once begun, the magazine never stopped; it is now being continued by his disciples and granddisciples and is published in over thirty languages.

Recognizing Srila Prabhupada's philosophical learning and devotion, the Gaudiya Vaisnava Society honored him in 1947 with the title "Bhaktivedanta." In 1950, at the age of fifty-four, Srila Prabhupada retired from married life, adopting the vanaprastha (retired) order to devote more time to his studies and writing. Srila Prabhupada traveled to the holy city of Vrindavan, where he lived in very humble circumstances in the historic medieval temple of Radha-Damodara. There he engaged for several years in deep study and writing.

He accepted the renounced order of life (sannyasa) in 1959. In Vrindavan, Srila Prabhupada began work on his life's masterpiece—a multi-volume annotated translation of the eighteen-thousand-verse Srimad-Bhagavatam (Bhagavata Purana). He also wrote essays such as "Easy Journey to Other Planets."

After publishing three volumes of the Bhagavatam, Srila Prabhu-pada came to the United States of America in September 1965 to fulfill the mission of his spiritual master. Subsequently, His Divine Grace wrote more than sixty volumes of authoritative annotated translations and summary studies of the philosophical and religious classics of India. When he first arrived by freighter in New York City, Srila Prabhupada was practically penniless. Only after almost a year of great difficulty did he establish the International Society for Krishna Consciousness (ISKCON) in July of 1966. Before his passing away on November 14, 1977, he guided ISKCON and saw it grow to a worldwide confederation of more than one hundred ashrams, schools, temples, institutes, and farm communities.

In 1968, Srila Prabhupada created New Vrindavan, a farm community in the hills of West Virginia. His students have since founded several similar communities in the United States and abroad.

In 1972, His Divine Grace introduced the Vedic system of primary and secondary education in the West by founding the Gurukula school in Dallas, Texas. Since then, under his guidelines, his disciples have established children's schools throughout the United States and the rest of the world, with the principal educational center now located in Vrindavan, India.

Srila Prabhupada also inspired the construction of several large international cultural centers in India. The center at Sri Dhama Mayapur in West Bengal is the site for a planned spiritual city, an ambitious project for which construction will extend over many years to come. In Vrindavana, India are the very popular Krishna-Balarama Temple, International Guesthouse, and Srila Prabhupada Memorial and Museum. There are also major cultural and educational centers in Mumbai (Bombay) and New Delhi. Other impressive centers have also been built in Ujjain and Tirupati, and others are planned in important locations on the Indian subcontinent.

Srila Prabhupada's most significant contribution, however, is his books. Highly respected by the academic community for their authority, depth, and clarity, they are used as standard textbooks in numerous college courses. His writings have been translated into over fifty languages. The Bhaktivedanta Book Trust, established in 1972 to publish the works of His Divine Grace, has thus become the world's largest publisher of books in the field of Indian religion and philosophy.

In just twelve years, in spite of his advanced age, Srila Prabhupada circled the globe fourteen times on lecture tours that took him to six continents. In spite of such a vigorous schedule, Srila Prabhupada continued to write prolifically. His books constitute a veritable library of Vedic philosophy, religion, and culture.

# An Explanation of the Hare Krishna Maha-Mantra

by His Divine Grace
A. C. Bhaktivedanta Swami Prabhupada

**Hare Krishna Hare Krishna Krishna Krishna Hare Hare
Hare Rama Hare Rama Rama Rama Hare Hare**

The transcendental vibration established by the chanting of Hare Krishna Hare Krishna Krishna Krishna Hare Hare, Hare Rama Hare Rama Rama Rama Hare Hare is the sublime method of reviving our Krishna consciousness. As living spiritual souls, we are all originally Krishna conscious entities, but due to our association with matter from time immemorial, our consciousness is now polluted by the material atmosphere. The material atmosphere, in which we are now living, is called maya, or illusion. Maya means "that which is not." And what is this illusion? The illusion is that we are all trying to be lords of material nature, while actually we are under the grip of her stringent laws. When a servant artificially tries to imitate the all-powerful master, this is called illusion. In this polluted concept of life, we are all trying to exploit the resources of material nature, but actually we are becoming more and more entangled in her complexities. Therefore, although we are engaged in a hard struggle to conquer nature, we are ever more dependent on her. This illusory struggle against material nature can be stopped at once by revival of our Krishna consciousness.

Krishna consciousness is not an artificial imposition on the mind; this consciousness is the original energy of the living entity. When we hear the transcendental vibration, this consciousness is revived. And this process is recommended for this age by authorities. By practical experience also, one can perceive that by chanting this maha-mantra, or the Great Chanting for Deliverance, one can at once feel a transcendental ecstasy coming through from the spiritual stratum. And when one is factually on the plane of spiritual understanding— surpassing the stages of senses, mind, and intelligence—one is situated on the transcendental plane. This chanting of Hare Krishna Hare Krishna Krishna Krishna Hare Hare, Hare Rama Hare Rama Rama Rama Hare Hare is directly enacted from the spiritual platform, and thus this sound vibration surpasses all lower strata of consciousness, namely sensual, mental, and intellectual. There is no need, therefore, to understand the language of the mantra, nor is there any need for mental speculation or any intellectual adjustment for chanting this maha-mantra. It springs automatically from the spiritual platform, and as such, anyone can take part in the chanting without any previous qualification, and dance in ecstasy.

We have seen this practically. Even a child can take part in the chanting, or even a dog can take part in it. Of course, for one who is too entangled in material life, it takes a little more time to come to the standard point, but even such a materially engrossed man is raised to the spiritual platform very quickly. When the mantra is chanted by a pure devotee of the Lord in love, it has the greatest efficacy on the hearers, and as such, this chanting should be heard from the lips of a pure devotee of the Lord so that immediate effects can be achieved. As far as possible, chanting from the lips of non-devotees should be avoided, just as milk touched by the lips of a serpent has poisonous effects.

The word Hara is the form of addressing the energy of the Lord, and the words Krishna and Rama are forms of addressing the Lord Himself. Both Krishna and Rama mean "the supreme pleasure," and Hara is the supreme pleasure energy of the Lord, changed to Hare in the vocative. The supreme pleasure energy of the Lord helps us to reach the Lord.

The material energy, called maya, is also one of the multi-energies of the Lord. And we, the living entities, are also the energy—marginal energy—of the Lord. The living entities are described as superior to material energy. When the superior energy is in contact with the inferior energy, an incompatible situation arises; but when the superior marginal energy is in contact with the superior energy, called Hara, the living entity is established in his happy, normal condition.

These three words, namely Hare, Krishna, and Rama, are the transcendental seeds of the maha-mantra. The chanting is a spiritual call for the Lord and His internal energy, Hara, to give protection to the conditioned soul. This chanting is exactly like the genuine cry of a child for its mother. Mother Hara helps the devotee achieve the grace of the supreme father, Hari, or Krishna, and the Lord reveals Himself to the devotee who chants this mantra sincerely.

No other means of spiritual realization, therefore, is as effective in this age as chanting the maha-mantra.

**Hare Krishna Hare Krishna Krishna Krishna Hare Hare
Hare Rama Hare Rama Rama Rama Hare Hare**

# Relevant Verses from the Srimad-Bhagavatam

*Narada Muni's Instructions to Vyasadeva*

### Srimad-Bhagavatam 1.5.19

*na vai jano jatu kathancanavrajen
mukunda-sevy anyavad anga samsrtim
smaran mukundanghry-upaguhanam punar
vihatum icchen na rasa-graho janah*

### Translation

My dear Vyasa, even though a devotee of Lord Krishna sometimes falls down somehow or other, he certainly does not undergo material existence like others because a person who has once relished the taste of the lotus feet of the Lord can do nothing but remember that ecstasy again and again.

### Purport

A devotee of the Lord automatically becomes uninterested in the enchantment of material existence because he is rasa-graha, or one who has tasted the sweetness of the lotus feet of Lord Krsna. There are certainly many instances where devotees of the Lord have fallen down due to uncongenial association, just like fruitive workers, who are always prone to degradation. But even though he falls down, a devotee is never to be considered the same as a fallen karmi. A karmi suffers the result of his own fruitive reactions, whereas a devotee is reformed by chastisement directed by the Lord Himself. The sufferings of an orphan and the sufferings of a beloved child of a king are not one and the same. An orphan is really poor because he has no one to take care of him, but a beloved son of a rich man, although he appears to be on the same level as the orphan, is always under the vigilance of his capable father. A devotee of the Lord, due to wrong association, sometimes imitates the fruitive workers. The fruitive workers want to lord it over the material world.

Similarly, a neophyte devotee foolishly thinks of accumulating some material power in exchange for devotional service. Such foolish devotees are sometimes put into difficulty by the Lord Himself. As a special favor, He may remove all material paraphernalia. By such action, the bewildered devotee is forsaken by all friends and relatives, and so he comes to his senses again by the mercy of the Lord and is set right to execute his devotional service.

In the Bhagavad-gita it is also said that such fallen devotees are given a chance to take birth in a family of highly qualified Brahmans or in a rich mercantile family. A devotee in such a position is not as fortunate as one who is chastised by the Lord and put into a position seemingly of helplessness. The devotee who becomes helpless by the will of the Lord is more fortunate than those who are born in good families. The fallen devotees born in a good family may forget the lotus feet of the Lord because they are less fortunate, but the devotee who is put into a forlorn condition is more fortunate because he swiftly returns to the lotus feet of the Lord, thinking himself helpless all around.

Pure devotional service is so spiritually relishable that a devotee becomes automatically uninterested in material enjoyment. That is the sign of perfection in progressive devotional service. A pure devotee continuously remembers the lotus feet of Lord Sri Krsna and does not forget Him even for a moment, not even in exchange for all the opulence of the three worlds.

# Prayers by Queen Kunti

### Srimad-Bhagavatam 1.8.25

*vipadah santu tah sasvat*
*tatra tatra jagad-guro*
*bhavato darsanam yat syad*
*apunar bhava-darsanam*

## Translation

I wish that all those calamities would happen again and again so that we could see You again and again, for seeing You means that we will no longer see repeated births and deaths.

## Purport

Generally the distressed, the needy, the intelligent, and the inquisitive, who have performed some pious activities, worship or begin to worship the Lord. Others, who are thriving on misdeeds only, regardless of status, cannot approach the Supreme due to being misled by the illusory energy. Therefore, for a pious person, if there is some calamity there is no other alternative than to take shelter of the lotus feet of the Lord. Constantly remembering the lotus feet of the Lord means preparing for liberation from birth and death. Therefore, even though there are so-called calamities, they are welcome because they give us an opportunity to remember the Lord, which means liberation.

One who has taken shelter of the lotus feet of the Lord, which are accepted as the most suitable boat for crossing the ocean of nescience, can achieve liberation as easily as one leap over the holes made by the hoofs of a calf. Such persons are meant to reside in the abode of the Lord, and they have nothing to do with a place where there is danger in every step.

This material world is certified by the Lord in the Bhagavad-gita as a dangerous place full of calamities. Less intelligent persons prepare plans to adjust to those calamities without knowing that the nature of this place is itself full of calamities. They have no information of the abode of the Lord, which is full of bliss and without trace of calamity. The duty of the sane person, therefore, is to be undisturbed by worldly calamities, which are sure to happen in all circumstances. Suffering all sorts of unavoidable misfortunes, one should make progress in spiritual realization because that is the mission of human life. The spirit soul is transcendental to all material calamities; therefore, the so-called calamities are called false. A man may see a tiger swallowing him in a dream, and he may cry for this calamity. Actually there is no tiger and there is no suffering; it is simply a case of dreams. In the same way, all calamities of life are said to be dreams. If someone is lucky enough to get in contact with the Lord by devotional service, it is all gain. Contact with the Lord by any one of the nine devotional services is always a forward step on the path going back to Godhead.

## Srimad-Bhagavatam 1.8.26

*janmaisvarya-sruta-sribhir*
*edhamana-madah puman*
*naivarhaty abhidhatum vai*
*tvam akincana-gocaram*

### Translation

My Lord, Your Lordship can easily be approached, but only by those who are materially exhausted. One who is on the path of [material] progress, trying to improve himself with respectable parentage, great opulence, high education and bodily beauty, cannot approach You with sincere feeling.

### Purport

Being materially advanced means taking birth in an aristocratic family and possessing great wealth, an education and attractive personal beauty. All materialistic men are mad after possessing all these material opulences, and this is known as the advancement of material civilization. But the result is that by possessing all these material assets one becomes artificially puffed up, intoxicated by such temporary possessions. Consequently, such materially puffed up persons are incapable of uttering the holy name of the Lord by addressing Him feelingly, "O Govinda, O Krsna." It is said in the sastras (scriptures) that by once uttering the holy name of the Lord, the sinner gets rid of a quantity of sins that he is unable to commit. Such is the power of uttering the holy name of the Lord. There is not the least exaggeration in this statement.

Actually the Lord's holy name has such powerful potency. But there is a quality to such utterances also. It depends on the quality of feeling. A helpless man can feelingly utter the holy name of the Lord, whereas a man who utters the same holy name in great material satisfaction cannot be so sincere. A materially puffed up person may utter the holy name of the Lord occasionally, but he is incapable of uttering the name in quality. Therefore, the four principles of material advancement, namely (1) high parentage, (2) good wealth, (3) high education, and (4) attractive beauty, are, so to speak, disqualifications for progress on the path of spiritual advancement. The material covering of the pure spirit soul is an external feature, as much as fever is an external feature of the unhealthy body. The general process is to decrease the degree of the fever and not to aggravate it by maltreatment. Sometimes it is seen that spiritually advanced persons become materially impoverished. This is no discouragement. On the other hand, such impoverishment is a good sign as much as the falling of temperature is a good sign. The principle of life should be to decrease the degree of material intoxication which leads one to be more and more illusioned about the aim of life. Grossly illusioned persons are quite unfit for entrance into the kingdom of God.

### Srimad-Bhagavatam 1.8.27

*namo 'kincana-vittaya*
*nivrtta-guna-vrttaye*
*atmaramaya santaya*
*kaivalya-pataye namah*

### Translation

My obeisances are unto You, who are the property of the materially impoverished. You have nothing to do with the actions and reactions of the material modes of nature. You are self-satisfied, and therefore You are the most gentle and are master of the monists.

### Purport

A living being is finished as soon as there is nothing to possess. Therefore a living being cannot be, in the real sense of the term, a renouncer. A living being renounces something for gaining something more valuable. A student sacrifices his childish proclivities to gain better education. A servant gives up his job for a better job. Similarly, a devotee renounces the material world not for nothing but for something tangible in spiritual value. Srila Rupa Gosvami, Sanatana Gosvami, and Srila Raghunatha dasa Gosvami and others gave up their worldly pomp and prosperity for the sake of the service of the Lord. They were big men in the worldly sense. The Gosvamis were ministers in the government service of Bengal, and Srila Raghunatha dasa Gosvami was the son of a big zamindar (landlord) of his time. But they left everything to gain something superior to what they previously possessed. The devotees are generally without material prosperity, but they have a very secret treasure house in the lotus feet of the Lord.

There is a nice story about Srila Sanatana Gosvami. He had a touchstone with him, and this stone was left in a pile of refuse. A needy man took it, but later on wondered why the valuable stone was kept in such a neglected place. He therefore asked him for the most valuable thing, and then he was given the holy name of the Lord. Akincana means one who has nothing to give materially. A factual devotee, or mahatma, does not give anything material to anyone because he has already left all material assets. He can, however, deliver the supreme asset, namely the Personality of Godhead, because He is the only property of a factual devotee.

The touchstone of Sanatana Gosvami, which was thrown in the rubbish, was not the property of the Gosvami, otherwise it would not have been kept in such a place. This specific example is given for the neophyte devotees just to convince them that material hankerings and spiritual advancement go ill together. Unless one is able to see everything as spiritual in relation with the Supreme Lord, one must always distinguish between spirit and matter. A spiritual master like Srila Sanatana Gosvami, although personally able to see everything as spiritual, set this example for us only because we have no such spiritual vision.

Advancement of material vision or material civilization is a great stumbling block for spiritual advancement. Such material advancement entangles the living being in the bondage of a material body followed by all sorts of material miseries. Such material advancement is called anartha, or things not wanted. Actually this is so. In the present context of material advancement one uses lipstick at a cost of fifty cents, and there are so many unwanted things which are all products of the material conception of life. By diverting attention to so many unwanted things, human energy is spoiled without achievement of spiritual realization, the prime necessity of human life.

The attempt to reach the moon is another example of spoiling energy because even if the moon is reached, the problems of life will not be solved. The devotees of the Lord are called akincanas because they have practically no material assets. Such material assets are all products of the three modes of material nature. They foil spiritual energy, and thus the less we possess such products of material nature, the more we have a good chance for spiritual progress.

The Supreme Personality of Godhead has no direct connection with material activities. All His acts and deeds, which are exhibited even in this material world, are spiritual and without affection for the modes of material nature. In the Bhagavad-gita the Lord says that all His acts, even His appearance and disappearance in and out of the material world, are transcendental, and one who knows this perfectly shall not take his birth again in this material world but will go back to Godhead.

The material disease is due to hankering after and lording it over material nature. This hankering is due to an interaction of the three modes of nature, and neither the Lord nor the devotees have attachment for such false enjoyment. Therefore, the Lord and the devotees are called nivrtta-guna-vrtti. The perfect nivrtta-guna-vrtti is the Supreme Lord because He never becomes attracted by the modes of material nature, whereas the living beings have such a tendency. Some of them are entrapped by the illusory attraction of material nature.

Because the Lord is the property of the devotees, and the devotees are the property of the Lord reciprocally, the devotees are certainly transcendental to the modes of material nature. That is a natural conclusion. Such unalloyed devotees are distinct from the mixed devotees who approach the Lord for mitigation of miseries and poverty or because of inquisitiveness and speculation. The unalloyed devotees and the Lord are transcendentally attached to one another. For others, the Lord has nothing to reciprocate, and therefore He is called atmarama, self-satisfied.

Self-satisfied as He is, He is the master of all monists who seek to merge into the existence of the Lord. Such monists merge within the personal effulgence of the Lord called the brahmajyoti, but the devotees enter into the transcendental pastimes of the Lord, which are never to be misunderstood as material.

# Notes on the Country of Armenia

As with most nations located at the border between Europe and Asia, there is relatively little popular knowledge about the unique culture and long history of the Armenian nation. Landlocked and shielded by Mount Ararat (the mountain peak where Noah's Ark was said to have come to rest), Armenian lands combine semi-desert with hills and fertile lowlands, where famous wines and cognac are produced. The cellar vaults of cognac-producing regions complement the ancient churches and historical sites as fascinating visitor destinations.

Armenia boasts one of the oldest continuous civilizations in the world, dating back around 3,000 years. The history of the Armenian nation is intertwined with periods of subordination to powerful neighbors as well as years of independence and strength. Armenia is surrounded by Muslim nations to the east, west, and south, yet it was the first country in the world to adopt Christianity.

The present-day Republic of Armenia emerged from the Soviet Union in 1991 and since then has been striving to build a multi-party democracy and maintain favorable ties with its neighbors, despite its recent conflict with Azerbaijan and historical tensions with Turkey.

Armenia is a state where minorities are well integrated, yet patriotic feelings are very strong. It is a highly educated country, where national history and culture are now emphasized in the curriculum at this time of movement away from Soviet-style education system.

# International Religious Freedom Report

By the Bureau of Democracy, Human Rights, and Labor
Released October 26, 2001 by the Bureau of Public Affairs, U.S.
Department of State.

## ARMENIA

The Constitution of Armenia provides for freedom of religion; however, the law specifies some restrictions on the religious freedom of adherents of minority faiths, and there were some restrictions in practice. There was no change in the status of respect for religious freedom during the period covered by this report. The Armenian Apostolic Church, which has formal legal status as the national church, enjoys some privileges not available to adherents of other faiths. Jehovah's Witnesses continue to have their application for legal recognition as a registered religion rejected and report individual acts of discrimination. Other denominations occasionally report acts of discrimination, usually by mid-level or lower level government officials.

Relations among religions in society are generally amicable; however, societal attitudes towards some minority religions are ambivalent, and antipathy towards Muslims remains a problem. The United States government discusses religious freedom issues with the government in the context of its overall dialog and policy of promoting human rights.

### Section I. Religious Demography

The country has a total area of 11,496 square miles, and its population is approximately two million.

The country is ethnically homogenous, with approximately ninety-five percent of the population classified as ethnic Armenian. About ninety percent of citizens belong nominally to the Armenian Apostolic Church, an Eastern Christian denomination whose spiritual center is located at the cathedral and monastery of Echmiatsin. Religious observance was discouraged strongly in the Soviet era, leading to a sharp decline in the number of active churches and priests, the closure of virtually all monasteries, and the nearly complete absence of religious education. As a result, the level of religious practice is relatively low, although many former atheists now identify themselves with the national church.

For many citizens, Christian identity is an ethnic trait, with only a loose connection to religious belief. This identification was accentuated by the conflict over Nagorno-Karabakh in 1988–94, during which Armenia and Azerbaijan expelled their respective Azeri Muslim and Armenian Christian minorities, creating huge refugee populations in both countries. The head of the Church, Catholicos Karekin II (alternate spelling Garegin) was elected in October 1999 at Echmiatsin with the participation of Armenian delegates from around the world.

In 2001, the Armenian Apostolic Church engaged in a dispute with its Moscow archbishop, who was removed from office and excommunicated in May. There are comparatively small, but in many cases growing, communities of the following faiths: Yezidi (a Kurdish religious/ethnic group which includes elements derived from Zoroastrianism, Islam, and animism, with some 50–60,000 nominal adherents); Catholic, both Roman and Mekhitarist (Armenian Uniate) (approximately 180,000 adherents); Pentecostal (approximately 25,000); Armenian Evangelical Church (approximately 5,000); Greek Orthodox (approximately 6,000); Baptist (approximately 2,000); Jehovah's Witnesses (approximately 6,000); unspecified "charismatic" Christian (about 3,000); Seventh-Day Adventist; Mormon; Jewish (500–1,000); Muslim; Baha'i; Hare Krishna; and pagan. Yezidis are concentrated primarily in agricultural areas around Mount Aragats, northwest of Yerevan. Armenian Catholic and Greek Orthodox Christians are concentrated in the northern region, while most Jews, Mormons, and Baha'is are located in Yerevan. There is a remnant Muslim Kurdish community of a few hundred persons, many of which live in the Abovian region; a small group of Muslims of Azeri descent live primarily along the eastern or northern borders. In Yerevan there are approximately 1,000 Muslims, including Kurds, Iranians, and temporary residents from the Middle East. Jehovah's Witnesses continue their missionary work fairly visibly and reported net gains in membership during 2000 and 2001. Evangelical Christians and Mormons also are engaged in missionary work.

### Section II. Status of Religious Freedom Legal/Policy Framework

The Constitution of Armenia provides for freedom of religion; however, the law specifies some restrictions on the religious freedom of adherents of faiths other than the Armenian Apostolic Church. The Constitution also provides for freedom of conscience, including the right either to believe or to adhere to atheism. The 1991 Law on Freedom of Conscience, amended in 1997, establishes the separation of church and state, but grants the Armenian Apostolic Church official status as the national church. A 1993 presidential decree, later superseded by the 1997 law, supplemented the 1991 law and further strengthened the position of the Armenian Apostolic Church.

The 1991 law requires all other religious denominations and organizations to register with the State Council on Religious Affairs. The State Council on Religious Affairs is a state agency under the prime minister, without cabinet level representation. The Council does not include representatives of minority religions in its activities. Petitioning organizations must "be free from materialism and of a purely spiritual nature," and must subscribe to a doctrine based on "historically recognized Holy Scriptures." To qualify, a religious organization must have at least two hundred adult members (increased in 1997 from the previous figure of fifty). A religious organization that has been refused registration may not publish newspapers or magazines, rent meeting places, broadcast programs on television or radio, or officially sponsor the visas of visitors. No previously registered religious group seeking re-registration under the 1997 law has been denied; however, the Council still denies registration to Jehovah's Witnesses.

Several other religious groups are unregistered, specifically the Molokhany, a branch of the Russian "Old Believers," and some Yezidis. According to an official of the State Council on Religious Affairs, those two groups, which number in the hundreds, have not sought registration. As of June 30, 2001, there were fifty religious organizations, some of which are individual congregations from within the same denomination, registered with the State Council on Religious Affairs. All existing denominations have been reregistered annually. Almost all existing denominations, except for the Hare Krishna's and Jehovah's Witnesses, have been reregistered. The Hare Krishna's do not have  enough members to qualify, as their numbers by 1998 had dropped below even the previous membership threshold of fifty. Although Jehovah's Witnesses have enough members, the State Council on Religious Affairs continues to deny them registration.

Current legislation permits religious education in state schools only by instructors appointed by the Armenian Apostolic Church. If requested by the school principal, the Armenian Apostolic Church will send priests to teach classes in religion and religious history in those schools. Other religious groups are not allowed to provide religious instruction in schools, although they may do so in private homes to children of their members.

As a result of extended negotiations between the government and the Armenian Apostolic Church, a memorandum was signed in April 2000 that provides for the two sides to negotiate a concordat, presently scheduled to be signed in September 2001, in time for the 1,700th anniversary celebrations of the country's conversion to Christianity. The document is expected to regulate relations between the two bodies, settle disputes over ecclesiastical properties and real estate confiscated during the Soviet period, and define the role of the Armenian Apostolic Church in such fields as education, morality, and the media.

In July 1998, President Kocharian created a Human Rights Commission, which has met with many minority organizations. The Law on Religion states that the State Council on Religious Affairs is to serve as a mediator in conflicts between religious groups; however, the Council has not yet done so.

### Restrictions on Religious Freedom

During the period covered by this report, most registered religious groups reported no serious legal impediments to their activities. However, members of faiths other than the Armenian Apostolic Church are subject to some government restrictions. In particular the 1991 law forbids "proselytizing" (undefined in the law) except by the Armenian Apostolic Church, and requires all other religious denominations and organizations to register with the State Council on Religious Affairs. The State Council on Religious Affairs continued to deny registration to Jehovah's Witnesses during the period covered by this report. The President's Human Rights Commission declined to intervene and recommended that Jehovah's Witnesses challenge their registration denial through the courts, as provided by law. Although Jehovah's Witnesses officials stated that they had filed such a legal challenge, it had not been heard by the courts by the end of the period covered by this report. An assembly of Jehovah's Witnesses approved slight changes to their charter in order to meet the country's legal requirements (for example, changing a commitment to "proselytize" into one to "witness"), but cautioned that they could not change fundamental articles of faith, such as opposition to military service. The court previously had stated that the denial was due to the group's opposition to military service. However, in 1999 and 2000 the Council defended its refusal to accept applications by the Jehovah's Witnesses by stating that the group cannot be registered because "illegal proselytism" is allegedly integral to its activities. Discussions between Jehovah's Witnesses and the Council temporarily were suspended in 2001 due to a lack of progress on this issue. According to Jehovah's Witnesses officials, Council representatives have met with them but have refused to assist in the group's efforts to gain registration.

Although the law bans foreign funding for foreign-based churches, the ban on foreign funding has not been enforced and is considered unenforceable by the State Council on Religious Affairs. The law also mandates that religious organizations other than the Armenian Apostolic Church need prior permission from the State Council on Religious Affairs to engage in religious activities in public places, to travel abroad, or to invite foreign guests to the country. However, in practice travel by religious personnel is not restricted. No action has been taken against missionaries, although groups such as the Mormons are allowed by the Council to have only a limited number of official missionaries present in the country. A 1993 presidential decree requires the State Council on Religious Affairs to investigate the activities of the representatives of registered religious organizations and to ban missionaries who engage in activities contrary to their status. However, the Council largely has been inactive, due in part to lack of resources, except for registering religious groups.

### Abuses of Religious Freedom

At the end of the period covered by this report, thirteen members of Jehovah's Witnesses still remained in prison charged with draft evasion or, if forcibly drafted, with desertion due to refusal to serve. During the year, fourteen were released but still under house arrest, and twenty-one more were free on probation. Two more were in detention pending trial, and seven had been released unconditionally and were not subject to future trials. A group estimated by an official of Jehovah's Witnesses to be approximately fifty members reportedly were in hiding from draft officials. Representatives of Jehovah's Witnesses officials said that the increase in the number of those imprisoned persons was due to the fact that members of Jehovah's Witnesses who had been called for military service were going directly to police and turning themselves in rather than waiting until induction to declare conscientious objection. As part of its required undertakings for joining the Council of Europe (COE), in January 2001, the government pledged to pass a new law conforming to European standards on alternative military service within three years.

Government officials stated that, according to their interpretation of COE regulations, those presently in prison as conscientious objectors were not required to be released until the new law was passed. However, COE officials stated that their interpretation was that the government's undertaking required immediate release of such conscientious objectors. As of June 2001, no alternative on military service was passed before Parliament.

There are reports that hazing of new conscripts is more severe for Yezidis and other minorities. Jehovah's Witnesses are subject to even harsher treatment by military and civilian security officials, because their refusal to serve in the military is seen as a threat to national survival. According to law, a religious organization that has been refused registration may not publish newspapers or magazines, rent meeting places, broadcast programs on television or radio, or officially sponsor the visas of visitors. Jehovah's Witnesses continue to experience difficulty renting meeting places and report that private individuals willing to rent them facilities are visited by police and warned not to do so. Lack of official visa sponsorship means that Jehovah's Witnesses visitors must pay for tourist visas. When shipped in bulk, Jehovah's Witness publications are seized at the border. Although members of Jehovah's Witnesses supposedly were allowed to bring in limited quantities of printed materials for their own use, Jehovah's Witnesses officials reported that "spiritual letters" from one congregation to another, which they said were meant for internal rather than proselytizing purposes, continued to be confiscated by customs officials.

In August 2000, the mayor and the council of the town of Talin, in the western part of the country, expelled two members of Jehovah's Witnesses after residents alleged that they were going from door to door preaching and disturbing residents.

Other than Jehovah's Witnesses who were conscientious objectors, there were no other reports of religious detainees or prisoners.

### Section III. Societal Attitudes

Relations among religions in society are generally amicable; however, societal attitudes towards some minority religions are ambivalent, and antipathy towards Muslims remains a problem.

The Armenian Apostolic Church is a member of the World Council of Churches and, despite doctrinal differences, has friendly official relations with many major Christian denominations, including the Eastern Orthodox churches, the Roman Catholic Church, the Anglican Church, and major Protestant churches. Catholicos Karekin II visited the Vatican in November 2000, and the Vatican announced that Pope John Paul II intends to visit the country in September 2001. Relations between forcign-based religious groups and the dominant Armenian Apostolic Church are also strengthened through cooperation in assistance projects. Various registered Christian humanitarian organizations are working with the Armenian Apostolic Church to distribute humanitarian assistance and educational religious materials.

Although such activities contribute to mutual understanding, they take place in an undercurrent of competition. Suppressed through seventy years of Soviet rule, the Armenian Apostolic Church has neither the trained priests nor the material resources to fill immediately the spiritual void created by the demise of Communist ideology. Non-traditional religious organizations are viewed with suspicion, and foreign-based denominations operate cautiously for fear of being seen as a threat by the Armenian Apostolic Church. After his election in October 1999, one of the first actions of Karekin II was to create a Secretariat for Ecumenical Outreach to other Christian denominations.

Societal attitudes toward most minority religions are ambivalent. Many citizens are not religiously observant, but the link between religion and Armenian ethnicity is strong. As a result of the Karabakh conflict with Azerbaijan, most of the country's Muslim population was forced to leave the country. Antipathy towards Muslims remains a problem, and the few Muslims remaining in the country keep a low profile, despite generally amicable relations between the government and Iran. There is no formally operating mosque, although Yerevan's one surviving 18th century mosque, which was restored with Iranian funding, is open for regular Friday prayers on a tenuous legal basis.

There was no officially sponsored violence reported against minority religious groups during the period. Yezidi children on occasion report hazing by teachers and classmates. Some observers report increasingly unfavorable attitudes towards Jehovah's Witnesses among the general population, both because they are seen as "unpatriotic" for refusing military service and because of a widespread but unsubstantiated belief that they pay money to the desperately poor for conversions. The press reported a number of complaints lodged by citizens against Jehovah's Witnesses for alleged illegal proselytizing. They are the focus of religious attacks and hostile preaching by some Armenian Apostolic Church clerics. Although it is difficult to document, it is likely that there is some informal societal discrimination in employment against members of certain religious groups.

## Epilogue

# Recent Problems in Armenia

Below, we chronologically document the more recent development of systematic harassment of Hare Krishna members by priests of the majority Armenian Apostolic Church, police, and local government officials.

On July 10th, 1992, the Hare Krishna temple in Yerevan was attacked by arsonists. Temple members managed to extinguish the fire, which damaged the temple building and two cars owned by ISKCON. ISKCON appealed to the Commission for Human Rights of the Supreme Council of Armenia and local police, but the complaint was ignored.

In June 1993, a few members of the Society went to the Republic of Nàgorno Karabakh to open a free food distribution center for local people. On June 12th, ISKCON members and Mr. L. Gulian, the head of the Department of Refugees and Humanitarian Aid reached an agreement to co-operate together in order to help the region's under-privileged. Mr. Gulian promised to provide ISKCON with premises for their free food distribution in Stepanakert city and other settlements in the R.N.K. In Stepanakert, ISKCON was granted facility to distribute free food on the premises of a former restaurant. Within a month of the program starting, a group of armed men broke into the premises and demanded, on behalf of the government, that our members leave the country within twenty-four hours.

ISKCON's members appealed to the State Minister Zirair Pogosian, who refused to help and actually declared support for the demands of the intruders.

On September 23, 1993, Mikhael Unjugulian, a Krishna devotee was severely beaten before the inhabitants in his village of origin, Oshakan. His assailant was a priest from the local Armenian Orthodox Church, a Father Gevork. A vain appeal for justice was made by the victim to the police in the Ashtrak region. His complaint was ignored. The incident was witnessed and can be verified by many inhabitants of the village.

In April 1994, thirty tons of religious books were dispatched from ISKCON in Moscow for the temple in Yerevan. The books were seized by the customs at Masis station before they reached Yerevan. Initially, the Council for Religious Affairs instructed the customs station not to release the books but later claims to have written to ask them to release them. It should be noted that religious books do not require customs clearance in order to be imported into Armenia.

After various attempts to secure possession of the confiscated books, ISKCON members heard from reliable political sources that the literatures had been burned. Further information suggested that the order to burn the books came from the head of the Armenian KGB, David Shahnazarian. They were reportedly burnt in the ovens of the thermal power plant in Yerevan, mixed with liquid fuel. Informants claim that this was done in reply to the international reaction to the reported persecution of Hare Krishna members in Armenia.

On the 16th of March, 1995, a committee was formed comprised of the president of ISKCON in Armenia, a representative of the U.S. Embassy in Armenia, the head of Customs, the head of the local police station, and the head of the railway station in Masis. This committee proceeded to unlock the container of books. The container was opened and it was found to be empty.

ISKCON in Armenia has lodged an official complaint regarding this but has been advised that it may not be wise to pursue the case seriously.

On April 18, 1994, Hare Krishna member Artur Khachatrian was attacked by a group of fifteen members of the Armenian Army in an Officer's Club in Yerevan. He was severely beaten and had to be hospitalized. The religious books he carried with him were burned. The case was reported to the police station in the Spandarian district of Yerevan. The appointed police investigator was a Captain Asatryan who decided not to question or arrest the offenders, although their names are known to the police.

On July 4, 1994, two female members of the Hare Krishna Society in Yerevan, Anaite Arzumanyan and Mariana Dorunz, traveled to the neighboring town of Sisyan to distribute religious literature and minister to local sympathizers. They were intercepted on route by two priests of the Armenian Apostolic Church, Father Narek from Sisyan and an American priest of the Avat Mission (a branch of the Armenian Apostolic Church), Father Zenob. Supported by soldiers of the Armenian Army, the priests confiscated more than 150 books and proceeded to light a bonfire with them, an act that attracted much local attention. The priests and their supporters then forcibly ripped the clothing off the women, twisted their arms, tore their religious beads off their necks, and threw these articles into the bonfire. This scene was witnessed by many of the local people. This incident was reported to Mr. Robert Patterson of the American embassy in Armenia, and to the special correspondent of Espress-chronika in Armenia, Michail Dabasian.

Krishna devotees appealed for justice in these cases to the Armenian Prosecutor and the Committee for Human Rights at the Armenian Supreme Soviet. The only response came from an investigator, Mr. Kroian, which consisted only of a threatening commitment to investigate all Hare Krishna activities in Armenia.

On July 26, 1994, another ISKCON member, Karo Mkrtchian, was seriously beaten and threatened with murder by six members of the Dashnaktzusyun Party (a nationalist political party). Again, any religious books or paraphernalia he carried were confiscated. He was also told that if he was seen again in the city after twenty-four hours, he would be killed on the spot.

On July 31, 1994, in the town of Goris, a live phone-in interview with the Patriarch of the South Armenian region, Bishop Abraham, was broadcast on the local state cable television. During the interview, a question was raised about the status of ISKCON. The bishop replied that it was all the work of Satan and that the books sold by ISKCON represent a real social danger, diverting people from the path of God. He claimed to have formed a committee in the local Cultural House for Youth with the aim of collecting all the ISKCON books from the population in exchange for free Bibles (this facility was also announced on local radio). He promised to burn publicly the collected literature.

On August 28, 1994, ten armed thugs stormed the Hare Krishna temple in Yerevan. They completely vandalized the place of worship, desecrated the altar, and severely assaulted the temple president, Ivan Dallakian. The attack lasted more than twenty minutes. During the attack, ISKCON members tried to report the attack to the police, who only sent a police patrol to the scene after four attempts at trying to contact them. The police car only stayed long enough for the police officer to declare, "We are not going to protect people like you." After the incident, Ivan Dallakyan himself called the police and asked for protection. He gave the police the names and addresses of the people who attacked the temple; but again, there was no sign of response from the police.

On the morning of August 31, 1994, the same people phoned and warned that they would come again at 7:00 pm. Temple members called the police at 5:00 pm and requested protection. A police patrol arrived after a short time and stayed only fifteen minutes, explaining that they had no time to wait. At the appointed time, four people arrived at the temple. They started to abuse the temple residents and threatened violence. Before long a scuffle ensued, and suddenly, after just a few moments, a fleet of fourteen police cars appeared on the scene. The policemen surrounded the temple and arrested all the residents. Seventeen Hare Krishna members were taken into custody. In the police station, the prisoners were abused and beaten.

Subsequently, sixteen of those arrested have been freed from the state prison. They were, nonetheless, forced to stay under house arrest for an unspecified investigation period. After a period of two months, the charges were dropped.

As a result of the attack on the temple, one Hare Krishna member, Boris Agagabyan, was hospitalized with head injuries and a severely damaged nose. Another member, Mkrtchyan Karo suffered severe head injuries, inflicted by a metal bar. Others also had to receive hospital treatment.

On September 3, 1994, a member called Grigoryan Kamo was arrested by the local police and taken into custody. During the night, he was severely beaten in his cell by the same policemen who had beaten the others on the 31st.

On the 6th September, Grigorian Kamo was transferred to a psychiatric prison hospital. He has since been released.

### Media Incitement

A mass media campaign was orchestrated against ISKCON in the last six months of 1994. The reportage was sensationalistic and sectarian. When Ara Akopian (an ISKCON member) recently asked Voskan Mamikonian, a correspondent from the Erkir newspaper, why he published blatant lies about ISKCON, the correspondent replied, "When a war is being fought against a political enemy, then all means are to be used, both honest and dishonest."

# APPENDIX III

# About the Author

Gagik Buniatyan (Sarvabhavana das) was born in a small town called Meghri on August 26, 1964 in a middle class family.

He had lovely parents who would sacrifice everything for their children's education and well being.

From early childhood he showed interesting qualities that made his parents think that he was not like the rest of the other children, and certainly was not going to be easily controlled by them or others.

He was a very active and energetic boy, becoming involved in many school activities such as sports, drama, etc. He was a "naughty but sweet boy" as his mother used to describe him to our friends or relatives. He was loved by his teachers and friends and showed respect and love to all of them.

He would always ask interesting questions, and sometimes teachers were bewildered and did not know what to answer. But they would always tell his parents that he was somewhat special in the class. They would always tell his parents that if he would work a little harder then he could be one of the best students in the school. Unfortunately from a very young age, due to his association, he started taking drugs (marijuana) and gaving up all other activities, he started his long journey with all kinds of books and available literature at that time. He was searching for knowledge about God but could not quench his thirst for it.

He liked very much Indian music, dance, movies, and philosophy from his early childhood, and India's greatest stars, such as Raj Kapoor, Lata Mangeshkar, Asha, Hema Malini, Dharmendra, and Amitabh Bhacchan, were his favorite characters. He says that they actually made him a devotee of Lord Krishna, and he owes them so much for that. Especially Hema Malini stood out from all of them. Gagik believes that she can change even the most stone-hearted person's life by her wonderful movies and her incredible dancing and acting.

However, time and circumstances took him different directions in life, and he became very interested in religion and Eastern philosophy. He was very compassionate towards his friends, animals, and birds, and from fifteen years of age chose to become strict vegetarian (details you can find in the book).

In 1981 he completed his high school education and from 1982 to 1984 he served in the Russian Army, this being mandatory at that time.

After returning from the army in 1984, by his good fortune he met the Hare Krishna devotees and found almost all of the answers to his questions. He took this path very seriously and started practicing bhakti-yoga with his new friends. Soon after joining, he was actively involved in publishing and distributing the holy scriptures of ancient India, like Bhagavad-gita and other books by Srila Prabhupada.

Soon he became one of the most active book distributors in Armenia, along with his good friend Sachisuta das. He was arrested by the police several times and persecuted by the KGB members.

As a result of this, on January 24, 1986 he was arrested for the last time and sentenced for two years imprisonment for illegal religious book publication and distribution in the territory of former USSR.

On March 25, 1986, under unique circumstances, he was formally initiated via letter by his spiritual master Harikesa Swami and received the name Sarvabhavana das.

From January 24, 1986 until January 22, 1988 he was tortured in Armenian and Russian jails for his missionary activities.

In June 1986 he was sent to a Sovetashen's psychiatric jail hospital for one month and tortured by the staffs. In July 1986 he was sentenced to two years imprisonment. He was asked many times to voluntarily give up practicing Krishna conscious activities, and he could have his sentence reduced by one third. But he refused, and as a result on August 26, 1986, his birthday, he was sent to a Russian jail where the police promised him that he would die from hunger.

On January 22, 1988 he was released from the prison camp two days early because Saturday and Sunday were the weekend and the office was closed. They were not allowed to keep him beyond his release date of the 24th.

On May 18, 1988 Sarvabhavana das married Dustrik Buniatyan (Dayanvisha devi dasi). Together they have three wonderful children— Sarkis (Sachisuta) 17, Rasa-lila 14, and Narek (Balaram) 9. They named their first son Sarkis (Sachisuta) as a respect and dedication to his very good friend Sachisuta das, who could not survive in the prison camp and left his body on December 26, 1987, less than one month before his release date.

In February 1989 Gagik Buniatyan visited India with the first group of fifty Russian Hare Krishna devotees. He met Rajiv Gandhi and traveled to holy places of pilgrimage for two months.

In 1990 he moved to India with his family, getting refugee status from the United Nations High Commissioner for Refugees (U.N.H.C.R.), and stayed seven long years in Sri Mayapur Dhama, India. His second and third children were born there. In 1998 he moved to the United States and stayed there for four years before returning back to his motherland, where he and his family are currently situated.

## Hare Krishna.

# History and Summary of the Abuse in Armenia

**1981** – first ISKCON members in Armenia meet together privately to worship.

**1985** – KGB orchestrates two court cases against Krishna followers.

**1986** – Martik Zhamkochian held in a psychiatric hospital and force-fed raw eggs and injected with large quantities of psycho-pharmacological drugs, dies at twenty-five years of age.

**1986** – seven members of the Hare Krishna movement are arrested. Four of them spend many months in the Sovetashens jail then in psychiatric hospitals, namely Suren Karapetyan (Sannyasa das), Karen Sahakyan (Kamalamala das), Armen Sahakyan (Atmananda das), and Armen Sargisyan. Three of them are charged with illegal distribution of religious literature, namely Sarkis Ohanjanian (Sachisuta das) two years imprisonment, Agvan Harutyunyan (Adwaita Acharya das) three years imprisonment, and Gagik Buniatyan (Sarvabhavana das) two years imprisonment.

**1987** – Sargis Ohanjanyan (Sachisuta das) 23, dies of tuberculosis and malnutrition in Soviet labor camp YU-25/B.

**1990** – ISKCON registers as an official religion during the post-Soviet period of reform.

**1992** – Yerevan temple is attacked by arsonists. Complaints to the Commission for Human Rights of the Supreme Council of Armenia go unanswered.

**July, 1994** – thirty tons of religious books, legally imported into Armenia, are seized by customs officials. They were later burnt in the ovens of the thermal power plant in Yerevan.

**August, 1994** – ten armed men attack and vandalize the temple, severely assaulting Ivan Dallakyan (Haridas Thakur das), temple president. Police declare, "We are not going to protect people like you."

**April, 1995** – the temple is attacked again by twenty armed men who destroy the altar, severely beat all the members, and steal everything of value. No police response.

And so on and on, not only in Armenia but regularly these kind of reports have been and continue to be given by the members of the movement throughout all former Soviet Union territory.

Hundreds of different horrible unwritten cases can be heard from different members of the Hare Krishna movement individually.

One of the most recent events took place in Kazakhstan on the 21st of November 2006 where illegally dozens of homes were destroyed by the state, using bulldozers. Women and children were left outside homeless in a cold winter.